ABOUT THE AUTHOR

On the eve of World War II, **John G. Stoessinger** fled from Nazi-occupied Austria to Czechoslovakia. Three years later, he fled again via Siberia to China where he lived for seven years. In Shanghai, he served with the International Refugee Organization.

Dr. Stoessinger came to the United States in 1947, received his B.A. degree from Grinnell College in 1950 and then went to Harvard where he earned his Ph.D. degree in 1954. He entered the teaching field immediately and has taught at Harvard, M.I.T., Columbia, Princeton, and the City University of New York. In 1969, he led the International Seminar on International Relations at Harvard University, and in 1970 he received an Honorary Degree of Doctor of Laws from Grinnell College, Iowa, and from the American College of Switzerland. He is now a Distinguished Professor of International Affairs at Trinity University in San Antonio, Texas.

Dr. Stoessinger is the author of ten leading books in international relations. *The Might of Nations: World Politics in Our Time* was awarded the Bancroft Prize by Columbia University in 1963 as the best book in international relations published in 1962. The tenth edition of the book was published in 1993. His other works include *The Refugee and The World Community* (1956); *Financing the United Nations System* (1964); *Power and Order* (1964); *The United Nations and the Superpowers* (1965, 1970, 1973, 1977); *Nations in Darkness: China, Russia, and America* (1971, 1975, 1978, 1981, 1986, 1990); *Why Nations Go to War* (1974, 1978, 1985, 1990, 1993); and *Henry Kissinger: The Anguish of Power* (1976). Dr. Stoessinger also served as Chief Book Review Editor of *Foreign Affairs* for five years and is a member of the Council on Foreign Relations. From 1967 to 1974, Dr. Stoessinger was acting Director of the Political Affairs Division at the United Nations.

Dr. Stoessinger's autobiography, *Night Journey*, was published in 1978. His latest book, *Crusaders and Pragmatists: Movers of Modern American Foreign Policy*, was published by W. W. Norton in 1979 and 1985.

Nations at Dawn
China, Russia, and America

NATIONS AT DAWN

China, Russia, and America

John G. Stoessinger

Trinity University
San Antonio, Texas

SIXTH EDITION

McGRAW-HILL, INC.
New York   St. Louis   San Francisco   Auckland   Bogotá
Caracas   Lisbon   London   Madrid   Mexico City   Milan
Montreal   New Delhi   San Juan
Singapore   Sydney   Tokyo   Toronto

This book is printed on recycled, acid-free paper containing a minimum of
50% recycled deinked fiber.

1234567890   DOC DOC 909876543

ISBN 0-07-061626-4

This book was set in Electra by Americomp.
The editors were Peter Labella and Fred H. Burns;
the production supervisor was Friederich W. Schulte.
The cover was designed by John Hite / Joan E. O'Connor.
R. R. Donnelley & Sons Company was printer and binder.

Library of Congress Cataloging-in-Publication Data is available:
LC Card # 93-30898.

For now we see through a glass darkly;
but then face to face:
now I know in part;
but then shall I know even as I also am known.

—ST. PAUL, First Epistle to the Corinthians

CONTENTS

PREFACE TO THE
SIXTH EDITION

More than two decades ago, in the depth of the cold war, I wrote the following sentence in the Preface to the First Edition of this book:

> There is a need to try to build bridges from America to Russia, from America to China, and from Russia to China—two way bridges between these nations which now hold the fate of the world in their hands.

Few such bridges existed then. Myths and misperceptions dominated the policies of all three nations. Since then, after a long and terrible night, the darkness has begun to lift. In China, the old men of Communism are on their last legs, defying their imminent mortality. Their latest definition of Communism is a form of capitalism without political freedom, a formula which is destined to be transitory. I believe that China now stands at a threshold of history similar to the Soviet Union's just before the emergence of Mikhail Gorbachev. In other words, just before the dawn.

Russia in this century has been the object of two historic experiments: the Bolshevik Revolution and its undoing seventy-five years later. The sixth edition of this book traces this historic arc and its impact on relations with the United States. Since the last edition of this book appeared, the Soviet Union has disappeared. For the first time in its tortured history Russia is groping for democracy. Amity and trust with the United States have begun to replace mistrust and hostility. Russia has come out of the night at last.

The enormity of these events has made the title of this book obsolete. Hence, *Nations in Darkness* has been replaced by *Nations at Dawn*. And I am grateful to have been dawn's chronicler.

McGraw-Hill and I would like to thank the following reviewers for their many helpful comments and suggestions: Jay Cobbledick, Eastern Connecticut State University; Richard Kranzdorf, Cal Poly, San Luis Obispo; James Mitchell, Cal State, Northridge; Benjamin Nimer, George Washington University; and Ken Rodman, Colby College.

John G. Stoessinger

PREFACE TO THE
FIRST EDITION

There are two fundamental ways in which a man can deal with tragic experience: he can get stuck in the past and do battle with its ghosts, or he can come to terms with it and try to fashion it into strength. This book represents an effort to take the latter course.

This is a deeply personal book. It has grown out of my life experience: youth as a Jew under Hitler, flight across Stalin's Russia, refugee life in China, and the chance to build a new life in America.

During the first twenty years of my life in Europe and in China, tragedy seemed to be the basic existential fact of life; during the second twenty years I discovered that America was still relatively innocent of tragedy—despite the Civil War, a depression, two world wars, and a growing inclination toward violence. There is a need to try to build bridges from America to Russia, from America to China, and from Russia to China—two way bridges between these nations which now hold the fate of the world in their hands.

Today it is no longer enough for nations to understand each other with their minds; they must learn to *feel* each other with their souls. Intelligence and knowledge alone cannot prevent catastrophe. Also needed is the kind of empathy that flows from the knowledge in one's mind that ultimate tragedy is truly possible and from the subsequent realization in one's heart that all men—in their brief and precarious journey through life—are truly brothers. Americans, I believe, still do not know that men can build both cathedrals and concentration camps. They still do not know, in other words, that everything is possible.

Many dear friends have helped me in this quest: Bernard E. Brown, Zbigniew Brzezinski, Inis L. Claude, Jr., Walter Kaufmann, Hans J. Morgenthau, Harrison Salisbury, Arthur M. Schlesinger, Jr., and Ethel Sherman. Two former students, now close friends, have been a steady source of strength: Brenda Forman and Robert

G. McKelvey. I have also been blessed with three fine and understanding editors: Susan Gilbert, Elizabeth Kaye, and Barry Rossinoff; and with valuable secretarial assistance from Pamela Nicholas.

John G. Stoessinger

Nations at Dawn
China, Russia, and America

Chapter One

Introduction

More than two thousand years ago, Plato, in the seventh book of his *Republic*, conjured up a melancholy scene. Inside a cave, a group of men are chained in such a way that they are unable to turn their heads and can only look at the wall before them. Behind them a fire blazes and, between them and that fire, other men walk up and down, some talking and some silent. The chained men can only see the shadows of their fellow-men. To them, the shadows are in fact the men, and the voices come from the passing shadows. To these chained men, in Plato's words, "The truth would be nothing but the shadows."

The shattering symbolism of this allegory has haunted mankind for generations. And well it might—because we still wear the chains of which Plato spoke. All too often we mistake shadows for men and dim echoes for their voices. In Plato's time such shadows did not have the power to obliterate the species. In our time they do. To draw attention to this danger is, in essence, the purpose of this book.

The last three decades of the twentieth century may well be dominated by the political constellation of the world's three great powers: the United States, China, and Russia. This work attempts to shed light on *one* facet of this constellation's history. It is my hope that the material uncovered may serve as warning for the future.

During the past century the struggles between the United States and China and those between the United States and Russia were not waged solely on the basis of objective reality. They were also fought in the realm of imagery and illusion. At times, great gaps existed in the realms of imagery and reality, and these gaps deeply exacerbated tensions and made more difficult the task of political accommodation.

The assumption underlying this thesis is that international relations are often what people think they are, or, to put it in other words, that under certain conditions, men respond not to realities but to fictions that they have themselves created. To say that there are no objective problems in Sino-American or Russo-American relations would, of course, be folly. But the stage of world politics lends itself all too easily to the development of wide gaps between what reality is and the way it is perceived. Because of this fact, perception probably plays almost as important a role in international relations as does objective reality itself.

Misperceptions among nations may have disastrous effects on policy decisions. Stereotyped images on one side may elicit similar ones on the other, compounding the distortion. Even worse, if one believes a stereotype long enough, it may become reality by setting in motion the mechanism of self-fulfilling prophecy. Thus, if a nation believes that another is its implacable enemy and reiterates this often enough, making it the guideline of its national policy, it will eventually be right.

The task of this book is to examine fifteen empirical case studies in which misperceptions had concrete and specific effects on policy decisions. Six of these deal with milestones in Sino-American relations. The first vignette looks at the earliest encounters between these two nations during the last decades of the Chinese empire; the second traces the complex relationship between Chiang Kai-shek and the United States; the third deals with the Communist Chinese intervention in the Korean War; the fourth examines the United States-Chinese relationship during the French phase of the war in Indochina; the fifth examines Sino-American relations during the Americanization of the Vietnamese war; and the sixth concludes with an analysis of the zigzags on the road to reality during the 1980s and 1990s.

The second set of studies examines the great watersheds in Russo-American relations. The first of these concerns the volatile relations between the United States and Czarist Russia in the days of Catherine, Alexander, and Nicholas; the second deals with the encounter between Woodrow Wilson and V. I. Lenin in the crucible of world war and the Bolshevik Revolution; the third examines Soviet-American relations leading to the establishment of diplomatic relations; the fourth traces the beginning of the cold war spiral and the division of Germany; the fifth analyzes the interaction between President John F. Kennedy and Premier Nikita Khrushchev during the Cuban missile crisis of 1962; the sixth deals with the descent into cold war during Ronald Reagan's first term; and the seventh examines the new Russo-American rapprochement during the Gorbachev era and beyond. Finally, I have made an attempt to subject the third side of the triangle—the Sino-Soviet relationship—to a similar perceptual analysis.

These fifteen case studies, drawn from three vital areas in world politics, provide valuable empirical material for conceptual conclusions about the effects of misperceptions on policy decisions. I am fully aware that anyone who purports to undertake the task of distinguishing illusion from reality in world politics may justly be accused of hubris, for he is venturing into areas that pose formidable problems of an epistemological and even metaphysical nature. Nevertheless, an attempt must be made to determine when perceptions are accurate, when they are partially false, and when they are completely false. I have made a determined effort to maintain a balanced and objective attitude and to adhere to a pragmatic approach. While perception is the main subject treated, it is only one factor among many. This work is not meant to be a single-factor analysis. But like any effort at theoretical innovation, it emphasizes *that* conceptual insight which is considered original and new. Unlike a photograph, the analysis does not attempt to reproduce every detail of the truth; more like a portrait, it tries to uncover a new truth.

I have attempted to analyze perception in terms of four distinct, yet interrelated, categories: first, each nation's *self-image*; second, each nation's perception of the *character* of its adversary; third, each nation's perception of its adversary's *intentions*; and finally, each nation's perception of the other's *power* and *capabilities*.

The methodology is traditional in that it avoids excessive quantification of data and complex behavioral jargon; but it is innovative in the sense that it refuses to compartmentalize the social sciences. Insights are drawn, wherever relevant, from the fields of political science, history, psychology, and philosophy.

The book is essentially a diagnosis. It tries to show how great nations struggle not only with each other, but also with their perceptions of each other. To move from diagnosis to prescription is yet more difficult. In the concluding chapter, I attempt to determine the conditions under which national leaders manage to correct their misperceptions. Finally, I have suggested some guidelines for building policies on the basis of reality.

Facts are usually quite complex. When one learns to respect them, nuances appear instead of black-and-white or good-and-evil categories. Nations, like people, must learn to think in color rather than in black and white.[1] Once again, man must escape from Plato's cave, from perceiving only shadows. Toward that end this book is dedicated.

[1] I am indebted for this phrase to Professor Walter Kaufmann's article, "Beyond Black and White: A Plea for Thinking in Color," *Midway* (Winter 1970), pp. 49–79.

Part One

THE ROLE OF PERCEPTION IN SINO-AMERICAN RELATIONS

Chapter Two

China and America: The Burden of the Past

History, in psychological terms, is the memory of nations. It is the repository not only of objective events, but also of illusions and misunderstandings that filter down to our own time. Many Americans are profoundly anxious about the course of Chinese-American relations, but far too few are aware of the psychological roots of the present encounter. These roots go deep and are grounded in a soil of misperceptions that have marred relations between China and America since the very beginning. Perhaps an analysis of this tragic past may better equip us to deal with the challenge of the present.

THE FIRST ENCOUNTERS

This is the first century in over 2,000 years in which China has not considered itself to be at the center of the universe. For two millennia the Chinese empire conceived of itself as the hub of civilization, the great school of the world—much as Athens had once considered itself the school of the ancient Mediterranean world. Although dynasties came and went, the political structure of the empire remained essentially stable: the emperor, aided by a small intellectual elite, controlled the government; he ruled by the Mandate of heaven; and his edicts had the authority of a philosopher-king. His vast realm, which stretched from Siberia to the tropics, was known as "everything under heaven."

7

The world beyond the Great Wall of China did not hold much interest, since, in the eyes of the Chinese, it was populated by barbarians. Hence, the foreign relations of the empire for 2,000 years were in essence tributary relationships: long caravans laden with gifts for the emperor would weave their way across the land to the Imperial Court at Peking; the envoy would kowtow before the Son of Heaven and present the tribute. The act of kowtow, for example, left no doubt as to the personal superiority of the emperor. The ritual consisted of three separate kneelings, each accompanied by three separate prostrations, all performed to the command of a court usher: "kneel," "fall prostrate," "rise to your knees." All envoys went through this calisthenic exercise, and its proper performance was regarded merely as good manners by the court. The Chinese believed that it was perfectly self-evident that their empire was a superior civilization and the act of kowtow was a symbolic recognition of this axiomatic truth.

This view of themselves made the Chinese a stay-at-home people. Since the empire contained everything of value, no one wanted to go abroad and thus be removed from civilization. There was no interest in the conquest of strange lands of lesser value; an Office of Barbarian Affairs handled all foreign, that is, tributary, relations. On reading the descriptions of "Western barbarians," one is struck by a fuzzy-minded, fairy-story quality not unlike that which dominated the descriptions of Western travelers to "Cathay." The barbarians were thought to inhabit small islands separated from civilization by "intervening wastes of sea." They were described as having skins of "dazzling white color," beaked noses, and flaming red hair. No distinction was made among the multifarious "tribes" of barbarians. In all cases, the Chinese attitude was a mixture of indifference and contempt.

The first attempt by a Westerner to pierce this curtain of ignorance took place in the sixteenth century. It was the attempt of a Jesuit Father—Matthew Ricci—to convert China to Catholicism. (Marco Polo's travels to China in the twelfth century had had a significant impact on Europe but almost none on China.) Ricci arrived in China in 1583, strongly influenced by the Catholic Counter Reformation, and engaged in a thirty-year effort to convert China from the top. This resourceful Jesuit mastered the Chinese language, dressed in the garb of a Confucian scholar, and adapted himself to the customs of the land. His knowledge of mathematics and astronomy earned him the respect of Chinese scholars and even got him an audience with the emperor. His first mission, as he saw it, was to show the Chinese that their view of the world was false:

> Their universe was limited to their own fifteen provinces, and in the sea painted around it they had placed a few little islands to which they gave the names of different kingdoms they had heard of. All of these islands put together would not be as large as the smallest of the Chinese provinces. With such a limited knowledge, it is evident why they boasted of their kingdom as being the whole world, and why they called it Thienhia, meaning, everything under the heavens. When they learned that China was only a part of the great east, they considered such an idea, so unlike their own, to be something utterly impossible. . . .[1]

Ricci's effort met with such resistance and even fury that the Jesuit had to settle for a tactful compromise. While he did include the Western empires on a map that he made, giving them Chinese names in the process, he retained China's central position:

> They could not comprehend the demonstrations proving that the earth is a globe, made up of land and water, and that a globe of its very nature had neither beginning nor end. The geographer was therefore obliged to change his design and, by omitting the first meridian, he left a margin on either side of the map, making the Kingdom of China to appear right in the center. This was more in keeping with their ideas and it gave them a great deal of pleasure and satisfaction.[2]

When Matthew Ricci died in China in 1610, his famous map did not long survive him. It had made a sufficient impact, however, to fix in the minds of the ruling Confucian scholars the names of the great Western empires, although their exact location in the world was soon forgotten. During the next two centuries, right up to the time of the Opium War, total confusion dominated Chinese perceptions of the outside world. Contemporary maps showed islands named France, Spain, Portugal, England, Italy, and America, rotating like satellites around the great sun of the celestial empire. Ricci's role had been to lift the veil briefly, but soon after his death it descended again, and the barbarians were relegated once more

---

[1] Matthew Ricci, *China in the Sixteenth Century: The Journals of Matthew Ricci: 1583–1610*, Louis J. Gallagher, S. J. (tr.) (New York: Random House, 1953), p. 166.
[2] *Ibid.*

to obscurity. Only vague memories of strange names connoting quaint and faraway places remained.[3]

When in 1793 Lord Macartney, leader of a trade mission from Great Britain, refused to perform the kowtow upon his arrival in Peking, he was denied an audience with the emperor, Ch'ien Lung, who sent the following rebuff to King George:

> You, O King, are so inclined toward our civilization that you have sent a special envoy across the seas to bring to our Court your memorial of congratulations on the occasion of my birthday and to present your native products as an expression of your thoughtfulness. On perusing your memorial, so simply worded and sincerely conceived, I am impressed by your respectfulness and friendliness and greatly pleased.
>
> The Celestial Court has pacified and possessed the territory within the four seas. Its sole aim is to do its utmost to achieve good government and to manage political affairs, attaching no value to strange jewels and precious objects. The various articles presented by you, O King, this time are accepted by my special order to the office in charge of such functions in consideration of the offerings having come from a long distance with sincere good wishes. As a matter of fact, the virtue and prestige of the Celestial Dynasty having spread far and wide, the kings of myriad nations come by land and sea with all sorts of precious things. Consequently there is nothing we lack, as your principal envoy and others have themselves observed. We have never set much store on strange or ingenious objects, nor do we need any more of your country's manufacturers. . . .[4]

The American Revolution, which occurred toward the end of Emperor Ch'ien Lung's reign, must have seemed to Ch'ien like an insignificant squabble between white barbarians somewhere in the outer darkness. Perhaps he never even heard of it. At any rate, when the first American ship, the *Empress of China*, reached Canton in 1784 "in the adventurous pursuit of commerce," her master, Captain John Green, was received as just another white barbarian, although he managed to sell for an enormous profit his cargo of furs, cotton, and ginseng weed, which, the Chinese believed, could restore lost virility. By 1789, the year George Wash-

---

[3] John K. Fairbank, *Trade and Diplomacy on the China Coast* (Cambridge: Harvard University Press, 1953), I:10.

[4] Quoted in John K. Fairbank and Ssu-yu Teng (eds.), *China's Response to the West: A Documentary Survey* (Cambridge: Harvard University Press, 1954), p. 19.

ington was inaugurated as President, fifteen American vessels were carrying on trade with China.

The first serious controversy involving Americans and Chinese clearly demonstrated the Chinese attitude. In 1821, a Chinese woman peddling fruit on board the ship *Emily*, anchored in Canton, fell overboard and drowned. The captain of the *Emily* claimed that the death was an accident, but the Chinese officials at Canton insisted that an American sailor, one Francis Terranova, had caused the woman's death by hurling a heavy object at her. They now demanded a life for a life and insisted that the sailor be handed over to them or all trade with the Americans would be stopped immediately. The Americans, in a quandary, refused to hand over Terranova but permitted the Chinese to try him on a murder charge aboard the *Emily*. The Chinese declared him guilty and demanded his custody for execution of the sentence of death by strangulation. The Americans reluctantly complied, and Terranova was executed by the local Cantonese authorities. Shortly after the sentence was carried out, an imperial edict reached the Americans that permitted them to continue their trading but left no doubt in their minds about the emperor's view of them. "As the dispositions of these foreigners are depraved by the education and customs of countries beyond the bounds of civilization," the edict read, "they are incapable of following right reason; their characters are formed; their perverse obstinacy is untameable; and they are dead to the influence of our renovating laws and manners."[5] The Son of Heaven was moved to compassion, however, by a people so dependent upon the products of the Celestial Dynasty that he was willing to permit them to continue their tribute-bearing activities.

These conditions prevailed until the year 1839 when the flourishing opium traffic off the China coast precipitated a major crisis between the British government and China. In the autumn of that year, the Chinese emperor was so disturbed about the ravages of the drug upon the Chinese population that he sent a stern protest to Queen Victoria:

> We find that your country is sixty or seventy thousand li (three li make one mile, ordinarily) from China. Yet there are barbarian ships that strive to come here for trade for the purpose of making a profit. I have

[5] Quoted in Foster Rhea Dulles, *China and America* (Princeton: Princeton University Press, 1946), p. 13.

heard that the smoking of opium is very strictly forbidden by your country; that is because the harm caused by opium is clearly understood. Let us ask, where is your conscience?[6]

The emperor then stated, in conclusion, that "the barbarians could not get along for a single day without two major Chinese exports, tea and rhubarb," and threatened Queen Victoria with an embargo: "If China cuts off these benefits with no sympathy for those who are to suffer, then what can the barbarians rely upon to keep themselves alive?"

The protest went unheeded, and finally the emperor appointed one of his officials, Commissioner Lin, to blockade British merchants at Canton and to destroy their opium. The British interpreted this seizure as an interference with freedom of trade and as an act of aggression. Instead of ending the smuggling of opium, Commissioner Lin had precipitated the Opium War. The war was little more than a skirmish during which the British destroyed the Chinese forts at Canton and imposed upon the empire the Treaty of Nanking of 1842. The Opium War, which signified the first violent encounter between China and a Western nation, came as a terrible shock to the Chinese. There was no room for this phenomenon in the Chinese universe. It was as if the world had suddenly been turned upside down. Strange and inferior people, known to them only through folklore and myth, had suddenly assaulted them out of nowhere and broken their ramparts with superior firepower. As one Chinese edict to the British put it, shortly before the Treaty of Nanking was signed: "Except for your ships being solid, your gunfire fierce, and your rockets powerful, what other abilities have you?"[7]

The Treaty of Nanking compelled the Imperial government to open not only Canton but four other Chinese ports—Amoy, Ningpo, Foochow, and Shanghai—to British trade. Moreover, Britain exacted from China a heavy indemnity and the cession of the island of Hong Kong. At the time the treaty was being signed, an American sea captain, Commodore Lawrence Kearney of the *Constellation*, was anchored in Canton. The captain sized up the situation and immediately demanded from Commissioner Chi-Ying, the Chinese negotiator, that "the trade and commerce of the

[6] Quoted in Fairbank and Teng, *op. cit.*, p. 25.
[7] Quoted in *ibid.*, p. 36.

United States be placed upon the same footing as the nation most favored."[8] This demand was granted, and shortly thereafter the first United States emissary to the Chinese empire, Caleb Cushing, a lawyer from Newburyport, Massachusetts, arrived with a naval squadron of four vessels to formalize the agreement. The first Chinese-American treaty that granted the United States equal privileges to those exacted by Britain was signed at Wanghia in July 1844.

The Chinese negotiators were simply defenseless in the face of Western guns. But they deeply believed in their own cultural superiority and the "backwardness" of the white barbarians in everything but firepower. Chi-Ying, before sitting down with the British and Americans, made it his business to study these strange tribes. A short excerpt from his discoveries is revealing:

> As to these various countries, although they have rulers, they may be either male or female, and they may rule variously for a long or short time, all of which is far beyond the bounds of any system of laws. For example, the English barbarians are ruled by a female, the Americans and the French are ruled by males, the English and French rulers both rule for life, while the ruler of the American barbarians is established by the campaigning of his countrymen, and is changed once in four years— after he leaves the position, he is of equal rank with the common people.[9]

Chi-Ying hoped that if the barbarians were exposed for a short period to the impact of a superior civilization, they would recognize this self-evident fact and depart from the soil of China with their profuse apologies. Hence, the correct way of dealing with the barbarians was to conciliate them and to play them off against each other. For example, Chi-Ying thought nothing of giving the Americans, in 1844, the right to try their own citizens who committed crimes on Chinese soil. An arrangement whereby the barbarians would administer justice to their own nationals and assume responsibility for their good behavior could only be of advantage to the Imperial government. Upon concluding the Treaty of Wanghia with Ambassador Caleb Cushing, Chi-Ying stated that "he could not restrain his spirit from delight and his heart from dilat-

---

[8] Lawrence Kearney, quoted in Dulles, *op. cit.*, p. 28.

[9] Chi-Ying, quoted in Fairbank and Teng, *op. cit.*, p. 39.

ing with joy."[10] This was the beginning of American extraterritorial rights in China.

Early American images of China were deeply colored by the Marco Polo story. At the time the *Empress of China* sailed into Canton harbor, Cathay was described as a great, ancient, and exotic culture devoted to the arts and sciences. By and large, Americans were much too busy with the affairs of revolution and the building of a nation to be concerned with an oriental potentate at the other end of the globe. But the early American writings that exist are permeated with a feeling of profound respect and admiration. The information that the Chinese had invented such things as paper, gunpowder, and the compass and had great sages and philosophers was known to the founders of the American republic. Symbolic of this period was the American conception of Confucius as a venerable Chinese sage who had developed a profound ethical system centuries before the West had become civilized. Actually Confucius had preceded Plato by a little over a century.

Once the seafaring Yankees of the Canton trade had established actual physical contact, American images of China changed drastically. Most of the Americans who came to China in these early days were interested either in making a profit, making converts, or both. Merchants and missionaries soon began to see China as a "backward" nation. The exotic now acquired a tinge of the inferior. In almost all of these early American travelogues there are stories about pigtails, bound feet, ancestor worship, female infanticide, and a host of other sinister practices. Life in China was no longer described as superior but as upside down. The people read from right to left, wrote their surnames ahead of their given names, made soup the last course of a meal, and made a gesture for "come here" when they meant "good-by." The respected Chinese became "Chinamen"; the bearers of a superior civilization became "teeming faceless millions"; and the originators of a profound ethical system became godless heathens. The attitude of superiority of Chinese officials toward Americans was perceived as grotesque arrogance. In Harold Isaacs' telling phrase, the Age of Respect was giving way to the Age of Contempt.[11]

The American reaction to the Terranova incident was already symptomatic of this transition. The murder trial was described as

---

[10] Chi-Ying, quoted in Dulles, *op. cit.*, p. 29.
[11] Harold R. Isaacs, *Images of Asia* (New York: Capricorn Books, 1962), p. 71.

a farce, and only the lack of effective protection by their own government, fear of losing their lucrative trade, and their helpless position in Canton made the Americans give up Terranova to the Cantonese officials. However, the captain of the *Emily* expressed the bitter feelings of the Americans in the following note to the Chinese government:

> We are bound to submit to your laws while we are in your waters, be they ever so unjust. You have, following your ideas of justice, condemned the man unheard. You have the power to compel us. We believe the man innocent, when he is taken from the ship; the commander strikes his colors.[12]

Twenty years later the Americans had reversed the balance of power.

Ambassador Caleb Cushing, who arrived in Canton in 1844 to formalize the Treaty of Wanghia, was to take no presents to the emperor so that no tribute would be inferred. Instead, a varied collection of scientific objects was assembled to impress upon the Chinese the technological achievements of the United States. A list of these objects is worth mentioning: a pair of six-shooters, models of a steam excavator and a steam vessel, a daguerreotype apparatus, a telescope, a barometer, and the *Encyclopedia Americana*. Cushing carried with him a letter of introduction from President John Tyler that addressed the Son of Heaven in a tone customarily reserved for petty American Indian chiefs:

> Great and Good Friend: I hope your health is good. China is a great empire, extending over a great part of the world. The Chinese are numerous. You have millions and millions of subjects. The twenty-six United States are as large as China. Our territories extend from one great ocean to the other. . . . I therefore send to your Court Caleb Cushing, one of the wise and learned men of this country. On his first arrival in China, he will inquire for your health. He has then strict orders to go to your great city of Pekin, and there to deliver this letter. . . .[13]

Cushing's mission, as we have seen, was a great success. The Americans received the most-favored-nation privileges they had come for, including extraterritorial rights. While these rights were granted by the Chinese in the hope of persuading the foreigners to withdraw after they realized their own inferiority, the Americans

---

[12] Quoted in Dulles, *op. cit.*, p. 15.
[13] John Tyler, quoted in *ibid.*, p. 26.

interpreted the Chinese concessions as appeasement stemming from weakness. They had come to force the Chinese to treat them as equals. In the process, American perceptions of China changed so greatly that the positions were completely reversed. It was now the Chinese who were treated as inferior. This first encounter between the nations was thus a surprise to both sides: the Chinese found themselves unable to eject the barbarians through moral persuasion; and the Americans encountered almost no effective military resistance.

* * *

The most striking observation about the early images that China and America held of each other is how little they resembled reality. This is not too surprising since nothing in the history of these nations prepared them for the violent encounter to follow. Matthew Ricci's effort to teach the Chinese about the outside world remained a ripple on the sea of illusions that had been placid for thousands of years. When Caleb Cushing's naval squadron entered Canton harbor, Confucian scholars had to learn about America like children in school. The first Chinese researcher on the United States, Hsu-chi-yu, wrote a primer in 1848 with the following description of Washington:

> There was a certain Wa-sheng-tun (Washington) born in 1731 (sic). When he was ten he lost his father, and his mother educated him and brought him up. He had cherished great ambitions in youth and was gifted in both literary and military matters. When the time came for the multitude of the people to revolt against the British, they urged Tun (Washington) to be their commander. . . .[14]

The Americans, on their part, brimming with ideas of innovation and revolution, quickly lost respect for a civilization that placed little value on expansion and technical progress. Admiration for a superior culture quickly changed to disdain for a backward people. Americans had little patience with a static bureaucracy that could not even defend itself.

Almost everything about the two societies was different. Ancient China venerated tradition above all else. All inspiration came

---

[14] Hsu-chi-yu, quoted in Fairbank and Teng, *op. cit.*, p. 44.

from the past, and history was the queen of the sciences. Early America, on the other hand, looked to the future. Age was a liability, not an asset. The earth's resources had to be harnessed, and the frontiers had to be explored.

What finally brought the two societies into contact in the nineteenth century was the coming of the new imperial age and the growing expansionary drive of America. The two nations met in a world in which one regarded itself as the bearer of tradition and the other became associated with the destruction of tradition. The expansion of Europe that created this new America had also destroyed the old China, and China made her stand against this modern world, stunned and bewildered.

It is reasonable to assume that had the West not forced open the Chinese door, China's perception of itself and of the West would have continued undisturbed. But given the dynamism of Western expansionism, the meeting between China and America was probably inevitable. What made it a tragedy, however, were the illusions that the main participants harbored about each other. The Chinese self-image left no room for learning from the outside world; barbarians would always remain barbarians. The Americans, on the other hand, held directly opposite views: they went to slay dragons in a land where the dragon stood for almost everything that was good. Thus, this first encounter, steeped in misperceptions on both sides, became the seedbed for the great conflicts to follow.

THE BOXER UPRISING AND THE OPEN DOOR

The story of China's dismemberment at the hands of the Western powers in the nineteenth century has often been told. Yet most Western accounts do not fully grasp the fact that this event was probably the greatest disaster that befell China in her entire history. A civilization that saw itself at the top was brought low by the gunboats of a group of assorted barbarians. After the Opium War, a scramble for concessions in China had taken place, considerably reducing China's sovereignty. By 1900, the British, the French, and the Japanese had all defeated China and exacted territories and spheres of influence. Russians and Germans had followed suit and carved out extraterritorial rights with the result that, in most of China's coastal cities, as well as in the capital of Peking, foreign laws reigned supreme, and the Chinese were treated as inferiors in their own country. I still recall how, upon arrival in Shanghai in 1941, I was shocked to see a sign affixed to a foreign club in the international settlement: "Chinese and dogs not permitted." The United States fought no colonial wars in China but benefited from all the concessions exacted by the other Western powers. She, too, enjoyed extraterritorial rights and all the special privileges accorded foreigners under the unequal treaties of the nineteenth century. While the British had brought the first gunboats into the harbor of Canton, Caleb Cushing had also brought his naval squadron. And in 1858, while British and French gunboats besieged Tientsin, an American emissary waited some distance up the river and then joined with the other envoys in signing a treaty that secured for America a share of Chinese territory.

What reduced the old China to dust was, of course, the superior firepower of foreign cannon. But if we are to understand the Chinese reaction at a deeper level, we must ask the question: Why were they so slow to respond? The answer can be found in the Chinese perceptions of themselves and of the West, particularly on the matter of physical force.

Throughout the entire history of the Chinese empire, the ultimate sanction of rule was virtue by example. The right conduct of the Son of Heaven would move all others to respect and obedience, and his virtue would command their loyalty. In all their foreign relations, the Chinese kept this myth intact, even when they were weak. When 3,000 Mongol horsemen threatened Peking, they were given lavish gifts by the emperor, but he insisted that their visit be called a tribute mission. Thus, the fiction of superiority was kept intact; and since the recorded "facts" substantiated the theory, it became self-perpetuating. Physical force seemed unimportant in this context.

Hence, when five major Western powers intruded into China, the one thing that could have stopped the assault was lacking in the Chinese attitude: the resolution to meet force with force. Instead, old techniques were applied to the new situation. The barbarians were conciliated or played off against each other, usually with disastrous results. The Chinese army was decades behind its Western counterparts. It was simply a rabble provided with bags of rice and an assortment of antiquated weapons, including umbrellas, fans, gaily colored flags, and heavy swords. There was no medical staff, and the wounded either died or recovered in the nearest ditch. Pay was unpredictable and the soldiers usually survived by living off the countryside. When they were not on the march, soldiers spent their time smoking, gambling, or prowling after women. Discipline was erratic, though officers thought nothing of beheading conscripts who incurred their displeasure. Men of good family would not join the army, since it was known everywhere that Confucius had held that "good iron is not used for nails and good men are not used for soldiery."

Until the scramble for concessions threatened to swallow up China altogether, Emperor Kuang Hsu was complacent in his conviction that the time-honored techniques would work. There were a few men who perceived reality more accurately, but they remained voices in the wilderness. One of these was Kang Yu-wei, a reformer who appealed to the emperor in 1895 urging a thorough overhaul of the empire if the situation was to be saved. His memorial is a poignant document:

> If Your Majesty will not decide, or will prefer to remain in the old grooves of the Conservatives, then your territories will be swallowed up, your limbs will be bound, your viscera will be cut up, and Your Majesty will scarcely manage to retain your throne or to rule over more than a fragment of Your ancient Empire.[15]

Unless China would modernize and develop firepower to expel the foreign devils, "she would sink in the earth, be buried in ruins, burst like an egg, and be torn to shreds." At the very thought of this, Kang concluded, he was so angry that his "hair stood on end, his eyes stared out of their sockets, and he was not able to endure it for a single day." Finally, in 1898, Kuang Hsu listened and attempted some reforms, but with little success. The resistance of the Confucian conservatives was too strong, and later that year the old Empress Dowager Tzu Hsi deposed him in a coup d'état and assumed control of the government. The short-lived reforms came

---

[15] Kang Yu-wei, quoted in William L. Langer, *The Diplomacy of Imperialism* (New York: Knopf, 1935), II: 677

to an abrupt end. The old empress nurtured a fierce hatred for the "foreign devils." In an edict of November 1899, she complained that "the various powers cast upon China looks of tiger-like voracity, hustling each other in their endeavors to be the first to seize upon her innermost territories."[16] Yet she refused to meet the challenge realistically, and when the old China finally did respond with violence, the result was a failure.

At about the time of the empress' edict, a popular movement began to flare up in northern China describing itself as the Fists of Righteous Harmony, to be known later and more popularly as the Boxers. These bands were held together by fierce hatred of the Westerners and their ceaseless pressure and interference with indigenous customs. Many of the Boxers believed, for example, that the foreign devils had built railroads and telegraph lines for the express purpose of murdering the good spirits of the harvest, for when it rained, the wires would rust and reddish drops would fall to the ground, obviously the blood of good spirits impaled on the wires. The barbarians had also built buildings steeper than any in China, obviously constructed so that benevolent spirits, flying low over the countryside, would crash to death. Worse, the foreigners had disturbed the ancestral burial grounds, desecrated holy places, and made a tourist attraction of the Temple of Heaven in Peking. By early 1900, armed bands roamed the countryside, burning foreign property and taking the lives of "secondary devils," Chinese converts to Christianity. By the spring, Peking was encircled by fanatical bands who robbed, pillaged, burned, and killed as they advanced. They no longer concealed their objective of driving all the barbarians into the sea. The empress, herself fiercely antiforeign, gave the movement her tacit and, at times, open support.

The story of the Boxers' siege of Peking is well known and will not be recounted here. What is less well known is the image the Boxers held of themselves that led directly to their disastrous defeat. They believed, in effect, that they were invulnerable, that Western bullets could not harm them, since right and justice were on their side. In April 1900, for example, placards appeared all over Peking proclaiming that God Himself had come down to earth to support the Boxers in their struggle:

[16] Tzu Hsi, quoted in *ibid.*, p. 693.

In a certain street in Peking some worshippers at midnight suddenly saw a spirit descend in their midst. The spirit was silent for a long time. Then a terrible voice was heard saying: I am none other than the Great Yu Ti (god of the unseen world) come down in person. Disturbances are to be dreaded from the foreign devils; everywhere they are erecting telegraphs and building railways. Their sins are numberless as the hair on the head. Therefore am I wroth and my thunders have pealed forth. I have given forth my decree that I shall descend to earth at the head of all the saints and spirits and wherever the I-ho Chuan (Boxers) are gathered together, there shall the Gods be in the midst of them. Therefore I expressly command you to make this known in every place. . . .[17]

Encouraged by their self-proclaimed invulnerability and "800,000 spirit soldiers," the Boxers burst into Peking in June 1900, assassinated the German and the Japanese ministers, and laid siege to the foreign legations. During the fifty-five days of the siege, the empress vacillated. One day she would send supplies to the beleaguered legations and on the next urge the Boxer leaders to destroy them. At any time, she could have lifted the siege or crushed the foreigners. But she did neither. One cannot be quite sure about the old lady's state of mind during those crucial days. But it is likely that her inaction stemmed from the conflict of her Confucian convictions against violence and her desire to get rid of the barbarians. At any rate, when the international relief expedition entered Peking in August and the siege was lifted, the empress had left the capital in headlong flight, leaving the responsibility of dealing with the victorious foreigners to a veteran Chinese diplomat, Li Hung-chang.

After the Boxer fiasco, China could not but agree to the harsh terms imposed upon her by the Western powers. The Boxer Protocol of 1901 included several items that were bitterly resented by the Imperial Court, but there was no alternative but to accept them. The leaders of the uprising were to be executed, and monuments to foreigners who had lost their lives were to be erected in each of the foreign settlements. The importation of arms and ammunition was to be prohibited for five years, and an indemnity of 450 million taels was imposed on the Chinese treasury. In the words of one thoughtful student of the period, the function of the

[17] Quoted in G. N. Steiger, *China and the Occident* (New Haven: Yale University Press, 1927), pp. 144–145.

Manchu government now became little more than a debt-collecting agency for the foreign penetration.[18]

At the time the Boxer rising was beginning to smolder in the Chinese countryside, the United States was deeply preoccupied with the Spanish-American War. But after Admiral George Dewey's victory and President William McKinley's famous decision, "after having walked the floor of the White House all night," to annex the Philippines, the attention of the United States government shifted to the Far East. The quest for concessions by the European powers worried American business interests who feared that they might be excluded from China altogether. Pressures for a more spirited United States Far Eastern policy mounted during 1899 and finally led to the famous American circular letter to the European powers known as the Open Door notes.

A great deal has been written about these notes and, hence, a brief summary will suffice here. What is interesting for our purposes is the astounding difference between what most American leaders at the time believed the Open Door to be and what it really was. Many of these misperceptions have lived down to the present day.

The Open Door notes of September 1899 are usually associated with the American Secretary of State John Hay. Actually, they were deeply influenced by two other men, one an American, the other a Britisher. When John Hay assumed the office of secretary of state in late 1898, he had no adviser on Far Eastern affairs. He had never been to China and had only a most cursory knowledge of the Far East. Thus, he brought with him to Washington an old friend, William W. Rockhill, who had served in the diplomatic corps in China. Rockhill, however, had not been to China in seven years and was somewhat out of touch with the rapidly changing events in that country. In June 1898, a friend of Rockhill's, the Englishman A. E. Hippisley of the Chinese Imperial Customs Service, then under the command of Sir Robert Hart, passed through Washington on his way to England. Hippisley was concerned about the threat of other European powers to British commercial interests in China. Britain controlled about 80 percent of Western trade with China and wanted to maintain the status

---

[18] Chester Tan, *The Boxer Catastrophe* (New York: Columbia University Press, 1955), pp. 215–236.

quo.[19] Hence, Hippisley urged Rockhill to persuade Hay to approach the European powers and to get from them an assurance that there would be no interference with foreign trade in each other's spheres of influence. Spheres of influence, he said, were here to stay and had to be treated as existing facts.[20] Rockhill sensed a congruence of British and American interests in China. He realized that an American initiative to the European powers would serve a double purpose: it would restate the most-favored-nation principle, which the United States had enunciated at the Treaty of Wanghia in 1844, but it would also put the United States on record as being against the further dismemberment of the Chinese empire. Hay was impressed and, after some initial reluctance to play into the hands of Great Britain, decided to go along with Rockhill's recommendation. The result was a circular memorandum dispatched on September 6, 1899, to London, St. Petersburg, and Berlin and a month later to Paris, Rome, and Tokyo, in which the United States asked the six powers concerned not to interfere in each other's treaty ports and spheres of influence and to observe trade equality for everyone. These were the original Open Door notes.

Upon close scrutiny, the notes did not amount to very much. First, they were inspired by a British subject and were in essence a restatement of British policy. William Langer asserts, in fact, that "the American position was exactly that of Britain."[21] Second, they represented no novel departure for the United States, but merely reasserted privileges claimed by, and granted to, the United States half a century earlier. Third, the replies of the six powers were evasive and noncommittal. The American ambassador at St. Petersburg, for example, warned Hay that the Russian government "did not wish to answer the propositions at all and finally did so with great reluctance."[22] Nevertheless, Hay announced on March 20, 1900, that he had received "satisfactory assurances from all the powers addressed" and that he regarded each as "final and defin-

---

[19] George F. Kennan, *American Diplomacy 1900–1950* (New York: Mentor Books, 1952), p. 27.

[20] *Ibid.*, p. 34.

[21] Langer, *op. cit.*, p. 687.

[22] Tyler Dennett, *John Hay* (New York: Macmillan, 1933), p. 294.

itive."[23] Finally, the notes had little if any impact on the fate of China. They were dispatched only a few months before the Boxer fiasco and its bitter consequences for the Chinese empire.

The interpretation put upon the Open Door notes by the American public at the time was very different. Almost without exception, the American press hailed the notes as a triumph of American diplomacy. The Chicago *Herald* declared that "there had never been a more brilliant and important achievement in diplomacy," and the New York *Evening Post* described the notes as a "noble work of peace." The two major political parties voiced their approval. The prevailing opinion was well summed up by one contemporary publicist:

> The "open-door" policy in China was an American idea. It was set up in contrast to the "spheres-of-influence" policy practised by other nations. . . .
> The "open-door" is one of the most creditable episodes in American diplomacy, an example of benevolent impulse accompanied by energy and shrewd skill in negotiation. Not one of the statesmen and nations that agreed to Hay's policy wanted to. It was like asking every man who believes in truth to stand up—the liars are obliged to be the first to rise. Hay saw through them perfectly; his insight into human nature was one of his strongest qualities.[24]

The gap between reality and the American perception of the Open Door is not difficult to explain. The Hay notes committed the United States to absolutely nothing. There was no sacrifice of any kind. Yet, the formula had a lofty and idealistic ring and sounded good at home. It made the United States appear as the arbiter among the self-seeking European powers and the protector of the weak. The very term "Open Door" conjured up rights of equal opportunity without fear or favor. And the United States was to be their guarantor.

Actually, the Open Door notes were quickly overtaken by events. Three months after Hay noted his satisfaction with the responses of the European powers, the Boxers laid siege to Peking.

---

[23] John Hay, quoted in A. Whitney Griswold, *The Far Eastern Policy of the United States* (New York: Harcourt, Brace, 1938), p. 78.

[24] Mark Sullivan, *Our Times: The Turn of the Century* (New York: Macmillan, 1926), p. 509.

On July 3, 1900, in the midst of the siege, Hay sent a follow-up circular note in which he reiterated the points made earlier and added that it was "the policy of the Government of the United States to seek to preserve Chinese territorial and administrative entity." Once again, the reaction of the American public was favorable, and the image of the United States as the protector of China permeated the contemporary American press. However, as George F. Kennan points out, this second set of notes had no practical effect outside the United States.[25] In fact, by August 1900, the international relief expedition was on its way to Peking. Of the 19,000 allied forces, 2,500 were American troops. Furthermore, the United States was one of the signatories of the Boxer Protocol of 1901.

While the United States government was hesitant at first to take an active part in the suppression of the Boxer rising, the siege of its legation in Peking tipped the scales. The American minister in Peking, K. H. Conger, encouraged legation guards to open fire on Chinese troops and called these actions "exhibitions of skill and courage that would serve as good object lessons."[26] Americans generally regarded the Boxers as ruffians who deserved the same treatment as ordinary criminals. Most contemporary American diplomats tended to regard the Protocol of 1901 as a lenient settlement for China.[27]

The final irony occurred in November 1900 when John Hay, the author of the policy of the Open Door, instructed his minister in Peking to seek to obtain for the United States a naval base and territorial concession at Samsah Bay in the province of Fukien, thus abandoning the basic premise of his entire policy. This American attempt to join in the scramble for concessions was thwarted by the Japanese government, which politely pointed out that Fukien was within its sphere of influence and noted its surprise that the United States, of all powers, should attempt to interfere. Hay abandoned the venture in disillusionment, and Rockhill, in a letter to Hippisley, expressed the hope that it would be "a long time

---

[25] Kennan, *op. cit.*, p. 38.

[26] K. H. Conger, quoted in Steiger, *op. cit.*, pp. 221–222.

[27] Edward Thomas Williams, *China Yesterday and Today* (New York: Thomas Y. Crowell, 1923), p. 424.

before the United States would get into another muddle of this description."[28] Thus ended the American policy of the Open Door in China.

The misperceptions that plagued the relations between China and America during the latter half of the nineteenth century added enormously to the tragedy of the encounter. Half a century separated Caleb Cushing's arrival in Canton from the Boxer rising. During that period, the leadership of the Chinese empire did not yield its self-image of moral and cultural superiority or its conviction that the barbarians would recognize these qualities and behave like the tribute-bearing missions of old. Nor did it recognize the Western cannon as a totally new factor to be reckoned with, but rather it preferred to meet physical force with the time-honored tactics of conciliation. Even extraterritorial concessions were not resented at first, but were seen by the Chinese as convenient devices whereby the barbarians would apply their own laws to their fellow barbarians without involving China. There was little if any feeling of Chinese nationalism in those early days.

As the European powers began to carve up China in earnest and the competition for concessions gathered speed, the Imperial government was forced to acquiesce almost without resistance. Only in 1900, when the capital itself was divided up and the hated barbarians had reached the Temple of Heaven, did the Boxer uprising take place. And even then, there was almost no awareness of reality. In the face of Western guns the Boxer myths of invulnerability and of countless armies of "spirit soldiers" led straight to their defeat. The self-image of the old China was only shattered on the rock of the Boxer Protocol.

The attitude of the United States toward the Chinese empire was also one of moral superiority. The Americans had not waged war against China, but they had received the same privileges as the European powers. Nevertheless, they wished to draw a clear distinction between themselves and the "imperialists." This the American government attempted to do through the Open Door notes. As we have seen, these circular memoranda of 1899 were little more than a free-trade "me too" claim, although those of 1900 made an unsuccessful

[28] William W. Rockhill, quoted in Griswold, *op. cit.*, p. 83.

effort to uphold the integrity of China. Yet the myth was established that "in this episode of the Open Door notes, a tremendous blow had been struck for the triumph of American principles in international society—an American blow for an American idea."[29] Neither their ineffectiveness nor American unwillingness to enforce the notes, nor in fact Hay's departure from the goals set forth in them—"none of these things succeeded in shaking in any way the established opinion of the American public."[30] The Americans saw the Chinese as their wards and themselves as superior to the petty power politics of the Europeans. To America, the Open Door was a democratic policy guaranteeing equal opportunity to all and at the same time protecting the integrity of China. To China, the Americans had arrived late at the Western holdup, but just in time to share in the spoils. The door of China had never opened voluntarily; it had been crashed in.

The Boxer rising was never perceived in the United States as a legitimate nationalist movement. Rather, the Boxers were seen as criminals and fanatics. One contemporary American diplomat describes the edicts of the empress dowager as "the cruel decrees of a selfish ruler" and the uprising itself as "the barbarity of a frenzied mob."[31] Hence, when the empire finally responded with force, the United States felt virtually betrayed by its protégé. So pervasive had the American self-image of the benevolent protector become that the Chinese attempt at self-assertion was met with fury. This explains why an American minister was able to order his troops to open fire on the Boxers "as an object lesson" and why another described the Boxer Protocol as "lenient." It also explains the United States participation in the suppression of the Boxer rising through force of arms.

Communist historians in China today describe the early relations between China and America in terms of a capitalist plot intended to victimize China, creating an image of victimization at the hands of a great evil force invading China. In the words of a leading scholar, "this makes for self-pity, resentment, and the need for an explanation of history in the terms of evil and injus-

[29] Kennan, *op. cit.*, p. 41.
[30] *Ibid.*
[31] Quoted in Williams, *op. cit.*, p. 423.

tice."[32] The Opium War and its aftermath left a more lasting impression on the present Communist leaders than on the apolitical peasants of the preceding century. The American response, on the other side of the gap, generally is a startled "Who, me?" when confronted with the historical data. The self-image of moral superiority coupled with one of benevolence toward China persists even today.

Reflection shows that neither the American nor the Chinese images tally with the facts. No one-dimensional, communist-devil theory showing how American capitalism attacked, betrayed, and exploited the Chinese people, diverting their otherwise "normal development toward Communism," will do. Nor is the typical American textbook history of the period any more satisfactory. It is true that in general the Western impact was a disaster for China and that the United States was a part of that impact. But this disaster was not the result of a plot; rather, it was the predictable result of Western civilization expanding and coming into contact with the last remaining separate, distinct, and isolated empire in the world, one that conceived of itself as superior to all others. Under this impact, the old China crumbled. As John K. Fairbank puts it: "circumstances made China the worst accident case in history."[33] The reciprocal images that accompanied these historical circumstances deepened the tragedy even further and made it echo down into the next century.

[32] John K. Fairbank, "Why Peking Casts Us as the Villain," *The New York Times*, May 22, 1966.

[33] Testimony of John K. Fairbank in U.S. Senate Committee on Foreign Relations, *U.S. Policy with Respect to Mainland China*, 89th Cong., 2nd sess. (1966), p. 102.

Chapter Three

Chiang Kai-shek and the United States

The twentieth century brought many profound upheavals in Chinese society. The shock of the Boxer defeat forced many Chinese intellectuals to reevaluate their positions in relation to the West. The year 1901 had demonstrated in the most explicit terms that whatever the barbarians' cultural inferiority might be, their firepower was overwhelmingly superior. Consequently, a whole new generation of students began studying the West in an entirely different light. They largely ignored its culture, its arts, and its literature. Instead, they carefully studied its science and technology for the express purpose of using this knowledge to expel the foreigners from China.

Accompanying this development was a widespread movement for political reform under the leadership of Sun Yat-sen. The Manchu dynasty was doomed, for although it had managed to survive the upheavals of the nineteenth century, it had lost an irretrievable amount of face with the Boxer defeat. In 1911, it succumbed to the revolutionary movement and the Republic of China was formally declared.

The republic, however, was beset by internal weakness. It had been born as a parliamentary democracy—with a representative legislature, an elected chief of state, and a judiciary—but with little of the requisite life force. There was no tradition of self-government on the national level, and the revolutionary party was a loosely organized group of intellectuals with little, if any, popular support. It fell prey almost immediately to factional strife within

29

its own ranks. Yuan Shih-k'ai, who had become the first president of China, attempted to declare himself emperor, and only his death in 1916 ensured his failure. The next seven years were a confused time of local revolt and internecine struggle within the revolutionary movement.

The revolution entered a new phase in 1923 when Sun Yat-sen embarked upon a complete reorganization of his party, the Kuomintang. His requests for aid from the West having been ignored, he turned to the Soviet Union for counsel. The USSR responded with material aid and expert advisers in the technique of revolution and helped to establish in 1924 a military academy at Whampoa to train officers for the Chinese army.

The next step was seen as the subjugation of various northern warlords entrenched in their respective satrapies. SunYat-sen died in 1925, however, and the northern expedition was carried out under the leadership of a young general who had risen rapidly in Kuomintang politics to become Sun's successor. This young man was Chiang Kai-shek, later generalissimo of China. His northern expedition was a success, but internal strains were soon evident within the Kuomintang. In 1927, Chiang Kai-shek purged all Communists from his party and spent the following years consolidating his power against recalcitrant dissidents and warlords. From 1931, moreover, he was under increasing pressure from the Japanese, who had begun their encroachments into Chinese territory.

During this time, Americans were largely unaware of events in China. American missionaries continued their efforts to convert China to Christianity and sent back periodic reports on their work to the faithful at home. The Western powers confined themselves to preserving their extraterritorial privileges in the face of the revolutionary turmoil in China, but there was little understanding even at the policy-making level of the nature of the revolution in which China was enmeshed. As for the public-at-large, it was dimly aware that China was the scene of considerable fighting, but the impression was one of general chaos in a remote land whose political impact on the United States was negligible.

Only the Sino-Japanese War brought China to the attention of the American public. The Japanese bombardment of Shanghai and the savage conquest of Nanking were greeted with horror in the United States, while China's continued resistance against heavy Japanese odds excited increasing admiration. As the 1930s drew to a close, the American people's image of China grew to heroic proportions—an image of a dogged, patient, indomitable people fighting with boundless determination against a brutal foreign intruder.[1]

This image was well described by an American who spent the war years in Chungking and several Chinese provinces:

> I had come back that summer [1940] with a full set of standard ideas about the Kuomintang's war, acquired from the American press: the gallant losing battles, the brave and clever guerrillas, the millions of determined refugees fleeing west; later, the firmly held fronts beyond which there would be no retreat, and behind them a new country a-building; the factories in the caves, the busy co-ops, the new roads and schools and hospitals, and looming over the whole united land, the massive figure of the Generalissimo, his attractive wife only slightly in the background. As a prewar visitor to China, when I read about such things in America I had marveled: "How different from the place I knew!" The idea that a new China was emerging from the war was one reason why I returned.[2]

Such images are frequently personified in an individual figure, particularly in moments of high historical drama, for strong feelings of admiration or horror are not easily applied to abstract entities such as nations; they run deep and require a human recipient. Thus, the Third Reich became "Hitler's Germany"; England was embodied in the formidable figure of Churchill; and it was only natural that the image of a heroic China was personified in the figure of the Kuomintang leader Chiang Kai-shek.

America's apotheosis of China between 1936 and 1945 came to be the apotheosis of the generalissimo. The image grew to extravagant dimensions, portraying Chiang as a hero, a soldier-saint, and savior of modern China. Above all, Chiang was shown as a defender of democracy—a tough and seasoned soldier whose fight was the same as that of America. "If the United States must face the Axis on two fronts," declared *Fortune* magazine in 1941, "it can do so for one reason: that a Free China is fighting the Battle of the Pacific.... The future history of China rests on him

---

[1] See Harold Issacs, *Images of Asia* (New York: Capricorn Books, 1962), chap. 7.

[2] Graham Peck, *Two Kinds of Time* (Boston: Houghton Mifflin, 1950), p. 35.

[Chiang]; and he has so far discharged his responsibility with superb skill."[3]

Time magazine designated Generalissimo and Madame Chiang "Man and Wife of the Year" in 1938 and asserted that the generalissimo "had remade China" and that "after centuries, the Chinese people had at last found a leader."[4] Much was also made of the fact that Chiang was a Christian, and the missionary press acclaimed him widely.

> To the missionaries, Chiang's acceptance of Christianity raised limitless hopes. Many even believed that China would now become a Christian nation. For the first time they could look forward to official support for their endeavors. And in return for this bright promise, the missionaries and their supporters at home gave Chiang Kai-shek and his wife, from 1930 on, their passionate and uncritical support.[5]

The hero image rose to even further heights. A pamphlet published by the Institute of Pacific Relations in 1942 compared Chiang Kai-shek to George Washington and drew analogies between the Chinese and American revolutions:

> As revolutionary America produced a great leader in war and peace— George Washington—so revolutionary China has produced a great leader—Chiang Kai-shek. Revolutionary China of today is not behind the revolutionary America of more than a hundred and fifty years ago. . . . Her war is a people's war and its impact has stimulated both the spirit and the practice of democracy in wartime China. . . . China is at last awake to modern techniques and modern ideas. She has acquired both chiefly from America. . . . Her future form of government will be an adaptation of Western democratic institutions to her own conditions and national genius.[6]

During the civil war between the Nationalists and the Communists in the late 1940s, Americans added yet another facet to the image of the generalissimo. Not only was Chiang Kai-shek a leading defender of democracy; he now became the United States'

---

[3] "China the Ally," *Fortune*, 24 (September 1941), 44, 49.

[4] *Time*, 31 (January 3, 1938), 14–15.

[5] Felix Greene, *A Curtain of Ignorance* (Garden City, N.Y.: Doubleday, 1964), p. 12.

[6] Robert W. Barnett, "China—America's Ally," *Far Eastern Pamphlet No. 5* (New York: Institute of Pacific Relations, 1942), pp. 24–25.

trusted friend in the common struggle against communism. Chiang Kai-shek, the Christian general, would fight side by side with America against the threat of atheistic communism. This image permeated American thinking during the 1940s and provided the basis for most decisions on China policy. A perusal of Chiang's record reveals a picture that is at great variance with the image described above. Let us first examine the extent of the Chinese leader's commitment to democratic rule.

Chiang Kai-shek's political model for the Kuomintang came not from the democratic West but from China's Confucian past. Once he was in complete power after the purge of the Communists in 1927, Chiang looked more and more for his inspiration to the example of Imperial China. In November 1928, he urged the officers of the Kuomintang army to delve into the Confucian classics in their leisure time. In 1931, he declared Confucius' birthday a national holiday, and Nationalist troops were ordered to give special protection to Confucian temples throughout China. In 1934, Chiang decreed the canonization of Confucius, and the Confucian temple at Kufow became a national shrine.

It is particularly significant that, after Confucius, the figure that Chiang Kai-shek admired most was Tseng Kuo-fan, the political architect of the T'ung-Chih Restoration, that short-lived decade in the 1860s described by a leading scholar as "the last stand of Chinese conservatism."[7] Tseng Kuo-fan made a last determined effort to renovate the Manchu dynasty, to restore the traditional Confucian virtues, and to prevent the massive Western incursions into China. The effort failed because the problems faced by Imperial China could not be solved by the restoration of the Confucian order. In essence, Tseng Kuo-fan was a political anachronism. Nevertheless, Chiang Kai-shek admired him as one of the greatest men in Chinese history.

It is easy to see that Chiang Kai-shek hardly fitted the American perception of the democratic leader. The Confucian leader governs by precept and example, not through elections; he stands at the top of a political pyramid whose hierarchy and structure he controls. The concept of a "loyal opposition" is unknown to him;

[7] Mary C. Wright, *The Last Stand of Chinese Conservatism* (Stanford: Stanford University Press, 1957).

he governs not by mandate of the people, but by the "Mandate of Heaven."

There is little wonder that a few leading Americans, upon close contact with Chiang, were shocked and surprised at what they saw. General Stilwell, for example, the United States military adviser to the Kuomintang, made the following entry in his diary on August 2, 1942:

> His [Chiang's] obstinacy refused description. He has lost all habit of discussion in fact because everybody around him is a yes-man. No one dares tell him an unpleasant truth because he gets mad. . . . He is not taking a single forward step, or doing anything concrete to improve the position of China, and so, incidentally, his own.[8]

Chiang Kai-shek was no enemy of democracy. He simply came from a completely different tradition, which he tried his best to restore and with which Americans had no empathy whatsoever.

The American perception of Chiang's violent anticommunism was equally far from the mark. While it is true that, after the purge of 1927, Chiang turned against the Communists, there is strong evidence that the origins of the Kuomintang and of the Communist party in China were almost the same. Both were conceived in the anti-Western reaction that swept China in the early 1920s. Chiang's political power base, at that time, was the Whampoa Military Academy of which he was the commander. He openly collaborated with the Communists, and many leading members of the Chinese Communist party occupied prominent posts in the Kuomintang. Mao Tse-tung's first significant appearance on the historical stage, for example, took place in 1924, when he was elected an alternate member of the Kuomintang Central Executive Committee. Stuart Schram, author of a leading political biography of Mao, observes that: "In this triangular relationship of Moscow, the Kuomintang, and the Chinese Communist Party, the position of Mao Tse-tung during the crucial years 1925–1927 was on the whole closer to that of the Kuomintang than to that of either Stalin or Chen Tu-Hsiu [the Head of the Chinese Communist Party]."[9] Schram also states that it is probable that "Mao

[8] Joseph W. Stilwell, *The Stilwell Papers*, Theodore H. White (ed.) (New York: William Sloane Associates, 1947), p. 133.

[9] Stuart Schram, *Mao Tse-tung* (New York: Simon and Schuster, 1966), p. 71.

was more at ease within the Kuomintang than within his own party."[10]

While these observations may seem startling to Americans, exposed for decades to the image of Chiang as an anti-Communist, the following excerpt from a speech he made in Changsha in 1926, provides revealing evidence of his views:

> Only after the overthrow of imperialism can China obtain freedom. In the present world revolution, there is the Third International, which can be called the general staff of the revolution. If we want our revolution to succeed, we must unite with Russia to overthrow imperialism. If Russia aids the Chinese revolution, does that mean she wants to oblige China to apply Communism? No, she wants us to carry out the national revolution. If the Communists join the Kuomintang, does this mean that they want to apply Communism? No, they do not want to do that either; they want to apply the Three People's Principles. I am persuaded that the Communists who have joined our party do not, at the present time, want to apply Communism, but want rather to carry out the national revolution. The Chinese revolution is part of the world revolution. We want to unite the partisans of the world revolution to overthrow imperialism.[11]

There is a striking similarity between these words and an article written by Mao Tse-tung in 1926, the first item of his *Selected Works*. Mao was in fact the head of the Peasant Institute of the Kuomintang in 1926, and, Lin Piao, his favorite disciple, was a student at the Whampoa Military Academy, which was supported with funds, advisers, and weapons by the Soviet Union.

All this is not to imply that Chiang Kai-shek was a Communist. It is merely to point out that, during the early part of his career, he made common cause with the Communists against Western imperialism in China. Chiang had suffered no harm at the hands of the Communists but he had witnessed the dismemberment of China by the Western powers. And to him that was a greater evil than communism. Most Americans perceived the Nationalists and the Communists as radically antithetical elements, with Chiang Kai-shek, the Christian general, battling the Communists on behalf of the forces of freedom and righteousness. This perception was at odds with reality. Chiang's desire to restore the Confucian

[10] *Ibid.*

[11] Chiang Kai-shek, quoted in *ibid.*, p. 83.

imperial tradition and Mao's goal of a Communist peasant revolution made them allies in the common cause of national self-assertion against the Western presence in China. The break between them in 1927 and the events that followed were essentially the manifestations of a struggle for power, not a conflict over ideological differences.

The progress of relations between China and America was further complicated by perceptual errors on the part of Chiang. These included Chiang's self-image, as well as his view of the United States.

In 1926, an American reporter named Lewis Gannett interviewed the young commander-in-chief of the Chinese Nationalist army. Gannett wanted to know what the general thought of America. The reply was revealing:

> Thinking men in China hate America more than they hate Japan. Japan talks to us in ultimatums; she says frankly she wants special privileges. . . . We understand that and we know how to meet it. The Americans come to us with smiling faces and friendly talk, but in the end your government acts just like the Japanese. And we, disarmed by your fair words, do not know how to meet such insincerity. This is what is behind the anti-Christian movement in China. Your missionaries write "charity" over their doors, and I do not deny that many of them are good men who do good work. But in the end they make it easier for American policy to follow that of the other imperialist powers. So because we have been deceived by your sympathetic talk, we end by hating you most.[12]

A year later, this same general, Chiang Kai-shek, purged the Communists from the Kuomintang and established his government at Nanking. Shortly thereafter, he became a Christian and, after the Japanese assault on Manchuria, a client of the United States. With the attack on Pearl Harbor, he became a full-fledged ally. Nevertheless, his perceptions of the United States had not changed significantly since that first interview in 1926. They emerge quite clearly from his book China's Destiny, first published in March 1943, especially since it was written at a time when the United States considered China a staunch ally and a loyal and steadfast friend. The book interprets China's history in the nineteenth century as the destructive result of Western penetration.

---

[12] Chiang Kai-shek, quoted in Harold Isaacs, "Old Myths and New Realities," Diplomat (September 1966), p. 45.

The unequal treaties forced upon the Manchu rulers during that time are given as the major cause of decay of all aspects of Chinese life, ranging from politics and law to ethics and psychology. Highly charged phrases, such as "national humiliation" and "the bondage of the unequal treaties," recur constantly.

> During the last hundred years, China's national position and the morale of the people deteriorated to such an extent that an unprecedented situation developed. . . . The oppression and bondage of the unequal treaties further undermined the Chinese state and the nation. . . . The national decay during the last hundred years reached a point unequaled in our history . . . until the basis of rebirth and recovery was almost destroyed.[13]

The second chapter of the book is entitled "The Origins of National Humiliation and the Sources of the Revolution." Its opening sentence sets the tone for the rest of the section: "The deterioration of China's national position and the low morale of the people during the last hundred years can be largely attributed to the unequal treaties. The implementation of the unequal treaties constitutes a complete record of China's national humiliation."[14]

America is not singled out for special recrimination, as in contemporary Chinese Communist historiography, but it is nowhere excluded from blame. At times, this omission is quite pointed: "Whenever one country obtained a new privilege from its treaty with China, all the other countries would, under the evil 'most-favored-nation' clause, enjoy the same benefits. The special privileges provided in a treaty were often amplified by the foreign interpretation of its terms."[15] It should be remembered that the United States had been one of the chief beneficiaries of the most-favored-nation policy in the nineteenth century.

Those who compared Chiang with George Washington and saw him as the West's firm ally might have been disturbed by his statement that "the main objective of the Nationalist Revolution was to escape from the bondage of the unequal treaties and especially to overcome the habits of arrogance, lawlessness, and the

---

[13] Chiang Kai-shek, China's Destiny, Philip Jaffe (ed.) (New York: Roy Publishers, 1947), p. 42.

[14] Ibid., p. 44.

[15] Ibid., p. 52. Italics added.

attitude of servile dependence upon foreign powers that had been fostered under the unequal treaties."[16] The anti-Western feelings of the author of China's Destiny are immediately apparent to the reader. Nor could these feelings be dismissed as the personal idiosyncrasy of Chiang, for the book was made a basic text in the training of all Kuomintang party members, government officials, and officer candidates. Yet after some negative editorial reactions in the United States, the book attracted little, if any, attention, while the myth of a firm Sino-American friendship lived on. Even Franklin D. Roosevelt, who harbored few illusions about the stability of Chiang's regime, retained the conviction that the two nations were united by a traditional rapport. At a private conference on China policy in Cairo on December 6, 1943, he remarked, "Well, now, we've been friends with China for a great many years. . . . They really like us and just between ourselves, they don't like the British."[17]

Much of this myth could be attributed to the American people's sincere feelings of goodwill toward China. We have seen how firmly the United States had come to believe in the benevolence of its historical role in China. And, being allies in a worldwide struggle, the two nations were commonly presumed to be united by bonds of friendship. To admit that the alliance was but a temporary congruence of national interests would have involved a total reconstruction of America's image of her relations with China. Hence, in order to maintain an internal coherence of outlook, it was necessary to presume that the Chinese were not only allies but friends as well. "By projection, this American benevolence toward China was transformed into an exaggerated notion of Chinese friendship for the United States. The extravagant idea of America's popularity in China influenced the estimate of the consequences of a Communist-controlled China for American interests in the Far East."[18]

Yet there were more deliberate elements that helped to solidify the myth. An English translation of China's Destiny did not appear in the United States until after the war. The United States

---

[16] Ibid., p. 69.

[17] Franklin D. Roosevelt, quoted in Stilwell, op. cit., pp. 251–252.

[18] Tang Tsou, America's Failure in China, 1941–1950 (Chicago: University of Chicago Press, 1963), p. 149.

State Department had made a translation for its own use but kept the document classified as "top secret" and refused to release it even in 1946, when a group of six congressmen requested to see it in connection with a major congressional debate on China policy. It was not propitious, the State Department said, to release the document at that time.[19] When a translation of the book finally appeared after the war, it was an "authorized" translation, with most of the anti-Western references that might have been offensive to the American reader deleted. Thus, in order to see what Kuomintang officers were reading in their training classes, one had to consult the unauthorized, but accurate, edition.

This official effort to "decontaminate" the real Chiang Kai-shek and to project an image of the "strong Christian general" to the American public must be understood against the larger background of United States-China relations.

One theme that recurs again and again in American accounts of United States' relations with China is the interpreting of events in a strongly moralistic light. Conflicts of interest and hard facts of power are often transmuted into conflicts between good and evil. The world is seen as divided into two camps of which one represents the force of righteousness and the other the forces of darkness. Thus, Americans since the Open Door, and even before, traditionally saw themselves as the benevolent guardians of China. The Chinese were generally seen as the object of American philanthropy, as wards—"devilishly exasperating wards sometimes, but still as wards."[20] The fact that the United States benefited from all the concessions exacted by the European powers was generally glossed over. Nor could it be admitted that the anti-Western passions of the new revolutionary Chinese leadership extended to the United States. Hence, the alliance with Chiang Kai-shek was not perceived in the United States as an arrangement brought about by the power alignments of the period, but rather as an alignment of the forces of justice in a moral battle. It was believed that Nationalists and Communists represented two completely opposite sets of motives and aspirations. Few Americans perceived the complex truth that the Nationalist and Communist

---

[19] Philip Jaffe, "The Secret of 'China's Destiny,' " in Chiang Kai-shek, *China's Destiny*, *op. cit.*, p. 18.

[20] Isaacs, "Old Myths and New Realities," *op. cit.*, p. 42.

revolutions were *both* essentially anti-Western and that the struggle between them was much more a struggle for power between competing forms of authoritarianism than a conflict between radically different ideologies.

A leading historian of American relations with China offers another perceptive insight:

> Americans are a funny folk. They applaud moral sentiment but they are rarely ready . . . to take the next step, to make effective the sentiment which they applaud. The time comes when they are asked to put up or shut up. They do neither. They will not put up the force without which sentiments in this wicked world are still sentiments only, but neither will they shut up. They keep talking about the sentiments as if wishes were horses.[21]

A. Whitney Griswold's classic study, *The Far Eastern Policy of the United States*, reaches similar conclusions. It suggests that American policy toward China had always swung like a pendulum from intense involvement to total lack of concern. Lofty rhetoric and commitments to moral principles were seldom backed up with military or economic sanctions. The Stimson doctrine of nonrecognition, proclaimed after the Japanese attack on Manchuria, is cited as one example among many.[22]

In the case of Chiang Kai-shek, the choice of "putting up or shutting up" had to be made during the Chinese civil war in the late 1940s. President Harry S Truman, true to the form described above, decided to do neither. He did not "put up" the necessary military force to prevent the Communist conquest of China, nor did he "shut up" and accept the fact that the Communists had won the civil war.

Most important for the purposes of this study, American policy, burdened by the Chiang Kai-shek image of the past, found itself unable, after the Communist victory, to make a realpolitik volte-face and deal pragmatically with the new rulers of China. One could not suddenly abandon the pro-American Christian gen-

---

[21] Tyler Dennett, "The Open Door as Intervention," quoted in *Historians and American Far Eastern Policy*, Dorothy Borg (compiler) (New York: Columbia University Press, 1966), p. 20.

[22] A. Whitney Griswold, *The Far Eastern Policy of the United States* (New York: Harcourt, Brace, 1938), *passim*.

eral and engage in commerce with the devil without dire domestic political consequences.

A number of leading American Foreign Service officers strongly urged a shift of policy, but to no avail. Thus, John Service wrote in October 1944: "Any new Chinese government under any other than the present reactionary control will be more cooperative with the United States and better able to mobilize the country."[23] And John Paton Davies wrote:

> But we must be realistic. We must not indefinitely underwrite a politically bankrupt regime. We must make a determined effort to capture politically the Chinese Communists rather than allow them to go by default wholly to the Russians. Furthermore, we must fully understand that by reason of our recognition of the Chiang Kai-shek government as now constituted we are committed to a steadily decaying regime and severely restricted in working out military and political cooperation with the Chinese Communists. . . . Power in China is on the verge of shifting from Chiang to the Communists.[24]

According to Tang Tsou, "Service's and Davies' hopes were shared by most of the foreign service officers in China." Nevertheless, the images of Chiang Kai-shek as the bastion of Christian morality and of the Communists as a godless evil ensured the very outcome that these experts in China warned against again and again.

When Chiang was driven to Formosa by the Communists in 1949, most Americans were not psychologically prepared to accept this fact. The forces of evil could not triumph in such a manner. The United States could not be so impotent. Thus, the myth developed that the United States had "lost" China as a result of the work of subversives in the American government. The loss of China was so unthinkable that only treason could explain it.

The rise of the Republican right wing on the American political scene in 1949 and the attacks on the State Department by Senator Joseph R. McCarthy in 1950 were symptoms of this psychological phenomenon. When Mao Tse-tung's armies swept across China toward victory in 1949, a number of American politicians began to mount a furious attack against the administration's China policy. On April 15, 1949, Senator Styles Bridges of New Hampshire demanded a congressional investigation of the State Department

---

[23] John Service, quoted in Tsou, *op. cit.*, p. 200.

[24] John Paton Davies, quoted in *ibid.*, p. 201.

and accused Secretary of State Dean Acheson of "what might be called sabotage of the valiant attempt of the Chinese Nationalists to keep at least part of China free."[25] On April 21, Senator William Knowland of California echoed the demand for an investigation and added: "If ever a government has had the rug pulled out from under it, if ever a non-Communist government in the world has reason to feel betrayed, that government is the Republic of China."[26]

When the State Department, in a white paper on China dated August 1949, attempted to present the administration's view of events, four senators immediately denounced the document as a "whitewash of wishful, do-nothing policy which has succeeded only in placing Asia in danger of Soviet conquest."[27] Patrick Hurley, the former United States ambassador to China, described the white paper as "a smooth alibi for the pro-Communists in the State Department who had engineered the overthrow of our ally, the Nationalist Government of the Republic of China, and aided in the Communist conquest of China."[28] Even Senator Robert A. Taft, known as "Mr. Republican" to millions of Americans and a man famous for his integrity, rose in the Senate to say, "The State Department has been guided by a left-wing group who obviously have wanted to get rid of Chiang and were willing at least to turn China over to the Communists for that purpose."[29] The furor culminated, of course, with the attacks by Senator Joseph McCarthy. For example: "When Chiang Kai-shek was fighting our war, the State Department had in China a young man named John S. Service. . . . He sent official reports back to the State Department urging that we torpedo our ally Chiang Kai-shek and stating, in effect, that Communism was the best hope of China."[30]

It is not within the purview of this study to examine the charges of subversion, but it must be noted that underlying these explanations of Chiang's defeat was the assumption that a handful of

[25] Styles Bridges, quoted in Allen J. Matusow (ed.), *Joseph R. McCarthy* (Englewood Cliffs, N.J.: Prentice-Hall, 1970), p. 8.

[26] William Knowland, quoted in *ibid.*

[27] Quoted in *ibid.*

[28] Patrick Hurley, quoted in *ibid.*

[29] Robert A. Taft, quoted in *ibid.*, p. 23.

[30] Joseph R. McCarthy, quoted in *ibid.*

Americans actually had the power to determine the fate of more than a half billion people in China. The spasm of McCarthyism finally passed, but many Americans continued to believe that China had been betrayed by the forces of evil.

Ironically enough, Chiang Kai-shek, too, felt betrayed by the United States. As late as 1942, after the United States had entered the war against Japan, he repeated his old accusation: "The American attitude toward China is in essence no different from that held by other nations. China is treated not as an equal but as a ward."[31] And, as many visitors to Taiwan have since testified, Chiang Kai-shek continued to see himself in large measure as a victim of American betrayal.

We can only speculate on the exacerbating effects of these distorted images. The record clearly shows that Chiang Kai-shek and the American leadership perceived each other through dark screens that often produced caricatures out of realities. It does not necessarily follow, of course, that if all these shadows had been cleared away, all the beasts would have become beauties. Objective conditions of conflict were real enough. The thrust of the new revolutionary China was anti-Western, and America was a part of the West. But there is little doubt that the opaque screens raised false hopes on both sides that, when shattered, led to only deeper disillusion. Even if Chiang Kai-shek had retained power on the mainland, it is unlikely that he would have remained allied with the United States for long. He might, in fact, have "reverted to type" and become its bitter enemy.

[31] Chiang Kai-shek, quoted in *ibid.*, p. 46.

Chapter Four

China's Intervention in the Korean War

The victory of the Communists on the Chinese mainland in 1949 ushered in a totally new period in Sino-American relations. Less than a year after the Communist takeover, American soldiers fought Chinese soldiers on the field of battle for the first time in history. This encounter radically changed the American view of China and deeply affected the Chinese view of America.

From the perspective of the United States, the Korean conflict marked the end of America's sentimental attachment to China, the end of the image of the Chinese as the heroic underdog, and the end to paternal interest and avuncular concern. In fact, the post-1950 American image of a hostile, menacing China dates from the Korean War.[1] The events of that period also confirmed the Chinese Communists in *their* view of the United States as an archenemy. These mutual perceptions, in turn, led to policy decisions of the most crucial consequence on both sides.

Let us briefly recapitulate the sequence of events. On June 25, 1950, North Korean troops attacked the Republic of South Korea and began a major campaign down the peninsula. The American response was swift: President Truman ordered American air and naval forces to the assistance of the hard-pressed South Korean armies; the Formosa Straits were "neutralized" by the dispatch of

---

[1] Harold Isaacs, *Images of Asia* (New York: Capricorn Books, 1962), chap. 10, esp. pp. 225–239; Allen S. Whiting, *China Crosses the Yalu* (New York: Macmillan, 1960), p. 167.

the United States 7th Fleet; and all available American ground forces in Japan were mobilized for action in Korea. At the same time, the United States took steps in the United Nations Security Council to place the conduct of the war under United Nations auspices, and so the Korean "police action" was launched.

By late September, the tide of battle had turned dramatically. The North Korean armies, which in the early days of the war had come close to conquering the entire peninsula, were turned around and then driven back across the thirty-eighth parallel, which marked the boundary between North and South Korea. By early October, the status quo antebellum had been restored, fulfilling the objectives announced by the United States at the beginning of hostilities.

At this point, however, the United States shifted its objectives and declared its intention to ensure a unified Korea. Thus, the United Nations forces did not halt their victorious advance at the thirty-eighth parallel. Instead, despite increasing warnings from the Chinese Communists that they would not tolerate the destruction of the North Korean government, South Korean troops crossed the parallel into the North on October 1, followed on October 7 by the United States 1st Cavalry Division.

The Chinese Communists had declared on October 2 that they would intervene if United States troops entered North Korea, but this warning had gone unheeded. The United Nations armies swept steadily northward, taking the North Korean capital of Pyongyang on October 19 and driving onward toward the Yalu River, which marked the international boundary between Korea and mainland China. On November 24, General Douglas MacArthur announced a final offensive: the troops, he declared, would be home by Christmas.

Late in October, however, a new participant entered the war. On October 26, 1950, United Nations troops began reporting contact with Chinese "volunteer" forces, and such clashes occurred more frequently in early November. Simultaneously, the tone of domestic Chinese propaganda became ominously anti-American. Yet the possibility of massive Chinese intervention in the Korean War was steadily discounted in the United States. In the opinion of American policy makers, the Chinese Communists would be foolhardy to intervene in a situation that would strain their resources and expose them to such punishing defeat.[2] Thus, even the explicit Chinese warning of October 2 went unheeded in Washington until November 26, when the Chinese unleashed a full-scale attack on the United Nations forces. This massive intervention resulted, in the words of General MacArthur, in an "entirely new war."

The Chinese attack was received with consternation in the United States. America had regarded the Korean conflict throughout as a Soviet-directed endeavor—part of the worldwide pattern of deepening tensions between the United States and the Soviet Union that had marked the postwar period. American policy makers had tried to discourage Chinese intervention by repeatedly stressing their benevolent intentions toward China. It was reiterated, for example, that the United States had no aggressive intentions upon the Chinese mainland, that neutralization of the Formosa Straits had been related only to events in Korea, and that the "traditional friendship" of the United States for the Chinese people held as firmly as ever. A report in The New York Times was a typical example:

> Secretary of State Dean Acheson said today that the United States was trying to discourage the Chinese Communists from entering the Korean war by making it plain in every possible way that this Government felt no hostility toward the Chinese and had no aggressive intentions in the Far East.
>
> The fact that the United States does not have aggressive designs on China . . . has been made repeatedly clear in his own statement, by the Voice of America and by President Truman himself.[3]

Yet these repeated assurances had failed to impress Peking. Instead, they were perceived as only further evidence of duplicity. Scornfully, the Chinese leaders replied that they had heard such rhetoric before. Had not the Americans declared that they would halt at the thirty-eighth parallel, and had they not crossed it? Had not the United States wanted it believed that they would not push their offensive up to the Yalu but would stop short of the river itself, and were not American troops now approaching the river? In the light of such past experience, what credence could be lent to

[2] Dean Acheson, "Foreign Policies Toward Asia—A Television Interview with Secretary Acheson," Department of State Bulletin, 23 (September 18, 1950), 463.

[3] The New York Times, August 31, 1950.

the new American assertions that they would not cross the Yalu into Chinese territory?[4]

In analyzing the Chinese decision to intervene, it is difficult, if not impossible, to assess the degree of Soviet influence. In his exhaustive and probably definitive study, *China Crosses the Yalu*, Allen Whiting reaches the conclusion that "China entered the war of her own free will":[5]

> It would seem that a Soviet *diktat* was not needed to bring the PRC [People's Republic of China] into the war. There may have been differences between the two allies as to the timing and extent of the move. . . . There undoubtedly were questions of mutual responsibility, some of which may have been resolved to the dissatisfaction of one or both partners. . . . But the final decision to fight appears to have been basically a Chinese decision, conditioned by Russian advice and encouraged by Russian support.[6]

The primary actors in the drama, then, were the United States and China. What, we must ask, was the nature of the misperceptions that led these two nations in the fall of 1950 to misjudge so seriously each other's actions?

The United States-Chinese relationship in late 1950 can be analyzed in terms of four distinctive, yet interrelated, factors: first, each nation's *self-image*; second, each nation's perception of the *character* of its adversary; third, each nation's perception of its adversary's *intentions*; and finally, each nation's perception of the other's *power* and *capabilities*.

In the matter of China's and America's respective self-images, it is important to note that both nations had strongly developed conceptions of their historical missions, and that these conceptions were perceived as antithetical. An atmosphere of conflict, therefore, existed that tended to exacerbate specific incidents. In this connection, one need hardly elaborate upon the United States' conception of itself as the "defender of democracy" or as the

---

[4] Editorial from Jen-min Jih-pao, November 6, 1950, quoted in Tang Tsou, *America's Failure in China, 1941–1950* (Chicago: University of Chicago Press, 1963), pp. 582–583. See also Peking's statement of November 17, 1950, *The New York Times*, November 18, 1950.

[5] Allen S. Whiting, *China Crosses the Yalu* (Stanford: Stanford University Press, 1960), p. 154.

[6] *Ibid.*, p. 160.

"bastion of the free world." Such rhetoric was far more current in the world of 1950, when Stalin was still alive, when the cold war was at its height, and when East-West relations were perceived in terms of the starkest opposition. The outlook was well conveyed by John Foster Dulles in an article for *The New York Times Magazine* of July 30, 1950:

> Now we are consciously enlisted in a great cause. We have enlisted voluntarily, as befits free men and women, and we sacrifice voluntarily. We do not work and sacrifice as slaves to any master save truth and righteousness. Our purpose is to join our strength with that of the other free members of the United Nations to preserve such human liberty as remains in the world. . . .
>
> We are engaged in the kind of crusade that Lincoln foresaw when he said, of our Declaration of Independence, that it promised "liberty, not alone to the people of this country, but hope for the world for all future time."[7]

But it is not enough to describe these quasi-religious, crusading elements in the American self-image. This would be too generalized and amorphous an approach. There is more empirical material at hand, and it is to be found abundantly in the personality of General MacArthur. For operational purposes, the perceptions of Douglas MacArthur, so long as he was in command of the Korean theater of war, *were* the American perceptions on which policy was based. Suffice it to say for the moment that MacArthur was frequently acclaimed, and probably believed himself to be, America's greatest living soldier. The startling success of the Inchon landing had made the general's confidence in his own military genius unshakable. Most United States political leaders considered the American cause in Korea to be just and right and America's most honored soldier believed the armed might of the United States to be invincible.

It is equally important to recognize that similar elements existed in Communist China's conception of itself. Where America conceived its mission to be the defense of democracy, Communist China considered itself to be the champion of Marxism-Leninism. The modern Chinese elite saw China as the proper and natural leader of all of Asia and themselves as the restorers of China's

[7] John Foster Dulles, "To Save Humanity from the Deep Abyss," *The New York Times Magazine*, July 30, 1950.

ancient glories and the redressers of the wrongs inflicted upon it by the West.[8] "He [Mao] . . . felt deeply as a historical thinker the injustices that European imperialism had inflicted on Asia. It seemed to be his view that Europe had unbalanced the life in Asia, and the work of this generation of liberators was to recover the balance."[9]

Mao Tse-tung's liberation image of Chinese Communism was directly linked to his perception of himself as a leading innovator in strategic thought, especially in the field of guerrilla warfare. There is ample evidence to support the view that Mao believed his guide *On Protracted War* to be the definitive work on the subject. The superiority of the peasant guerrilla over the "paper tiger" of American atomic power was relentlessly drilled into new recruits of the Chinese People's Liberation Army. If Mao's image of the new China as a great power dominated his political thinking, the peasant guerrilla constituted his most formidable military weapon against the imperialist West. As General Nieh Jung-chen put it: "They [the Americans] may even drop atom bombs on us. What then? They may kill a few million people. Without sacrifice, a nation's independence cannot be upheld. . . . After all, China lives on the farms. What can atom bombs do there?"[10]

Thus, both the United States and China saw themselves as the foremost proponents of similarly crusading, but deeply divergent, ideologies, both buttressed by weapons that were deemed invincible. On the eve of the Korean War, these self-images created a particularly explosive atmosphere in which incidents could escalate rapidly, signals could easily be misinterpreted; overt conflict became all too possible.

When we compare each nation's perception of the *character* of its adversary, certainly the Chinese image of the United States must make startling reading in America. It was a real devil image, a picture of unequaled malevolence. In the summer of 1950, the Chinese Communists launched an intensive domestic propaganda campaign portraying the United States not merely as the enemy of

[8] Tsou, *op. cit.*, p. 563.

[9] K. M. Panikkar, *In Two Chinas* (London: Allen & Unwin, 1955), p. 81.

[10] Nieh Jung-chen, quoted in Samuel B. Griffith, II, *The Chinese People's Liberation Army* (New York: McGraw-Hill, 1967), p. 118.

the moment, but as China's historical archenemy. The deepening Korean crisis was interpreted not as an isolated incident, but as one more example of America's longstanding hostility toward China. Je-min Jih-pao, for example, published a chronology of "American Aggression Against China," which enumerated almost annual examples of aggression—political, economic, and moral— throughout the entire period from 1839 to 1950.[11] To this chronology of overt conflict, there was added the element of moral corruption. The United States was depicted as a

> paradise of gangsters, swindlers, rascals, special agents, fascist germs, speculators, debauchers and all the dregs of mankind. This is the world's manufactory and source of all such crimes as reaction, darkness, cruelty, decadence, corruption, debauchery, oppression of man by man, and cannibalism. . . . Here the criminal phenomena that issue forth defy the imagination of human brains. . . . Everyone who does not want the people of his beloved fatherland contaminated by these criminal phenomena is charged with the responsibility of arising to condemn her, curse her, hate her and despise her.[12]

In early November, the Chinese government launched a fierce propaganda campaign under the slogan, "Resist America, Aid Korea, Preserve Our Homes, Defend the Nation." The population was bombarded with anti-American propaganda from loudspeakers, radios, and platforms. Countless mass meetings were organized in every community, school, factory, and commune. At these, the United States, President Truman, and General Mac-Arthur were described as mad dogs, bloodstained bandits, murderers, rapists, and savages. The American leaders were depicted as bloodthirsty or poisonous animals in innumerable cartoons. The virulence of the campaign lashed more than half a billion people into a frenzy of hate and fear.

These were the lurid tones of a Cotton Mather sermon warning of the perils of commerce with the devil. The image projected was one of an opponent with whom there can and must be no com-

---

[11] *Hate America Campaign in Communist China* (Washington, D.C.: Department of State, 1952?), pp. 36–43. There are, incidentally, interesting parallels between this interpretation of the history of Sino-American contacts and that of Chiang Kai-shek in *China's Destiny,* Philip Jaffe (ed.) (New York: Roy Publishers, 1947).

[12] "Look, This Is the American Way of Life," supplement to *Nan Fung Jih Pao,* CCP official organ, December 1950, in *Hate America, op. cit.,* p. 184.

promise, whose very touch brought contamination and defilement. It implied, in short, bottomless hate and contempt.

On the American side, there was also an element of semireligious ardor. John Foster Dulles referred to the South Korean government as a "moral salient in the otherwise solid Communist despotism of North Asia."[13] General MacArthur wrote in November 1950 that "the Chinese people have thus become militarized in their concepts and in their ideals. . . . This has produced a new and dominant power in Asia, which . . . has become aggressively imperialistic, with a lust for expansion and increased power normal to this type of imperialism."[14]

Despite the fact that MacArthur characterized Communist China as a power lusting for expansion, he had a curious contempt for the Chinese soldier. He equated the highly indoctrinated and well-disciplined Communist soldier of 1950 with the demoralized Nationalist soldier of 1948. To be blunt, he did not respect his enemy, and this disrespect was to cost him dearly.

A nation's perception of its adversary is closely related to its estimation of the adversary's *intentions* toward the nation itself. Here we encounter the most clear-cut divergence in perceptions between China and the United States in 1950. The United States believed that the Chinese Communists neither would nor could intervene in Korea and relied on frequent pronouncements of America's nonaggressive intentions to reassure the Chinese leaders. The Chinese Communists, on the other hand, regarded the United States as the heir to Japan's imperialist ambitions in Asia[15] and became increasingly convinced that only powerful intervention in Korea would prevent the United States from invading China. Two quotations will serve to point up the contrast:

The United States government has taken this series of aggressive actions [in Korea] with the purpose of realizing its fanatical devotion of dominating Asia and the world. One of the master-planners of Japanese aggression, Tanaka, once said: to conquer the world, one must first conquer Asia; to conquer Asia, one must first conquer China; to conquer China, one must first conquer Korea and Taiwan. . . . American impe-

---

[13] Dulles, *op. cit.*, p. 5.

[14] Douglas MacArthur, *Reminiscences* (New York: McGraw-Hill, 1964), p. 367.

[15] Tsou, *op. cit.*, p. 577.

rialism . . . plagiarizes Tanaka's memorandum, and follows the beaten path of Japan's imperialist aggressors![16]

I can give assurance that we . . . have never at any time entertained any intention to carry hostilities into China. . . . Because of our . . . longstanding friendship for the people of China we will take every honorable step to prevent any extension of the hostilities in the Far East. If the Chinese Communist authorities or people believe otherwise, it can only be because they are being deceived by those whose advantage it is to prolong and extend hostilities in the Far East against the interests of all Far Eastern people.[17]

Thus, American policy makers chose to view the tension between America and China in 1950 as a passing phenomenon, and they felt that assurances of goodwill toward China would suffice to insulate the Korean conflict from Chinese intervention. The Chinese Communists, on the other hand, viewed the Korean conflict as yet another incident in a longstanding pattern of American hostility toward China. These preconceptions helped fashion each side's interpretation of the other's actions. As one scholar of Chinese-American relations has noted:

While Secretary Acheson was talking about the traditional friendship of America, the Chinese Communists were teaching their compatriots that from the early nineteenth century onward the United States had consistently followed an aggressive policy toward China which culminated in her support for Chiang Kai-shek in the civil war and her present actions in Korea and Taiwan. The Chinese people were told to treat the United States with scorn . . . because she was a paper tiger and "certainly" could be defeated.[18]

Operating upon the assumption of longstanding Sino-American friendship, United States policy makers were deeply astonished at the violence of the Chinese response in October 1950. They did not see the intervention coming, either from the specific warning conveyed on October 2 by Chou En-lai to Indian Ambassador K. M. Panikkar in Peking[19] or from the increasingly hostile tone of Chinese domestic propaganda during the two preceding

---

[16] Chinese Communist spokesman in United Nations, Security Council (SC/PV/527), 5th Session, 527th Meeting (November 28, 1950), pp. 23–24.

[17] Statement by President Harry S Truman, November 16, 1950.

[18] Tsou, *op. cit.*, p. 578.

[19] Whiting, *op. cit.*, pp. 108–109.

months.[20] That the illusion of a firm Sino-American friendship underlying a Communist veneer persisted in the face of considerable evidence to the contrary suggests that the United States was not yet prepared to take China seriously. Her warnings were not as yet considered credible. It suggests, in fact, that the United States still tended to look upon China as the immature "ward" it had so long considered her.

A detailed examination of the Chinese warning to Ambassador Panikkar and the American response to it is quite revealing. Chou En-lai clearly told Panikkar on October 2 that, if American troops crossed the thirty-eighth parallel, China would enter the war.[21] Prime Minister Jawaharlal Nehru, in a parliamentary speech, repeated the substance of the Chinese warning in the following terms:

> The Chinese government clearly indicated that if the 38th parallel was crossed, they would consider it a grave danger to their own security and that they would not tolerate it. We did, as a matter of fact, convey our views to the governments of the United Kingdom, the United States of America, as well as to some governments in Asia.[22]

Neither President Truman nor General MacArthur took this warning seriously. Truman viewed it as "a bold attempt to blackmail the United Nations" and later observed in his *Memoirs* that "Mr. Panikkar had in the past played the game of the Chinese Communists fairly regularly, so that his statement coud not be taken as that of an impartial observer."[23]

On October 7, United Nations forces crossed the parallel and began their sweep toward the Yalu River. On October 10, Chou En-lai repeated his warning and announced that the Chinese people would not "stand idly by in this war of invasion." Once again, it received only passing attention in Washington and Tokyo and was dismissed as just another example of Chinese bombast.

On October 15, Truman and MacArthur met on Wake Island, and the President wanted to know the general's opinion of the

---

[20] *Ibid.*, pp. 84–85, 88–89.

[21] Cited in Panikkar, *op. cit.*, p. 110.

[22] Jawaharlal Nehru, quoted in Griffith, *op. cit.*, p. 120.

[23] Harry S Truman, *Years of Trial and Hope, Vol. II: Memoirs* (Garden City, N.Y.: Doubleday, 1956), p. 362.

possibility of Chinese intervention. MacArthur considered this possibility remote:

> Had they interfered in the first or second month, it would have been decisive. We are no longer fearful of their intervention. We no longer stand hat in hand. The Chinese have 300,000 men in Manchuria. Of these, probably not more than 100 to 125,000 are distributed along the Yalu River. They have no Air Force. Now that we have bases for our Air Force in Korea, if the Chinese tried to get down to Pyongyang there would be the greatest slaughter.[24]

Four days later, when MacArthur's forces entered Pyongyang, the State Department also came to the conclusion that Chinese intervention in Korea was "unlikely." In the opinion of one leading authority:

> This assessment was by no means confined to the department over which Acheson presided. It was shared alike by the President, the Joint Chiefs of Staff, members of the National Security Council, General Walter Bedell Smith, Director of Central Intelligence, prominent senators, congressmen, and political pundits of all hues. If questioned, that amorphous character "the man in the street" would have expressed the same opinion.[25]

Nevertheless, at the very time that the American leadership, virtually without exception, denied the possibility of Chinese intervention, the Chinese 4th Field Army crossed the Yalu and penetrated the rugged mountain terrain of North Korea.

Truman, MacArthur, and the State Department perceived a China that no longer existed. "The conviction that China would not intervene represented an emotional rather than an intellectual conclusion, an ascription to the enemy of *intentions* compatible with the desires of Washington and Tokyo."[26] This misperception prepared the ground for a military disaster of major proportions.

If the Americans misperceived Chinese intentions by refusing to take them seriously, the Chinese erred in the opposite direction. The world as viewed from Peking presented a picture of implaca-

[24] U.S. Senate, *Military Situation in the Far East,* Hearings before the Committee on Armed Services and the Committee on Foreign Relations, 82nd Congress, 1st sess. (1951), p. 3483.

[25] Griffith, *op. cit.,* p. 124.

[26] *Ibid.,* p. 125. Italics added.

ble American hostility. Not only were American troops marching directly up to the Korean border at the Yalu River, but the United States was protecting the hated Nationalist regime on Taiwan and was aiding the French against the revolutionaries in Indochina. In addition, the United States was rehabilitating and rearming Japan. Hence, the Chinese leadership reasoned, the intention of the United States

> [was] to make use of Taiwan as a springboard for the invasion of the Chinese mainland. . . .
> Her plan is to invade China after her complete occupation of Korea. . . .
> The U.S. is now arduously rebuilding and rearming Japan. . . . The aim of the U.S. is to utilize Japanese military force as the U.S. advance guard in the American invasion of the Far East. . . .
> Apart from open aggression, the U.S. also tries to work against us from the inside. . . . According to statistics collected in the Southwest, 60% of the principal bandit groups in the Southwest had their training under the U.S. and Chiang.[27]

> We Chinese people are against the American imperialists because they are against us. They have openly become the arch enemy of the People's Republic of China by supporting the people's enemy, the Chiang Kai-shek clique, by sending a huge fleet to prevent the liberation of the Chinese territory of Taiwan, by repeated air intrusions and strafing and bombing of the Chinese people, by refusing new China a seat in the U.N., through intrigues with their satellite nations, by rearing up again a fascist power in Japan, and by rearming Japan for the purpose of expanding aggressive war. Is it not just for us to support our friend and neighbor against our enemy? The American warmongers are mistaken in thinking that their accusations and threats will intimidate the people of China.[28]

With this kind of outlook, it was hardly surprising that the Chinese regarded verbal protestations of goodwill on the part of the United States as a mockery.[29]

---

[27] "How to Understand the United States," in *Hate America, op. cit.*, pp. 50–52.

[28] Quote from Jen-min Jih-pao, September 25, 1950, in Whiting, *op. cit.*, p. 106; see also Tsou, *op. cit.*, p. 577.

[29] It is interesting to note in this respect that hostility toward America and suspicion of its intentions toward China were not exclusively characteristic of the Chinese Communists. The uproar in the Chinese press over the Peiping Rape Case in the winter of 1946–1947 shows how deep anti-Americanism ran in Chinese life well before the Communist victory. See Thurston Griggs, *Americans in China: Some Chinese Views*

The most crucial category of all, however, is the fourth—that of each nation's perception of the other's *power* and *capabilities*. At no time prior to October 25, 1950, did American policy makers seriously consider the possibility of Chinese intervention in the Korean conflict. The Chinese leaders, it was believed, would not be so foolhardy as to risk their meager resources against the over-whelming military forces of one of the world's superpowers.[30] That Peking might feel so endangered by the Korean action as to believe it had no other course but to intervene was not considered at all likely. Her warnings, therefore, were viewed as mere bluff. The United States' failure to credit these warnings was probably attrib-utable to its having considered China as the "sick man of Asia" for too long to be able suddenly to abandon its paternalistic attitude.

The United States, moreover, had no doubt as to its ability to defeat any military force that the Chinese might send into Korea. General MacArthur expressed his conviction to this effect at the Wake Island Conference.[31] Indeed, one of the major shocks of the Korean War was America's sudden realization that the Chinese soldier, hitherto regarded with a degree of contempt, was a tough opponent when well equipped and trained.[32] Speaking in this connection of the Korean soldier, Hanson W. Baldwin of *The New York Times* made some remarks that might as easily have applied to American attitudes toward the Chinese:

> We tended prior to Korea, despite the hard lessons taught us by the Japanese in World War II, to look down upon the Koreans as an inferior race. It was with this attitude of patronizing contempt that we went into

---

(Washington, D.C.: Foundation for Foreign Affairs, 1948), pp. 7–15. Later in 1947, some Chinese newsmen were maltreated and insulted by American personnel while covering the withdrawal of United States troops from Tangku. In reporting the inci-dent, the Peiping *Shih Pao*, a Kuomintang paper, remarked on April 23, 1947: "We are led to doubt that such incidents are really isolated and accidental. . . . That these foreigners . . . should build a sense of racial superiority . . . on the grounds of China's weakness and poverty and need for foreign troops . . . is a serious matter." (Quoted in *ibid.*, p. 29.) Griggs gives several other illustrations of this current of anti-Americanism in China well before the Communist takeover.

[30] Tsou, *op. cit.*, pp. 574, 579.

[31] Leland M. Goodrich, *Korea: A Study of U.S. Policy in the United Nations* (New York: Council on Foreign Relations, 1956), p. 136; see also John Spanier, *The Truman-MacArthur Controversy and the Korean War* (Cambridge: Harvard University Press, 1959), p. 105.

[32] Isaacs, *op. cit.*

action in Korea. We quickly discovered that the "gook" was a tough soldier. . . .[33]

This line of analysis, incidentally, casts some light upon General MacArthur's insistence on crossing the thirty-eighth parallel, for the general, far from regarding the Chinese as equals, insisted that "the pattern of the Oriental psychology [is] to respect and follow aggressive, resolute and dynamic leadership, to quickly turn on a leadership characterized by timidity or vacillation. . . ."[34] MacArthur's paternalistic and contemptuous view of the military power of the new China led directly to disaster in October and November 1950. The story is worth examining in some detail.

On October 26, to the accompaniment of fierce bugle calls, shrill whistles, and blasts on shepherds' horns, the Chinese launched a surprise attack on South Korean and American forces some fifty miles south of the Chinese border. The results were devastating. Several United Nations regiments were virtually decimated. Nevertheless, Major General Charles A. Willoughby, MacArthur's main intelligence officer, still voiced the opinion on the following day that "the auspicious time for Chinese intervention [had] long since passed" and that "there [was] no positive evidence that Chinese Communist units, as such, [had] entered Korea."[35] On November 1, the Chinese initiated a massive attack against the United States 3rd Battalion and virtually tore it apart. Then, after shattering the United States 8th Cavalry, the Chinese abruptly broke contact and withdrew.

MacArthur's reaction to these events demonstrates how difficult it is for an old, but stubbornly entrenched, misperception to yield to the facts. On the day of the Chinese disengagement, his estimate of total Chinese strength in Korea was between 40,000 and 60,000 men.[36] In fact, as of October 31, the Chinese had deployed, in utmost secrecy and within short distances of the American forces they were about to strike, almost 200,000 men.[37] Some of these had crossed the Yalu before the Wake Island meeting between Truman and MacArthur.

[33] Hanson W. Baldwin, *The New York Times*, October 31, 1950.

[34] Douglas MacArthur, Message to Veterans of Foreign Wars, August 28, 1950.

[35] *Military Situation in the Far East, op. cit.*, p. 3427.

[36] Griffith, *op. cit.*, p. 134.

[37] *Ibid.*, p. 129.

The Chinese troops had done what MacArthur had deemed impossible. They had moved by night in forced marches, employed local guides and porters, and used the barren and hostile terrain of the North Korean hills to their advantage. Then they launched their assault on MacArthur's unsuspecting army. When the Chinese temporarily withdrew, MacArthur immediately ascribed this turn of events to the heavy casualties the enemy had sustained. The Chinese needed to rest, in MacArthur's view, and, hence, a golden opportunity was at hand for a second and victorious American drive to the Yalu.

In retrospect, it is clear that

> The Chinese withdrawal in early November was designed to encourage the enemy's arrogance; to lure the UN forces deeper into North Korea, where their tenuous supply lines could be interdicted and where units separated from one another by the broken terrain could be isolated and annihilated. This was the nature of the deadly trap which P'eng, at his Shenyang headquarters, was setting for the overconfident general in the Dai Ichi Building in Tokyo.[38]

Thus, MacArthur, believing that he was faced with 40,000 instead of 200,000 Chinese soldiers and believing that these soldiers were badly in need of rest after their encounter with the American army, advanced northward again for the "final offensive." The Chinese watched for three weeks and, finally, on November 27, attacked in overwhelming force, turning the American advance into a bloody rout. Thus, a peasant army put to flight a modern Western military force commanded by a world-famous American general. In one bound, China had become a world power, and the image of the Chinese ward, almost half a century in the making, was finally shattered, at a cost of tens of thousands of battle casualties on both sides. MacArthur, incredibly enough, did not learn much from the experience. In the words of his aide-de-camp, Major General Courtney Whitney, the general "was greatly saddened as well as angered at this despicably surreptitious attack, a piece of treachery which he regarded as worse even than Pearl Harbor."[39] The stark truth was that MacArthur had blundered into the trap of his own misperceptions.

---

[38] *Ibid.*, p. 134.

[39] Courtney Whitney, *MacArthur: His Rendezvous with Destiny* (New York: Knopf, 1956), p. 394.

The paternalistic attitude of American leaders toward Communist China died hard. It remained extremely difficult for the United States to admit that the new China was growing in power and was fiercely hostile and that this attitude was more than a passing phenomenon. Many rationalizations were invoked to explain this disturbing new presence on the world scene. Communism was viewed as somehow "alien" to the "Chinese character." It would pass, leaving the "traditional friendship" between China and America to reassert itself—although the paternalism implicit in this "traditional" relationship was never admitted.[40] At other times, Chinese hostility to the United States was explained as the result of the evil influence of the Soviet Union:

> On November 27, immediately following Mr. Vyshinsky's statement of charges of aggression against the U.S., the United States representative in this Committee [one of the United Nations], Ambassador Dulles . . . with a feeling of sadness rather than anger, said one could only conclude that the Soviet Union was trying to destroy the long history of close friendship between China and the United States and to bring the Chinese people to hate and, if possible, to fight the United States.[41]

One of the more bizarre examples of this attempt to maintain old attitudes in the face of bewildering new facts was the brief flurry in the press during December 1950 concerning the possibility of a United Nations military action in China—directed not against the Chinese people, but against the Mao faction, which was presumed to be their oppressor. A headline in the New York Herald Tribune proclaimed "Declaration of State of War Against Mao's Faction Urged" and stated in the text that "So far as can be determined now, the action of the UN will not be one of war against China or the Chinese people but against one faction in China, namely the Communists."[42] How this distinction was to be put into effect on the battlefield was never made clear, and apparently the utterly unrealistic nature of the proposal led to its early death. Nevertheless, the distinction between the Chinese people and their Communist leaders persisted for some time. On December 29, 1950, in a statement for the Voice of America, Dean

---

[40] See Whiting, op. cit., pp. 169–170.

[41] United Nations, United States Mission, Press Release, No. 1129, February 2, 1951.

[42] "Declaration of State of War Against Mao's Faction Urged," New York Herald Tribune, December 6, 1950.

Rusk, then Assistant Secretary of State for Far Eastern Affairs, accused the Chinese Communists of having plotted the North Korean assault. The press reported, "As all American officials have done consistently, Mr. Rusk drew a distinction between the Chinese people, for whom the United States has a long tradition of friendliness, and their Communist rulers."[43] By denying that the new government of China had a power base and a measure of popular support, the United States tried to maintain intact its old illusions about the historical relationship between the two nations. But that relationship had been a predatory one, and it was precisely this that was never admitted.

Indian Ambassador Panikkar detected this blind spot in the American picture of China. He noted that in the early days of the Korean War, the Western military attachés in Peking had been utterly confident that Chinese troops could not possibly stand up to the Americans. The American defeat in late November, he noticed, came as a profound shock to them, and their attitude thenceforth was very different.[44] In a good summation of the problem, he stated: "China had become a Great Power and was insisting on being recognized as such. The adjustments which such a recognition requires are not easy, and the conflict in the Far East is the outcome of this contradiction."[45]

The Korean crisis provides a good illustration of the practical, operational consequences of divergent perceptions in world affairs. These perceptions are, in effect, definitions of the situation at hand. Once the situation has been defined, certain alternatives are eliminated. One does not conciliate an opponent who is perceived as implacably hostile; hence, the Chinese Communists felt in the end that they had no resort but to intervene in Korea. One does not credit the threats of an opponent whose power one feels to be negligible; hence, the United States perceived even specific Chinese warnings as bluff. One does not compromise with an opponent whose ideology is perceived as antithetical to one's own values; hence, the United States and China remained poised on the brink of potentially disastrous conflict, neither one accepting the other's perception of its world role as legitimate.

[43] New York *Herald Tribune*, December 30, 1950.

[44] Panikkar, *op. cit.*, p. 117.

[45] *Ibid.*, pp. 177–178.

Yet, paradoxically, the violent clash between the United States and China in 1950 might in one sense have contributed in the long run to some future improvement of relations between the two nations, for the effectiveness of China's intervention in Korea established it as a power to be reckoned with. It shattered once and for all the attitude of patronization that, until then, had characterized the United States' view of China. To the extent that nations can admit their past mistakes, and are able to learn from them, the likelihood of war between them will diminish. Verbal threats may continue and various forms of indirect conflict will survive. But to the degree that each remembers the other's power, it will refrain from provocations beyond the point of no return.

Chapter Five

The United States, China, and the War in Indochina: The French Phase

The main thesis of this chapter is that the American perception of Ho Chi Minh underwent profound changes between 1946 and 1954. In 1946, most Americans saw Ho Chi Minh as an ardent nationalist fighting against French colonialism; four years later most Americans perceived him as the front man for Chinese communism. The point here is that this change was *not* the result of rational analysis or of objective changes in the political character of Ho Chi Minh, but of irrational, largely extraneous perceptions that Americans superimposed upon the situation in Indochina. Similarly, the Communist Chinese leaders superimposed their own perceptual "grid" upon the United States. To them, the world was divided into "imperialists" and "oppressed," and America was viewed as the embodiment of all evil. This devil image on both sides led to operational consequences in the foreign policies of both China and America that in turn made the hostility between them even more implacable.

In 1946, the United States considered itself merely a detached observer in Indochina. Hostilities erupted there, but they were regarded as France's problem. Indeed, many Americans tended to believe that they were just what the French deserved for their colonial ambitions. "Colonial war, then, is back in Indochina," said *The Saturday Evening Post* on November 30, 1946, and the *Christian Science Monitor* on December 24 described Ho Chi Minh's fight as "part of the world struggle of colonial peoples for liberation from foreign influence or control. . . . The peoples of Indochina joined the forward march toward independence more than six years ago and the present clashes are an unpleasant phase of this struggle."

This perception was very much in line with that of President Franklin D. Roosevelt during World War II. Roosevelt had openly opposed the return of French power to Indochina and had advocated some form of international trusteeship for the area.[1] If the fighting in Indochina was a colonial war, it naturally followed that the United States should remain disapproving of France. This was precisely American policy. The United States even urged France to end the war[2] and resisted all appeals for assistance, insisting, for example, that American-produced propellers be removed from the British aircraft given by Britain to the French troops fighting against Ho Chi Minh.[3]

The American view of Ho Chi Minh paralleled the American view of the war as a whole. On February 6, 1946, the *Christian Science Monitor* called him a moderate, and on January 9, 1948, remarked that "Ho Chi Minh's present Government is mixed and does not give the appearance of being Communist dominated." The entire American press showed considerable skepticism toward French claims that Ho was an outright Communist. On the whole, "United States policy decidedly favored Ho Chi Minh."[4] "An American OSS officer who had worked closely with Ho for several months prior to V-J Day had described him as an 'awfully sweet guy' whose outstanding quality was his 'gentleness.' "[5]

When American perception did change, it was not based on actual events in Indochina, but on developments altogether outside the area. In 1948 America's conception of its world role

[1] Victor Bator, *Vietnam: A Diplomatic Tragedy* (Dobbs Ferry, N.Y.: Oceana Publications, 1965), p. 206

[2] *The New York Times*, June 17, 1947.

[3] Bator, *op. cit.*

[4] *Ibid.*

[5] Bernard B. Fall, *The Two Vietnams* (New York: Praeger, 1964), p. 82.

changed profoundly. Crisis followed crisis, in Berlin, in Greece, and in Czechoslovakia. The division between East and West crystallized and hardened. The imagery of the "iron curtain" and of "containment" came to pervade the entire American view of foreign affairs. The chasm between Eastern and Western camps appeared deeper by the day, and the United States, architect of the North Atlantic Treaty, began to see itself as the leader of an embattled "free world" resisting the expansion of a ruthless totalitarianism.

The threat in Europe was undeniably real, and the American response to it was, on the whole, not exaggerated. The ramifications of this new outlook, however, were less rational, for the new definition of the European situation spilled over to encompass the entire globe. Having recognized a mortal threat in the heart of Europe, American leaders soon came to redefine *all* conflicts throughout the world as part of the same struggle.

Inexorably, the United States came to believe that the "frontiers" of the free world included Asia as well. In October 1948, the House Foreign Affairs Subcommittee on World Communism issued a report calling China the active theater in the cold war. The report said the Communists were using China as a testing ground for tactics they might use to take over the world and recommended a "guarantee of territorial and political integrity" to the Chinese Nationalists.[6]

This shift in outlook implied an American redefinition of the "true" nature of Ho Chi Minh as well:

> In this country, *it is only now beginning to be understood* that in any Asiatic nationalist movement connected with Moscow through its leadership, the totalitarian-imperialist trend must inevitably kill native nationalism. . . . His [Ho's] Indochinese independence has become a means to another end: Russian conquest of the Southeast Pacific.[7]

The New York *Herald Tribune*, on June 17, 1949, stated flatly that "Ho Chi Minh is a Comintern agent whom the French rate as an authentic political genius." The redefinition did *not* coincide with any *objective* developments in the Indochinese conflict. It coin-

---

[6] U.S. House Foreign Affairs Subcommitte on World Communism, *China and U.S. Far East Policy, 1946–1966*, 80th Cong., 2nd sess. (1967), p. 45.

[7] Andrew W. Green, "Are You a Middle of the Roader?" *Plain Talk*, 3 (April 1949), 35. Italics added.

cided instead with an extraneous event: the Communist victory in China. The sense of betrayal that the American public felt over the loss of China intensified the anxieties arising from the cold war. Thus, peril in Europe, compounded by betrayal in China, produced a strongly emotional reevaluation of the United States relationship to Southeast Asia.

Hence, American failure in China was attributed to the machinations of a worldwide conspiracy. From 1949 onward, the American press reflected an inexorable trend by which the perceptual grid of cold war categories was superimposed upon the older conflict in Indochina. This grid gradually eclipsed all awareness of the nationalist origins of the Ho Chi Minh insurgency. It even erased American recollections of the colonial conditions that had sparked the revolt, until finally, the original disapproval of France as an imperial power disappeared altogether in a redefinition of the French as "defenders of the West."

"Indochina: 'Greece' of 1950?" *U.S. News and World Report* asked on February 24, 1950. "Indochina . . . is in the process of becoming the Greece of Asia, now that the 'cold war' has turned to the East. All of a sudden, with the Communist victory in China to the north, Indochina is out front in the power struggle between Russia . . . and the Western world." On February 2, 1950, the *Department of State Bulletin* asserted that the recognition of Ho Chi Minh by the USSR, China, North Korea, and the Eastern European nations had brought an end to speculation as to the fate of Vietnam under Ho, who was now described as a lifelong servant of world communism.

One by one the ambiguities disappeared. "Nationalist rebels" were steadily amalgamated with the Communist threat. Bao Dai, once referred to as the "nightclub emperor" and as a man irretrievably tainted by his close association with the French colonial regime, was now officially considered as offering "more opportunity to the Vietnamese people to develop their own national life than a leader who . . . must obey the orders of international Communism."[8]

By September 1951, it was considered axiomatic that the rest of Southeast Asia could not be held if Indochina "fell to Moscow-

---

[8] Policy statement by Ambassador Loy W. Henderson, *Department of State Bulletin*, 22 (April 10, 1950), 565.

Peiping directed Communist rule,"[9] and by the middle of 1952, the State Department spoke of "the common recognition that the struggle in which the forces of the French Union and the Associated States are engaged against the forces of Communist aggression in Indochina as an integral part of the world-wide resistance by the Free Nations to Communist attempts at conquest and subversion."[10]

Now that the deadly enemy was seen at work in Southeast Asia, the United States was eager to keep the French in Indochina. If the United States was to reconcile French presence there with its conception of itself as firmly anticolonialist, however, France's role in Indochina would have to be perceived quite differently. This did in fact happen. "That the French are making a tremendous effort to hold it [Tonking] for the free world is *better understood now than it was a short time ago*" stated *The New York Times* in an editorial on September 24, 1951.[11] The reevaluation was even made retroactive: "A bitter and bloody struggle *between Communist forces and French Union troops* has been racking Indochina for *six years*," declared *Background* in 1951.[12] And in March 1952, a State Department official stated that "In this battle to preserve their country from Communism, France is contributing financially and militarily. . . . French soldiers and resources have borne the brunt of this brutal attack."[13] Thus, what had been regarded as a colonial war was now fully redefined as a brutal attack by an outside enemy, while France was recast as the defender, not the opponent, of Asian independence.

By early 1952, the cold war grid was firmly in place. "The great power struggle in Asia now appears to be moving inevitably and dangerously into a new theatre—Southeast Asia," stated the *Christian Science Monitor* on January 25. No longer was Southeast Asia viewed as the arena of an anticolonial revolt; it had now become part of the East-West power struggle. The same editorial

---

[9] *Christian Science Monitor*, September 11, 1951.

[10] U.S. Department of State, "Communiqué of Talks on Indochina," Press Release, No. 476, June 18, 1952.

[11] *The New York Times*, September 24, 1951. Italics added.

[12] U.S. Department of State, Office of Public Affairs, *Background* (October 1951). Italics added.

[13] U.S. Department of State, statement by Robert E. Hoey, Officer in Charge of Vietnam-Laos-Cambodia Affairs, Press Release, No. 178, March 8, 1952.

continued that "no one planned that, after a stalemate in Korea, there should be a new trial of strength in the southward projection of Asia," thus implying that the Indochinese conflict had begun *after* the outbreak of the Korean War. The editorial concluded by imposing the cold war dichotomy in full force: "It [Indochina] is a place which is bound to be occupied eventually either by East or West. The strategic prizes are so great that the issue must be joined and eventually settled." Any claim of the Vietnamese to the right to determine their own destiny disappeared in the chasm of East-West divisions.

Thus, the record shows that the American perception of the war in Indochina changed radically in the years between 1949 and 1952. Since the definition of what was going on changed, it was only natural that there should be a related shift in ideas of what should be done. This correlation was, in fact, strikingly close. In May 1950, the Griffin mission recommended an aid program of $23 million in economic assistance and $15 million in military aid to the French in Indochina.[14] In June, the first shipments of aircraft were made to Indochina, and $119 million in military aid was made available to France under the Mutual Defense Assistance Program. This aid increased to $300 million in 1952, then to $500 million in the following year; and by 1954, military assistance had reached the $1 billion mark. By then, the United States was paying over half of the total cost of the Indochinese war.[15]

This policy was rooted in the new American perception of the Vietnamese war, brought strikingly into focus in *Atlantic* magazine in June 1951: "Our support of Bao Dai means the support of a democratically minded native government of the Vietnamese people against a rebellious horde led by known Communists. . . . *On these premises, our present position became inevitable.*" *The New York Times* echoed this sentiment editorially when it stated in February 1953: "The French and the Vietnamese are fighting for the free world in Indochina just as the United Nations force is fighting for it in Korea."

Hence, the American involvement in Vietnam antedates the French defeat in Dienbienphu in 1954. Material aid was consid-

[14] Miriam S. Farley, *United States Relations with Southeast Asia, With Special Reference to Indochina* (New York: Institute of Pacific Relations, 1955), p. 4.

[15] *Ibid.*; see also *Department of State Bulletin*, 28 (January 5, 1953), 13.

erable as early as 1952, and psychologically the United States was deeply involved as early as 1950. The American perception of Vietnam, in effect, was "fixed" a full four years before the Geneva Conference. As early as May 14, 1950, *The New York Times* said editorially that "before Indochinese Nationalism can express itself, a real military victory must be won over Ho Chi Minh's regular army and the hard core of his movement either destroyed or driven out of the country. . . . The United States now seems committed to that belief and policy."

It is this emerging sense of *personal* peril that makes American policy in Indochina a case study in United States-Chinese perceptions, for after Mao Tse-tung's victory in 1949, the menace that American leaders saw in Indochina was China herself—a new and threatening China acting as the instrument of Soviet expansionism. China, now lost to the West, had apparently been "won" by the East, and the subsequent reversal of American policy in Indochina was a reaction to what the United States viewed as a sudden and frightening increase to the resources and manpower of international communism.

Large segments of the American public fully expected a Chinese military intervention on the side of Ho Chi Minh, especially after Chinese troops had entered the Korean War. Thus, the New York *Herald Tribune* stated editorially on January 3, 1951, that "Ho Chi Minh has either agreed or submitted to a plan of Chinese invasion. The date when the Chinese will move is generally set within this month," and *The New York Times* reported on December 29, 1951, that "observers foresee an increase in participation by Peiping in the Indochina war in 1952."

Most Americans tended to agree with the evaluation of President Dwight D. Eisenhower, who declared that "the struggle . . . began gradually, *with Chinese intervention*, to assume its true complexion of a struggle between Communist and non-Communist forces rather than one between a colonial power and colonists who were intent on attaining independence."[16]

The expectation of a Chinese invasion was so powerful that it defied all evidence to the contrary. Neither the fact that the anticipated invasion failed to materialize nor the lack of evidence

[16] Dwight D. Eisenhower, *Mandate for Change 1953–1956* (Garden City, N.Y.: Doubleday, 1963), p. 167. Italics added.

that it was actually planned lessened American apprehensions. Instead, the very strength of the expectation produced its own substantiation. Time and again, quite unfounded rumors were accepted as proof of impending intervention. The result was a recurrent pattern of false alarms. Typical of these was a headline in *The New York Times* on April 11, 1951, which reported that a "Chinese Unit [was] said to join [the] Vietminh." Secretary Dulles repeatedly stated that the Chinese were directly engaged in battlefield operations. On April 5, 1954, during the siege of Dienbienphu, he claimed that Chinese troops were actually participating in the battle for the French fortress.[17]

Thus, American involvement in the Indochinese war in the early 1950s was largely intended to counter an impending Chinese military invasion of Indochina. The towering shadow of Mao Tsetung was seen by most Americans as hovering over the figure of Ho Chi Minh. The evidence suggests that the threat of Chinese military intervention existed more in the American mind than in reality. The Chinese did aid Ho in the early 1950s but only with light arms and transport vehicles as well as with some technical and advisory personnel.[18] If viewed from the Chinese side, such a level of assistance was certainly no more provocative than the third of a billion dollars given by the United States to France in 1952 for the prosecution of the war.

The hypothesis thus arises that the initial decision to involve the United States in Indochina was based on elements that had little to do with the objective conditions that then prevailed in Indochina. The danger of responding to phantoms in this fashion is that such responses tend to set in motion the mechanism of the self-fulfilling prophecy. A phantom, if endowed in the mind of the beholder with reality, may gradually assume a more concrete shape and ultimately become a real threat. American fear of Chinese aggression led to the United States' aid program to France, which enabled France to continue the war after 1950. Ho Chi Minh, in turn, sought Chinese economic and technical aid, which helped him to continue the fight. Thus, the initial American perception dictated a policy of escalation, not accommodation. The United

---

[17] John Foster Dulles, cited in Bator, *op. cit.*, p. 210.

[18] Harold C. Hinton, *China's Relations with Burma and Vietnam* (New York: Institute of Pacific Relations, 1958), p. 18.

States failed to respond to at least two peace feelers from Hanoi in 1953, because as Secretary of State Dulles remarked, he "never thought there was much sincerity" in them.[19] The same American fear that China stood behind Hanoi militarily brought the United States close to a massive military intervention on the side of France at the time of the French disaster at Dienbienphu in 1954 and helped to persuade the Eisenhower administration to dissociate the United States from the Geneva Accords.[20] In essence, then, the American perception of an expected Chinese intervention prolonged and intensified the war in Indochina.

The facts, in all cases, were quite different from the perceptions. First, Ho Chi Minh was neither a Vietnamese nationalist alone nor a Communist alone. He was essentially both in equal measure. Second, the relationship between China and North Vietnam was a great deal more complicated and ambivalent than the simplistic American image suggested. And finally, Chinese military intervention on the side of the Vietminh forces never materialized. Instead the Chinese used the Vietminh as their proxy.

Ho Chi Minh is probably one of the most complex political figures of modern times. He was a product of the cross-fertilization of Vietnamese nationalism and European communism. The Vietminh forces that he led were Vietnamese nationalists with Communist leadership cadres. Nationalism and communism were always linked in Ho's mind as mutually supportive, never as mutually exclusive.

Ho Chi Minh's commitment to Vietnamese nationalism is described admirably by Harold Isaacs, one of the few Americans who knew him personally. Isaacs visited Ho when the latter had just become president of the provisional government of the Republic of Vietnam. "My party is my country," Isaacs quotes him as saying, "my program is independence."[21] Neither the Russians nor the Americans could be trusted. In Isaacs' words: "The Annamite Communists I met were men bitten deeply with the bitterness of having been abandoned by their ideological comrades overseas.

---

[19] *China and U.S. Far East Policy, op. cit.,* p. 66.

[20] For a full account of the events during this period, see John G. Stoessinger, *The Might of Nations: World Politics in Our Time,* 4th ed. (New York: Random House, 1973), pp. 173–180.

[21] Ho Chi Minh, quoted by Harold R. Isaacs, *No Peace for Asia* (Cambridge: M.I.T. Press, 1967), p. 165.

They had consequently taken refuge in a pure and simple nationalism. Ho Chi Minh was making no idle phrase when he said: 'My party is my country.' "[22]

The Russians were described as being "nationalists for Russia first and above all." As far as the United States was concerned, Isaacs' description of Ho Chi Minh's reaction is revealing:

> For the only indication of America's role in their [the Vietminh's] struggle came in the form of lend-lease weapons and equipment being used against them by the French and British, and the stunning announcement of an American deal with France for the purchase of $160 million worth of vehicles and miscellaneous industrial equipment for the French in Indochina. . . . This looked like American underwriting of the French reconquest. The Americans were democrats in words but no help in fact, just as the Russians were Communists in words but no help in fact. "We apparently stand quite alone," said Ho Chi Minh simply. "We shall have to depend on ourselves."[23]

As an exponent of Vietnamese nationalism, Ho Chi Minh was a great deal more persuasive than Bao Dai. In the words of one observer: "Bao Dai's white sharkskin suits, fluent French, clumsy Vietnamese, and corpulent fondness for French cooking contrasted sharply with Ho's wispy frame and plain clothes of black or khaki."[24]

Ho's commitment to communism is equally clear. In 1920, he had become a founding member of the French Communist party by voting with the Communist wing against the socialists. He had worked for the French Communists and, for a time, for the Comintern in Europe. Bernard Fall described him as a "dedicated Communist with Vietnamese reactions."[25]

The basic point here is that, in the American perception, nationalism and communism were regarded as almost mutually exclusive. A man was more of a nationalist only if he was less of a Communist. In Ho Chi Minh's mind, however, communism and nationalism were so intertwined that they had become virtually inseparable. This peculiar mixture made Ho Chi Minh's name symbolic for North Vietnam in the same way that the name of

[22] *Ibid.*, p. 174.

[23] *Ibid.*, pp. 174–175.

[24] Claude A. Buss, *Asia in the Modern World* (New York: Macmillan, 1964), p. 596.

[25] Fall, *op. cit.*, p. 90.

Charles de Gaulle had become symbolic for the Fifth Republic of France.

So far as Ho's relations with China are concerned, once again there is a wide gap between the American image and the facts. Ho Chi Minh was always somewhat suspicious of China. In Fall's words, he was "probably equipped with an instinctive Vietnamese fear of Chinese domination," no matter what its political coloration, just as to a Russian, *any* Germany might be slightly suspect.[26] His policy was essentially one of balance, of maintaining the independence and integrity of his movement, vis-à-vis both China and the Soviet Union, while accepting as much aid as could safely be accepted from both.

Chinese aid to Ho Chi Minh was at times considerable, but never decisive. It consisted mostly of light weapons, trucks, and radios, largely of American manufacture, that had been captured from the Chinese Nationalists some years before.[27] In view of economic needs at home and the burdens imposed by the Korean War, China could hardly afford to become a bottomless reservoir of military assistance for the Vietminh forces. The best analysis of the Chinese relationship with Ho Chi Minh has probably been provided by Robert Guillain, the front-line correspondent for *Le Monde* in Indochina: "China adheres to a very simple principle: that the balance of power never inclines in any permanent direction toward the French side. There is no need—and this is the difference from what has happened in Korea—of direct intervention, of an invasion."[28] Thus, when France received more American aid following the outbreak of the Korean War, the Chinese stepped up their own aid program just enough to reestablish a rough equilibrium. As Melvin Gurtov put it: "The Indochina campaign eventually became a crude game in which the French could never permanently regain the high ground."[29]

By 1954, largely as a result of their perceptions, the Americans were fighting a proxy war in Indochina. The battle for Dienbienphu almost changed this into a direct American war of interven-

[26] *Ibid.*, p. 90.

[27] Melvin Gurtov, *The First Vietnam Crisis* (New York: Columbia University Press, 1967), p. 14.

[28] Robert Guillain, *La Fin des Illusions: Notes d'Indochine* (Paris: Centre d'Etudes de Politique Etrangère, 1954), p. 39.

[29] Gurtov, *op. cit.*, p. 15.

tion. On March 20, 1954, General Paul Ely, commander of the French forces in Indochina, informed President Eisenhower that, unless the United States intervened, Indochina would be lost. Admiral Arthur W. Radford, chairman of the Joint Chiefs of Staff, recommended military intervention, and Vice-President Richard M. Nixon backed him in a statement on April 16, declaring that "if the United States [can] not otherwise prevent the loss of Indochina, then the Administration must face the situation and dispatch troops."[30] President Eisenhower overruled his Vice-President and the Chairman of the Joint Chiefs of Staff and decided not to intervene. He feared that the French had engendered too much popular antagonism to win the war and also felt that his administration would get little backing from the Congress and from Great Britain for a military intervention. Thus, on the American side the war remained by proxy for a little while longer, but by a narrow margin.

How did China perceive the situation in Indochina and the role there of the United States? The evidence reveals that the Chinese superimposed their own perceptual grid upon the situation. Their dichotomies were as sharp and their expectations of hostile intent as firm as the cold war categories of the United States. The Communist Chinese leadership perceived the entire modern history of China as "nothing but a history of the imperialist invasion of China and of obstruction by it of the path of Chinese independence."[31] It saw itself in deadly peril of renewed imperialist encroachment by the United States from the very beginning. In 1949, for example, Mao Tse-tung told the Preparatory Committee of the New Political Consultative Conference that "the imperialists . . . would not take their defeat in this land of China lying down . . . they may even send part of their armed forces to encroach on China's frontiers. . . . We must decidedly not . . . relax our vigilance toward the wild retaliatory plots of imperialist elements and their running dogs."[32]

It is quite revealing to trace the parallel features in the Chinese

---

[30] Richard M. Nixon, quoted in Chalmers M. Roberts, "The Day We Didn't Go to War," *The Reporter*, September 14, 1954.

[31] Quoted from Mao Tse-tung, *On the New Democracy*, in H. Arthur Steiner, "Mainsprings of Chinese Communist Foreign Policy," *American Journal of International Law*, 44 (January 1950), 77 ff.

[32] *China Digest*, June 28, 1949, p. 4.

and American perceptions of one another. Each pictured the other, a priori, as implacably hostile. Given this axiomatic assumption, the interpretation of each new event was almost predetermined. The American conviction of hostile Chinese intent caused even vague rumors to be taken as hard evidence of an imminent invasion of Indochina. Similarly, the Chinese conviction of hostile American intent caused each American action in the early 1950s to be taken as hard evidence of a concerted American policy of strangulation. In 1951, for example, the Chinese declared that it was

> part of the American imperialist plan of aggression to use Vietnam as one of the chief bases for military encirclement and attack on the new China. Having suffered a deplorable fiasco in their invasion of Korea, the American imperialists are sparing no efforts to carry out disturbances and sabotages against China from different directions.[33]

The Chinese view of American intent imparted a sinister pattern to the entire range of American actions in the Far East. United States intervention in Korea in 1950, the peace treaty with Japan in 1951, the increased military aid to Thailand, the commitment to Chiang Kai-shek on Taiwan, the presence of the American 7th Fleet in the Formosa Straits, and, of course, the deepening involvement in Indochina—all these were seen as a clear-cut pattern of hostile encirclement of the new China. Obviously, the Americans were "now stepping into the shoes of the Japanese,"[34] and "American interventionists would not voluntarily abandon their scheme to conquer Vietnam in preparation for aggression against China,"[35] for they were "intending to usurp the world alone . . . and convert Southeast Asia into a military base for aggression against China and the Soviet Union."[36]

Thus, on both sides a vicious circle was created. Each began with the a priori assumption of the other's implacable hostility; the power of this conviction caused actions to be interpreted as confirming the validity of the original assumption; hence, the adversary was found to be hostile a posteriori as well, since his actions

---

[33] *Survey of China Mainland Press,* 47 (Hong Kong: American Consulate General, January 12, 1951), 5.

[34] *Survey of China Mainland Press,* 166 (September 2–4, 1951), 18.

[35] *Survey of China Mainland Press,* 236 (December 14–15, 1951), 10.

[36] *Survey of China Mainland Press,* 334 (May 13, 1952), 25.

had "proved" that the original assumption was correct. The very actions that the Chinese perceived as an American plot to encircle them were perceived by the Americans as necessary measures to forestall Chinese aggression. Confronted by a series of American policies that appeared to prove American enmity, the Chinese embarked upon an increasingly virulent Hate America campaign that the United States in turn took as proof of implacable hostility. What seemed patently provocative to one appeared obviously defensive to the other. In this tragic spiral of reciprocally negative reinforcement, the border line between real and imagined threats tended to blur and finally to disappear altogether.

It is easy to see why political accommodation would be almost impossible under such conditions. On a deeper psychological level, such mirror devil images are the stuff that holy wars are made of, for to each side in the conflict, the enemy is not quite human and it becomes difficult, if not impossible, to identify with any part of him. Hence, each adversary is left with his fears and terrors, which are in no way allayed by their failure to materialize. But such fears can call forth a reality as terrible as the most anguished nightmare. This was the peril of the encounter between China and America during the first decade of the war in Indochina.

Chapter Six

The United States, China, and the Vietnamese War: The American Phase

The Chinese-American encounter in Vietnam during the presidency of Lyndon B. Johnson never exploded into armed conflict. It is the thesis of this chapter that this was the result of valuable lessons that the two antagonists drew from the Korean War. In that conflict, misperceptions on both sides played a significant role in hastening the day of Chinese intervention. In Vietnam, on the other hand, the Chinese initiated specific military moves in order to signal Washington of their intentions, rather than relying entirely on verbal warnings and diplomatic channels. Similarly, the United States not only announced to China that American goals did not include the destruction of the Hanoi government or an attack on China, but also refrained from military actions such as amphibious landings or large reconnaissance raids into North Vietnam that might have triggered a Chinese response in the way the American crossing of the thirty-eighth parallel in Korea had done. Thus, two nations that had suffered grievously as a result of policies based on misperception were capable of learning and growing from the experience.

The Geneva Conference of mid-1954 and the formation, a few weeks later, of the Southeast Asia Treaty Organization (SEATO) marked the end of French military involvement and the beginning of an American military presence in Indochina. The Geneva Conference resulted in the signing of several agreements to cease hostilities in Indochina and to establish three independent sovereign states: Laos, Cambodia, and Vietnam. The accords on Vietnam provided for a "provisional military demarcation line" at the seventeenth parallel. Vietminh forces were to regroup north of the line, while the forces of the French Union were to regroup to the south. The line was to have military significance only, and the political unification of Vietnam was to be brought about through a general election two years hence under the supervision of a neutral three-power International Control Commission consisting of Canada, India, and Poland.

France had little choice, but her exit was made somewhat more graceful. Ho Chi Minh's Vietminh forces were dominant in more than three-quarters of Vietnam and were poised to overrun considerably more. To Ho, the terms of the accords were acceptable, since he was convinced that the general election of 1956 would win him all of Vietnam. From his point of view, the certainty of a military victory was simply replaced by the certainty of a political victory. Both the Soviet Union and Communist China, reflecting their recently adopted line of "peaceful coexistence," applied pressure on Ho to accept the terms of the accords, reassuring him that his victory at the polls was certain.

The United States never signed the Geneva Accords. But, in a unilateral declaration at the end of the Geneva Conference, the United States government pledged to "refrain from the threat or the use of force to disturb" the settlement and added that it would view any violation of the accords with grave concern.

The general American position at the conference remained ambivalent, since on the eve of a congressional election campaign, the maintenance of Eisenhower's domestic appeal as peacemaker in Asia was of great importance. Moreover, to block a peaceful settlement of the Indochina war would also have jeopardized French participation in European defense plans. These conflicting considerations led the Eisenhower administration to dissociate the United States from the Geneva Accords and to seek another solution that would prevent any further territory in Asia from falling under Communist control. The answer was the creation of SEATO. Secretary of State Dulles declared that now that the war had ended, the United States could make arrangements for collective defense against aggression and build up "the truly independent states of Cambodia, Laos, and South Vietnam." On the day the treaty was signed at Manila, in an additional protocol, its eight members designated the states of Cambodia and Laos and "the free territory under the jurisdiction of the state of Vietnam" to be under SEATO protection. The United States thus created SEATO to offset the results of Geneva. It also decided to consider South Vietnam as a separate state.

The Vietminh, on the other hand, regarded SEATO as a clear violation of the spirit of the Geneva Accords. Ho Chi Minh saw the American position as an effort to deprive the Vietminh in the political arena of what it had gained militarily on the battlefield. Nevertheless, Ho withdrew his forces from the South, assuming that he would get enough votes there in 1956 to emerge with a clear national majority at election time. His election in the North would be a certainty, and if only a minority would support the Vietminh in the South, his election would be assured. President Eisenhower, too, thought that elections, if held on the basis of the Geneva Accords, would lead to a Communist victory. As he put it in 1954, "Had elections been held as of the time of the fighting, possibly 80 percent of the population would have voted for the Communist Ho Chi Minh as their leader rather than Chief of State Bao Dai."[1]

In the meantime, Ngo Dinh Diem, an American-backed Roman Catholic from a Mandarin family, began to challenge Emperor Bao Dai in the South. The United States strongly supported Diem in his bid for power, and in October 1955, Diem proclaimed the establishment of a Republic of Vietnam, with himself as president.

Hence, Geneva and the SEATO treaty meant the end of French power in Indochina and the beginnings of the American effort to enter the struggle with its own military presence. As yet, there were no significant military encounters between Vietminh and American forces. But the issue was joined. The Vietminh saw the Americans as following the path of French imperialism, and the Americans perceived Geneva as a well-laid Communist trap to

---

[1] Dwight D. Eisenhower, *Mandate for Change 1953–1956* (Garden City, N.Y.: Doubleday, 1963), p. 372.

engulf all of Vietnam. The end of a colonial war merely signified the beginnings of a war between Americans and Communists.

As the East-West conflict superseded the colonial war, the pace of battle gradually intensified. A pattern of escalation emerged in which every diplomatic failure to achieve negotiations paved the way for yet another upward step on the scale of violence.

The first such discernible moves after Geneva were the American effort between 1954 and 1956 to strengthen President Diem's military establishment and Ho Chi Minh's visit to Moscow and Peking in 1955 to negotiate aid and friendship treaties with the two Communist powers. Diem declared in July 1955 that, since South Vietnam had not signed the Geneva Accords, he was not prepared to permit elections under the conditions specified by them. He also added that there was no freedom in the North to campaign for any opposition to Ho Chi Minh. The American government supported this view, and July 1956, the date scheduled for general elections in the accords, passed without elections being held. Ho, in retaliation, began to train Communist cadres for guerrilla warfare in the South. He also became the recipient of aid from the Soviet Union and China for the purpose of shoring up the economic base of the North Vietnamese state.

On December 20, 1960, a National Liberation Front (NLF) was created in South Vietnam. The front announced a ten-point program calling for the overthrow of the incumbent Saigon government and the removal of American military advisers.

During the remaining years of the Eisenhower administration, the United States continued to support the increasingly unpopular President Diem with military advisers. The second level of escalation was reached in January 1961, when Hanoi announced its endorsement of the National Liberation Front in South Vietnam.

The three years of the Kennedy administration were years of gradually deepening, though always limited, American involvement. By the time of President John F. Kennedy's death, the United States had approximately 17,000 advisers in Vietnam, though there was no direct American participation in actual combat. The situation was further complicated by the increasingly oppressive nature of Diem's regime, which was ultimately overthrown by a military coup in November 1963. Kennedy always tried to draw a distinction between American assistance to South Vietnam and Americanization of the war. "In the final analysis," he said, "it is their war. They are the ones who have to win it or lose it."[2] In the meantime, Communist insurgency in the South was growing rapidly. The resurrected Vietminh, now called Vietcong by the Americans, infiltrated the South in increasing numbers. The National Liberation Front built a highly efficient network of political cadres, which began a campaign of terror and assassination in South Vietnamese villages. By late 1963, both sides had raised the stakes and the United States, though not yet directly involved in combat, began to establish the necessary logistical base for further action.

Another threshold was crossed in the summer of 1964. In July, the new South Vietnamese prime minister, General Nguyen Khanh, delivered a major address, the keynote of which was "to the North." Two days later, Nguyen Cao Ky, the commander of the South Vietnamese air force, announced that he was prepared to bomb North Vietnam at any time. In early August, North Vietnamese torpedo boats allegedly launched attacks on two American ships in the Gulf of Tonkin. President Johnson retaliated by bombing oil depots and other facilities in North Vietnam. On August 10, the President secured the passage of the Tonkin Gulf Resolution in Congress, which authorized him "to take all necessary measures to repel any armed attack against the forces of the U.S. and to prevent further aggression." The air war had gone north of the seventeenth parallel for the first time.

The next step in the escalation was reached in February 1965. On February 7, the Vietcong staged a night raid against American barracks at Pleiku, killing 8 Americans and wounding 126. Twelve hours later, American jets attacked North Vietnam in what was to be the first of an almost uninterrupted series of daily air attacks against the North. In the South, marines were introduced into the ground war, which was now rapidly becoming Americanized. By 1966, United States fighting units were frequently suffering higher casualty rates than were their South Vietnamese allies. The National Liberation Front responded to these events with its harsh five-point manifesto of March 1965, in which it refused to enter into negotiations until after American troops had been withdrawn. Three weeks later, however, Hanoi published its own four-point program, in which it did not rule out the possibility of negotia-

2 *Department of State Bulletin*, 49 (September 30, 1963), 498–499.

tions. In mid-May, the United States stopped bombing the North for five days, but no talks ensued—and the air attacks were resumed.

In February 1966, President Johnson met with the South Vietnamese leader, Air Marshal Ky, at Honolulu, where the two men underlined their solidarity against "the aggression from the North." In mid-1966, Johnson announced that guerrilla infiltration from the North had increased at an alarming rate and that further American retaliatory action might be necessary. In June, the United States bombed the North Vietnamese capital of Hanoi and its largest port, Haiphong. In the South, American manpower had risen from 17,000 to 500,000 by 1968. There was no evidence, however, that this policy of "strategic persuasion" had deterred the Hanoi regime from sending more guerrillas to the South or the National Liberation Front from attempting to infiltrate the countryside. The war had escalated in ever more violent bursts, but no decisive change had occurred in the balance of power among the main belligerents.

By this time, a deep division had occurred within the United States over the American commitment in Vietnam and the future course of American foreign policy in Southeast Asia. The administration defended its policy in Vietnam on the following grounds: first, the air attacks were not only seen as strategic persuasion of the North to leave its neighbors to the South alone, but they were also designed to boost the morale of the South Vietnamese fighting forces. Moreover, the bombing raids raised the costs of aggression and made it more difficult to send guerrillas to the South via the Ho Chi Minh Trail. Second, a withdrawal would signify a tremendous victory for the Chinese view on wars of liberation, reinforcing a view of the United States as a paper tiger and encouraging stepped-up aggressive moves by communism elsewhere in the world. Third, "aggression must be stopped at the source"—Hanoi stood behind the National Liberation Front, and China stood behind Hanoi; hence, China had to be contained on her periphery as the Soviet Union was twenty years earlier. A withdrawal, on the other hand, would produce a "row of falling dominoes" and bring to an end the American presence in Southeast Asia.

Critics of the administration pointed to the experience of 400,000 French troops in Indochina and wondered whether the

United States could fare better in a counterinsurgency war in which a ten-to-one troop ratio in favor of the United States might be necessary for victory over the Vietcong. Opponents of the war also accused the United States of destroying the social fabric of South Vietnam—the very nation it had set out to save from communism—through air bombardments and ground warfare. In addition, the danger of Chinese or Soviet intervention on Hanoi's side took a prominent place in the view of most critics. Finally, opponents asserted that the United States still behaved as if communism were a monolithic force that had to elicit an American response whenever a Communist regime appeared. Communism, the argument continued, was now much more diffuse, and each such regime should be evaluated in a specific and pragmatic manner by the United States, rather than seen automatically as an attempt to extend the design of world communism. Thus, while the American involvement in Vietnam would have made sense twenty years earlier, as did the formation of NATO in Europe, in the 1960s a strategic United States commitment in Southeast Asia was at best an anachronism and, at worst, a catastrophe. These differing perceptions of the nature of communism lay at the heart of the dialogue between "hawks" and "doves" in the United States.

By early 1968, the impasse over negotiations among the main belligerents—the National Liberation Front and North Vietnam, on one side, and the United States and South Vietnam, on the other—had crystallized into a single issue: the bombing of North Vietnam. Hanoi and the NLF demanded the cessation of bombings as a precondition to talks; the United States and South Vietnam demanded an end to Communist infiltration into the South as a prerequisite to the cessation of air attacks on the North. On March 31, 1968, President Johnson decided to stop all bombings north of the nineteenth parallel. Shortly thereafter, peace talks began in Paris between the United States and North Vietnam. At these talks, the North Vietnamese negotiators insisted on a total halt to the bombings; the United States in turn insisted on the simultaneous reduction of guerrilla infiltration into South Vietnam as an act of reciprocity. On October 31, President Johnson ordered the complete cessation of the bombings. The Paris peace talks were broadened to include South Vietnam and the National Liberation Front. But as in Korea, the peace talks did little to mitigate the ferocity of war.

The Chinese-American relationship during the Korean War had suffered from distortions in each of our four main analytical categories: self-image, perception of the other's character, perception of the other's intentions, and perception of the other's power and capabilities. In Vietnam, a considerable degree of distortion was evident in the first three categories, but there was little, if any, in evidence in the last. Both nations had a realistic assessment of each other's power, and this realism prevented a direct military clash between them. Let us first recall the sequence of events in Vietnam that affected United States-Chinese relations during the Johnson administration.

The first significant Chinese action to counter American operations in Vietnam reflected the experience of the Korean War in 1950. At that time, diplomatic warning to the United States not to cross the thirty-eighth parallel had proved ineffective. Peking then ordered the dispatch of troops across the Yalu to stop the advance of the United Nations forces. In the autumn of 1964, however, the Chinese response to American attacks on North Vietnamese PT boat bases was to make a specific military gesture. The Chinese quietly deployed several units of MIG jet fighters, 50,000 railroad construction troops, and some antiaircraft detachments to North Vietnam and began to construct military air bases in South China. This was a clear signal to Washington that China would not remain unengaged in hostilities directed specifically against North Vietnam.[3] There had been no such military "signal" in Korea. During the next few months, no major escalation took place either on the American or the Chinese side. In February 1965, however, the United States began the bombardment of North Vietnam and committed an increasing number of troops to combat operations in South Vietnam. As the number of American ground forces in South Vietnam rose steadily during 1966 and 1967, tensions with China increased as well. On April 26, 1966, an aerial dogfight took place between two American F-4C Phantom fighters and a Chinese MIG-21 fighter. The United States denied a Chinese assertion that the MIG was shot down over China. On May 27, 1966, the State Department chose "not to challenge" a Chinese report of May 12 that five American aircraft had crossed the Chinese

[3] This was first revealed publicly by Dr. Allen Whiting, former Director of Intelligence and Research for East Asia, U.S. Department of State, in an article entitled "How We Almost Went to War with China," Look Magazine, April 29, 1969.

border and had shot down a MIG-17. In August 1966, American bombs fell within ten miles of China, and "American, North Vietnamese and Chinese fighters flew ever closer to each other, with Communist planes relying on the sanctuary of bases in China."[4] These events marked the high point of United States-Chinese brinkmanship during the Vietnamese war. Even during these tense months, however, when the number of American ground troops crept up toward the half million mark, considerable prudence and restraint characterized the policies of both sides. President Johnson was reliably reported to have said that "Russia doesn't want war, China doesn't want to get into a war, and you know damned well that we don't want to get into the big war."[5] On the other side, Chou En-lai stated repeatedly that "China [would] not take the initiative to provoke a war with the United States."[6]

The cessation of the American bombing of North Vietnam and the beginning of the Paris peace talks also reduced tensions between China and America. The Chinese leadership, while continuing its verbal attacks on the United States, reduced its manpower commitments in Vietnam. During 1969, the 50,000 railroad construction troops that had been sent to North Vietnam in 1964 and 1965 were quietly pulled back to China.

The American self-image during the war in Vietnam retained most of the features that had characterized it during the Korean War. Once again "defender of democracy" and "bastion of the free world" were phrases that appeared regularly in President Johnson's speeches. In addition, honor and the sacredness of a commitment were frequently hailed as American ideals in the war. The image of the United States as "world policeman" emerged with even greater force in Vietnam than it had in Korea. In his address at Johns Hopkins University in 1965, for example, President Johnson justified the American involvement in Vietnam in the following terms:

> We are also there to strengthen world order. Around the globe, from Berlin to Thailand, are people whose well-being rests, in part, on the

---

[4] *Ibid.*

[5] Lyndon B. Johnson, quoted in Hugh Sidey, A *Very Personal Presidency* (New York: Atheneum, 1968), p. 238.

[6] Chou En-lai, "Four-Point Statement on China's Policy Toward the United States," *Peking Review*, May 13, 1966.

belief that they can count on us if they are attacked. To leave Vietnam to its fate would shake the confidence of all these people in the value of American commitment, the value of America's word. The result would be increased unrest and instability, and even wider war.[7]

And even more clearly, he said: "History and our own achievements have thrust upon us the principal responsibility for the protection of freedom on earth."[8]

Similarly, on the Chinese side, many of the self-images that prevailed during the Korean War carried over to the Vietnamese experience. Once again, Peking spoke of its revolutionary mission and the need to make China a "secure base for world revolution." The split with the Soviet Union that had developed since the Korean War, of course, deeply colored Peking's view of itself. The self-image of China as the true and only torchbearer of militant communism injected a Messianic zeal into the statements of the Chinese leadership that far exceeded those that had been made during the Korean War. Marshal Lin Piao, in an article published in September 1965, conceived of China as the revolutionary base of the "world countryside" of Asia, Africa, and Latin America as it prepared to surround and ultimately defeat the "world cities" of Europe and North America.[9] The practical operational consequences of this article have been the subject of much discussion. Some scholars saw it as a blueprint for world conquest, while others interpreted it in a much more modest light. In any case, the article no doubt projected a self-image of China as the last stronghold of militant, unspoiled communism and the world's last hope of obtaining communism's universal ideals.

At about the same time, yet another internal development helped to fuel China's self-image as the standard-bearer of revolutionary ideas: the Cultural Revolution. In 1966, the beginnings of this furious internal struggle became increasingly apparent. Mao Tse-tung, anxious that China might follow the "revisionist" example of the Soviet Union, made a concerted effort to reinfuse China's masses with the revolutionary fervor of the old Yenan

[7] Speech by President Lyndon B. Johnson at Johns Hopkins University, April 7, 1965, cited in *The Vietnam Reader*, Marcus G. Raskin and Bernard B. Fall (eds.) (New York: Vintage, 1967), p. 345.

[8] Lyndon B. Johnson, quoted in *The New York Times*, February 13, 1965.

[9] Lin Piao, "The International Significance of Comrade Mao Tse-tung's Theory of People's War," *Foreign Language Press* (Peking, September 1965), pp. 42–59.

days. Toward this end, hundreds of thousands of young Red Guards were mobilized to spread Mao's slogans across the land. Universities were closed and Chinese intellectuals suspected of foreign sympathies were purged and persecuted. The American bombing of North Vietnam, so close to the Chinese border, may have increased the ferocity of Mao's anti-Western purge. At any rate, through this campaign of terror and intimidation, China tried to perpetuate her "revolutionary purity."

Thus, the self-images of both major powers had changed somewhat since the Korean War. Both China and America saw themselves as even more on the side of right, truth, and justice than they had fifteen years earlier. A greater degree of rigidity and self-righteousness had begun to color their perceptions of themselves. And each now harbored an almost passionate sense of mission to spread its truth and justice beyond its borders.

The mirror devil image that had characterized each nation's perception of its adversary's character during the Korean War was even more intensely manifest in Vietnam. The Chinese viewed the Americans as "aggressors and imperialists," and the United States leadership regarded China as "aggressive and expansionist." Each side compared the other's character to that of Hitler's Germany. China was the first to make the comparison in an editorial published in the *Peking Review* on April 30, 1965, entitled "Escalation Means Getting Closer and Closer to the Grave":

> The tactics used by the Johnson Administration are very similar to Hitler's gradual expansion of aggression before World War II. The aim is nothing less than to slacken the vigilance of the world's people, so that they will be faced with a "fait accompli" by the US aggressor before they know it.[10]

In the United States, Marshal Lin Piao's article was seen by numerous high officials as the Chinese blueprint for world conquest, comparable to Hitler's *Mein Kampf*. Secretary of State Dean Rusk stated repeatedly that the aggression in Vietnam was backed by China, that it was similar to Hitler's aggression in Europe, and that appeasement in Vietnam would have the same consequences as appeasement in Munich. President Johnson struck the same note when he said: "Retreat leads to retreat, just as aggression leads to

---

[10] Cited in Marvin Gettleman (ed.), *Vietnam* (New York: Fawcett, 1965), p. 428.

aggression in this still primitive international community."[11] The American image of China's character conjured up a predatory beast poised to unleash hordes of faceless millions bent upon overrunning first Asia then, possibly, the rest of the world. In fact, numerous statements made by leading American statesmen brought to mind Kaiser Wilhelm's view of the "yellow peril." The racist "yellow" had yielded to the ideological "red," but otherwise all the old devil images remained intact. The Chinese view of the United States was equally one-dimensional and uncompromising. America was still the old imperialist nation bent upon trampling underfoot the yearnings of the peoples of Asia for independence. Driven by an economic engine that fed upon others like a parasite and powered by a vast military and industrial establishment that hungered for even further conquest, the United States was the aggressor incarnate.

Perceptions of the intentions of the adversary were complex and ambivalent on both sides. Although the Chinese press repeatedly described the American purpose in South Vietnam to be the enslavement of that nation and later an invasion of China, this was not the only view expressed. In January 1965, Mao told Edgar Snow that domestic pressures would soon precipitate an American withdrawal, but Anna Louise Strong, an authoritative voice from Peking, wrote that "The further the US escalates the more it will be entangled. Even now it is hard to tell whether the US ruling class really wants the long war which the experts say it will take to subdue South Vietnam, or whether they are on a tiger and cannot dismount."[12] Thus, at times the United States was portrayed as intent upon the conquest of Vietnam and a subsequent attack on China; at other times, the United States was depicted as about to withdraw and later to collapse internally from the domestic pressures and bewilderment over its involvement in the Vietnamese war. This ambivalence over American intentions characterized Chinese perceptions during the entire term of the Johnson administration.

On the American side, a dual image of Chinese intentions prevailed as well. The more widespread view was frequently artic-

[11] Lyndon B. Johnson, *The Choices We Face* (New York: Bantam, 1969), p. 27.
[12] "When and How Will China Go to War?" *Supplement to Letter from China*, 38 (April 25, 1966).

ulated by elected officials and the mass media. It envisioned a militant and aggressive China actively seeking to conquer its Asian neighbors and, ultimately, to dominate all nonindustrial nations of the world. This view was reinforced by Rusk, who frequently asserted his belief that the war in Vietnam was directed from Hanoi and inspired from Peking. This "Militant China" school saw confirmation of its views in the previously mentioned article by Lin Piao. The following passage served as evidence: "Everything is divisible and so is this colossus of US imperialism. It can be split up and defeated. The peoples of Asia, Africa, and Latin America, and other regions can destroy it piece by piece, some striking at its head and others at its feet."[13] Parallels to Hitler's *Mein Kampf* were repeatedly drawn from these lines.

A second school viewed in Lin Piao's article as clever rhetoric masking Peking's unwillingness or fear to intervene directly in the Vietnamese war. Limited MIGs, antiaircraft weapons, construction workers, and supplies would be the extent of China's tangible involvement in the Vietnamese struggle. This view was suggested in an analysis by the Rand Corporation in November 1965, entitled "People's War, China Takes a Second Look at Vietnam." A similar interpretation of Lin's article was given by Donald S. Zagoria in *Vietnam Triangle*.[14] Zagoria argued that the article was in reality a veiled exhortation to Hanoi to do the job of national liberation itself, without military assistance from China. Thus, Lin Piao's article provided the raw material for both the *Mein Kampf* and the "do-it-yourself" images of China's intentions. The Rorschach ink blot quality of the article suggests that, in the absence of hard information about the adversary's intentions, Americans tended to perceive what they wanted to perceive. But the view that ultimately prevailed among the policy-making elite during the Johnson administration was that of a militant China.

There is no doubt that for China and the United States the crucial difference between the Korean and the Vietnamese encounters lay in the two nations' perceptions of each other's power and capabilities. Despite the extremity of the perceptions described above, Korea remained a restraining memory for both sides. President Johnson had a high respect for China's military power.

---

[13] Lin Piao, *op. cit.*, quoted in *The New York Times*, January 19, 1966.
[14] Donald S. Zagoria, *Vietnam Triangle* (New York: Pegasus Press, 1967), *passim*.

He said, "We know there are about 200 million in the Chinese Army. . . . Think about 200 million Chinese coming down those trails. . . . No, Sir, I don't want to fight them."[15] This was a far cry from Douglas MacArthur's view of the Chinese army in 1950. In addition, China's explosion of nuclear bombs in October 1964 and in February 1965 helped to alter the American view of Chinese military "backwardness."

A similar process of reevaluation went on in China after the Korean War. Despite China's self-image of virtual invincibility and countless references to the United States as a paper tiger, a good measure of respect for American power often showed through the rhetoric. For example, in 1967, *People's Daily* warned that "the United States is very powerful; it is the strongest country in the world."[16] The Chinese leadership also paid close attention to American statements on the disposition of combat forces and the dispatch of arms and strategic aircraft, and it seems that most such statements were believed and taken at face value. Peking in fact exercised a great deal of caution. Mao's policy seems to have been to provide as much Chinese aid as possible to North Vietnam and to act as its rear area of support, but to avoid any involvement that might provoke American attacks on China. The possibility of the use of nuclear weapons no doubt acted as an additional deterrent.

Of course, the Korean War was not the only reason that a greater degree of realism entered Sino-American views of each other's power. The international constellation had changed dramatically since the conclusion of the Korean War. The most momentous change, of course, was the rift in Sino-Soviet relations. During the Korean War, the Soviet Union and China were on friendly terms and had just concluded a formal alliance in which they had agreed that, in case of attack on one, the other would use all means available to provide immediate military assistance. By 1966, the hostility between them had become so intense that Peking accused the Soviet Union of having "aligned [itself] with US imperialism in a holy alliance against China."[17] Moreover, the Vietnamese war, far from healing the Sino-Soviet rift, had tended

---

[15] Lyndon B. Johnson, quoted in Philip Geyelin, *Johnson and the World* (New York: Praeger, 1966), p. 197.

[16] *People's Daily* (Peking), April 5, 1967.

[17] *Associated Press*, March 24, 1966.

to exacerbate it further.[18] In addition to the Sino-Soviet split, both China and the United States had to face internal traumas during the course of the Vietnamese war that made them doubly anxious to avoid a military clash. In the United States, a wave of violence was rampant, and the pressures against the war in Vietnam finally became so powerful that they drove President Johnson from office in 1968. China not only was wracked by her "cultural revolution," but her foreign policy suffered severe setbacks in Indonesia, on the Asian rimland, and in Africa. All these changes in the balance of world power tended to inject a greater degree of caution into the policies of China and the United States vis-à-vis each other.

A comparison of the Korean and Vietnamese encounters between China and America permits a number of suggestive conclusions. The extreme images of self and of adversary that were evident during the Korean War persisted during the Vietnamese experience. In the latter case, they were even more extreme and one-dimensional. Images of the adversary's power, however, which had been seriously distorted in the Korean War, exhibited a remarkable degree of realism in the Vietnamese war. The conclusion is inescapable that the Korean experience served as an important corrective during the Johnson presidency. Thus, even when extreme images of one's own country's rectitude and the enemy's evil character and intentions continue to persist, disastrous consequences can be avoided if images of the enemy's power and capabilities tend to conform roughly to reality. One cannot, of course, answer with certitude the question of whether China and America would have gone to war over Vietnam in the 1960s if they had not fought in Korea. But in a broader sense, the melancholy answer that this analysis suggests is that the most efficient corrective to war may continue to be the memory of war itself.

[18] Zagoria, op. cit., passim.

Chapter Seven

The Winding Road to Reality

When Mao Tse-tung took control of China in 1949, there were few objective quarrels between him and the United States that could not have been resolved through a policy of compromise. There was no defense treaty with Chiang Kai-shek, there were no American ships in the Formosa Strait, there was no Korean conflict, and the Indochina war was years away. But Americans and Chinese had memories of each other that prevented compromise. More than a century of tragic history made reconciliation difficult. The Chinese remembered America's policy of the Open Door as a pretext for plunder and exploitation. They had never opened the door, they thought, but rather the Americans had crashed it in. Americans in turn, believed that they had played the role of China's benevolent guardian, and now China had been lost—as if China had been America's to lose. Both nations thus felt utterly betrayed and regarded each other as deadly enemies. It would take more than twenty years of hate, two bitter wars on Asian soil, and suffering on a horrendous scale, before China and America were to make fact, not fear, the basis of their policy.

For an entire generation, two great nations perceived each other through dark screens that often produced caricatures out of realities. They learned to fashion images that were based upon their deepest fears. To both Chinese and Americans during the 1950s and 1960s, "the other side" was not quite human. There were times when these fears conjured up a terrible reality.

In the matter of respective self-images, it is important to recall that both nations had quasi-religious, almost crusading views of themselves. Each side's view of the other's character came close to Cotton Mather's conception of the Devil. The image projected on each side was that of an opponent with whom there can, and must, be no compromise and whose very touch brings contamination and defilement. When, for example, Secretary of State John Foster Dulles encountered China's Premier Chou En-lai in Geneva in 1954, he refused to shake hands with the Chinese statesman. Little wonder that these images created an atmosphere of conflict that tended to exacerbate specific incidents. If you believe long enough and hard enough that the other side is your enemy, you will eventually be right.

Perceptions of each other's intentions always conjured up the worst. Thus, in 1950, the Chinese leadership came close to believing that General Douglas MacArthur was planning a full-scale invasion of China. The Chinese intervention in Korea and the bloody war that followed were perceived in China, at least in part, as defensive actions. Two years later, the Americans expected a Chinese intervention, on the Vietminh side, against France in Indochina. This expectation was so powerful that it defied all evidence to the contrary. Neither the fact that the anticipated invasion failed to materialize nor the lack of evidence that it was actually planned lessened American apprehensions. Instead, the very strength of the expectation led to its own substantiation. Time and time again, quite unfounded rumors were accepted as proof of impending intervention. The result was a recurrent pattern of false alarms. Thus, the American support of France in the Indochina war in the early 1950s was at least partially intended to counter an impending Chinese military intervention.

Finally, misperceptions of the power of the other side courted disaster. General MacArthur, as we have seen, seriously underestimated the strength of the Chinese forces and doubted China's readiness and ability to intervene in the Korean War. This lack of respect led to disastrous consequences: in late 1950, the Chinese attacked in overwhelming force and turned the American advance to the Yalu River into a bloody rout.

The Chinese and American peoples were not encouraged to learn new facts about each other. Instead, they had to offer up their bodies in defense of shadows. For two long decades, there was little creative statesmanship. Shop-worn slogans dominated policy. For more than twenty years, the history of China and America was written in ignorance, tragedy, and blood.

The roots of rapprochement on the American side lay in the decisions by Richard Nixon and Henry Kissinger, upon entering the White House in 1969, to reexamine America's China policy and to "Vietnamize" the war in Indochina. The new administration realized the sterility of past China policy and saw the need to deal with China on the basis of present facts rather than old fears. Moreover, the reestablishment of relations with China would thrust the United States into the role of balancer between China and the Soviet Union so long as the hostility between the two great Communist powers continued to exist. America, in short, would be wooed by both leading powers of the Communist world. On the Chinese side, the conviction gradually crystallized that the United States was a less formidable threat than the Soviet Union. After all, Americans were withdrawing from Asian soil while Soviet troops were massing on the Chinese border. Rapprochement with the United States would eliminate the danger of a two-front cold war. Thus, to the Chinese leadership, détente with the United States became a matter of national security.

Henry Kissinger had been Richard Nixon's teacher on how to build détente with the Soviet Union. In contemplating an American opening to China, however, both men reached similar conclusions at approximately the same time. Nixon, in October 1967, had written in *Foreign Affairs*, that "any American policy must come urgently to grips with the reality of China. There is no place on this small planet for a billion of its potentially most able people to live in angry isolation." He also was the first to see the possibility of levering the widening rift between China and the Soviet Union to the advantage of the United States. One week after Inauguration Day, Nixon sent a memo to his new assistant for national security affairs, asking him to explore discreetly the possibility of rapprochement with China. Kissinger promised to do so, though he believed that it might take some time to build a bridge to China.

In March 1969, shooting broke out along the Ussuri River, at the Chinese-Soviet border. Tensions over disputed territory had been escalating for some time, and they finally erupted into open conflict. The "fraternal unity" of the two colossi of the Communist world now lay shattered in ruins.

Kissinger's view of China was fundamentally affected by these events. He had always thought that China was more likely to attack Russia than Russia was to attack China. But then he learned that the Soviet Union had developed a formidable military build-up on the Chinese border, complete with missiles, tanks, and air power. In view of the Russian invasion of Czechoslovakia less than a year before, it was not impossible that the Soviet Union might be planning a surprise attack against the Chinese nuclear installations.

Kissinger came to believe that China's fear of Russia might be greater than her fear of the United States and that China, therefore, might respond to an American gesture of reconciliation. It was not until 1967 that Kissinger considered such an opening a realistic possibility. But once he was sure, he quickly made it the core of his entire policy. Rapprochement with China would give the United States enormous leverage over the Soviet Union.

Kissinger decided, as an initiative, to resuscitate the Sino-American talks that had taken place in Warsaw before being suspended in January 1968. The talks had never been productive, but instead had often degenerated into mutual insults. Kissinger cabled the American ambassador in Warsaw, Walter J. Stoessel, Jr., instructing him to contact the top Chinese official in the Polish capital and to propose a resumption of the Warsaw talks. In January 1970, the talks resumed. The atmosphere was businesslike and even cordial, far from the "stupefying boredom" that, according to Kissinger, had characterized the talks in earlier years. At a second meeting, in February, the Chinese announced that the American delegation would be welcome in Peking. Kissinger considered the proposal seriously, but his new interest in China was deflected temporarily by the invasion of Cambodia, which began on April 30. A third Warsaw meeting, scheduled for May, was canceled by the Chinese three weeks after the invasion had begun.

Nixon was now concerned that Mao Tse-tung and Chou En-lai might interpret the Cambodian "incursion" as a hostile action aimed at China. Accordingly, he reassured the Chinese leadership privately, through "third party" channels, that the United States had not changed its intention of leaving Indochina and of improving relations with Peking. A number of minor unilateral concessions had already been approved by Nixon. Scholars, journalists, and students were now permitted to travel to China; naval patrols in the Formosa Strait had been suspended; and a one-hundred dollar ceiling on the purchase of Chinese goods by Americans had been rescinded. The president emphasized that these concessions would be allowed to stand and that others were under active consideration.

During the summer of 1970, the power struggle in the Chinese leadership between Premier Chou En-lai and Defense Minister Lin Piao came to a head. Chou urged moderation in domestic policy and favored rapprochement with the United States. He believed that the Americans were sincere in their intention to withdraw from Asia, while the Soviet Union, in his view, was determined to remain in occupation of Chinese territory. Lin Piao regarded the Americans as the greater peril and urged reconciliation with the Soviet Union. Mao Tse-tung leaned toward Chou's more pro-American position and, on China's National Day, October 1, 1970, chose as his honored guest in the reviewing stand atop the Gate of Heavenly Peace in Peking an old American friend, Edgar Snow. Snow had formed a friendship with Mao during the bitter fighting days in the 1930s, when the Chinese Communists were living in the caves of Yenan. The American journalist had been so impressed with their staying power and determination that he had predicted their ultimate victory in his *Red Star over China*, a book destined to become a classic. Now, the two aging men stood side by side once more, a signal to Nixon and Kissinger that China still desired reconciliation.

Kissinger used the occasion of the United Nations' twenty-fifth birthday to convey a confidential message to Mao. He told President Nicolae Ceauşescu of Rumania that the United States would be interested in considering talks "at a high level" with the Chinese in Peking. On the occasion of a reception given at the White House for Ceauşescu, Nixon delivered a toast to Rumania's good relations with the United States, the Soviet Union, and the *People's Republic* of China. When Soviet Ambassador Dobrynin asked Kissinger whether Nixon's unprecedented phrasing had any special significance, he received an evasive answer. After all, the Russians, too, were referring to China as the People's Republic, Kissinger replied.

Kissinger also informed Yahya Khan, the president of Pakistan, of his new interest in China. During the next few months, Yahya Khan served as Kissinger's confidential courier to Peking. The

Pakistani president was received by Mao in November 1970. Kissinger received unsigned notes from Peking at periodic intervals, all handwritten on white paper with blue lines and each more cordial than the preceding one. Edgar Snow's memoirs revealed that Mao and Chou openly discussed the possibility of an American presidential visit to Peking. "Mao would be happy to talk with Nixon," Snow reported, "either as a tourist or as president."

In February 1971, the Indochina war interfered once more with these delicate maneuvers. Nixon had just approved a South Vietnamese invasion of Laos. Since Laos had a common border with China, Mao and Chou became alarmed. For six weeks no handwritten notes from Peking reached Kissinger. The Chinese leaders instead announced a military alert. MacArthur's drive to the Yalu River twenty years before was still a troubling memory for them. Perhaps another American general might try to escalate the war despite Nixon's good intentions. Nixon decided to reassure the Chinese leaders. On February 17, he declared that the Laos operation "should not be interpreted by the Communist Chinese as a threat to them." Two weeks later, Chou informed the Hanoi leadership that China would not intervene in the Indochina war because Peking believed that the Americans were sincere in their promise to withdraw from Indochina. The exchanges via Pakistan resumed. Finally, in March 1971, another unsigned handwritten note was delivered to Kissinger by Pakistan's ambassador. The note extended an invitation for an American envoy to come to Peking. Two names were mentioned in the note: one was Rogers, the other Kissinger.

There was never any question in Nixon's mind that it would be Kissinger who would go to China. While the two men were discussing plans for the trip, taking careful precautions to prevent any leaks, the Chinese decided to make their first public gesture of conciliation. On April 6, 1971, during the finale of the international table-tennis competition in Japan, the Chinese team invited the American team to visit China. Four days later, the U.S. players crossed the border into China, the first official American group to do so in twenty-two years. The Americans, after being received by Premier Chou En-lai, reciprocated by inviting the Chinese team to the United States. Later that month, Nixon hinted that the United States might change its twenty-two-year-old posture in the United Nations from all-out support for Taiwan to a two-China policy. In the meantime, Kissinger asked the CIA to send him full biographies of Mao Tse-tung, Chou En-lai, and other Chinese leaders. Late at night, after the day's work was done on SALT and Indochina, Kissinger tried to fill the gap in his education by avidly reading about China.

Indochina threatened at one point to interfere again with Kissinger's plans. In June, *The New York Times* began its publication of *The Pentagon Papers*, a classified history of the American involvement in Indochina through early 1968. Kissinger feared that the disclosures would jeopardize the trip, since the Chinese might feel that they could not rely on American discretion. His apprehensions, however, turned out to be groundless. The Chinese, much more fearful of the Soviet military threat than of possible American indiscretions, firmed up the date for Kissinger's visit to China: July 9 to 11, 1971.

Kissinger left Washington on July 1, allegedly on an around-the-world trip. Yahya Khan, who was privy to his plans, helped him camouflage the real purpose of his global tour. When Kissinger arrived in Islamabad, the Pakistani capital, it was announced that he had come down with a slight case of intestinal flu and would have to rest for a few days in a mountain resort near the capital. Actually, Kissinger was in excellent health. Shortly after 3:00 A.M. on July 9, a Pakistani International airlines jet took off from Islamabad's airport for China. Kissinger was on board, scheduled to arrive in Peking at noon.

Kissinger spent more than twenty hours of his two-day visit in conversations with Chou En-lai. The experience had a profound and lasting effect on both statesmen. Kissinger and Chou En-lai discovered very quickly that, despite the gulf of time and culture that separated them, they were very much alike. Both had powerful intellects, with a penchant for philosophy and history. They engaged in a wide-ranging discussion of Sino-American relations, without attempting to place blame on either side for the two decades of estrangement and hostility. Both men shared an elitist disdain for bureaucracy and mediocrity, though they recognized the importance of pragmatic adjustments to reality. Both men had had their share of domestic opposition. During the Cultural Revolution in 1966, Chou En-lai's residence had been besieged by 100,000 Red Guards, who had accused him of being a "cosmopolitan traitor." Chou had debated with the students for forty-eight hours before the throng had finally dispersed. Kissinger had his own memories of debates with students and professors during the Cambodian invasion a year before. Finally, both men survived adversity and achieved great power. Chou En-lai had been a member of the "Long March," which had decimated the Chinese Communists to a remnant of 10,000 soldiers seeking refuge in the dank caves of Yenan in the 1930s. Kissinger's own refugee background and meteoric rise from obscurity to power gave him a measure of empathy for the Chinese leader.

Thus, Kissinger and Chou En-lai developed a genuine respect for each other, and this became the basis for a real friendship. Insofar as two world leaders separated by light years of culture and tradition can become friends, Kissinger and Chou En-lai formed such a bond. As Kissinger told the Senate at the confirmation hearings on his appointment as secretary of state in September 1973: "I have been accused of perhaps excessive admiration for Prime Minister Chou En-lai, and it is true that I have very high regard for him." When the older man succumbed to a long illness in January 1976, Kissinger felt a keen sense of loss. "There is turmoil under the heavens," Chou En-lai had said to him in 1971. "And we have the opportunity to end it." Certainly that first encounter began the process of reconciliation. Fact gradually began to replace fear as the major cornerstone for America's China policy.

During that first visit, only a single specific agreement was reached between Kissinger and Chou. Chou extended an invitation to Nixon to visit China early in 1972. Beyond that, the two negotiators reached a meeting of minds in two important areas that had caused Sino-American tensions in the past. They agreed in principle that Taiwan should be considered a part of China and that the political future of the island should be settled peacefully by the Chinese themselves. The precise circumstances of such a future settlement were purposely left ambiguous. Kissinger, who knew when to be precise but also when to be ambiguous, proposed that he and Chou avoid adopting a specific plan for Taiwan and content themselves with an agreement that the process of change be a peaceful one. Chou En-lai agreed to this vague formulation and expressed his admiration for Kissinger by saying, only half in jest, that his American visitor had a "Chinese mind." The second principle on which the two men managed to agree was that the political future of South Vietnam would have to be settled by the Vietnamese, without outside intervention.

When Kissinger prepared to leave Peking, on July 11, he did so with a feeling of elation and accomplishment. Chou En-lai, too, was greatly pleased. Taiwan was important to the Chinese, and the United States was about to revise her policy. Vietnam was important to the United States, and China might now be induced to help end the Indochina war. Finally, the agreement on a Nixon visit in 1972 was important to both countries, since it would provide further leverage over Russia—for China, as well as for the United States.

At 10:00 P.M. on July 15, Nixon made the following historic surprise announcement to the nation.

> Premier Chou En-lai and Dr. Henry Kissinger, President Nixon's Assistant for National Security Affairs, held talks in Peking from July 9 to 11, 1971. Knowing of President Nixon's expressed desire to visit the People's Republic of China, Premier Chou En-lai on behalf of the Government of the People's Republic of China has extended an invitation to President Nixon to visit China at an appropriate date before May 1972. President Nixon has accepted the invitation with pleasure. The meeting between the leaders of China and the United States is to seek the normalization of relations between the two countries and also to exchange views on questions of concern to the two sides.

The response to the announcement was almost uniformly favorable in the United States. Kissinger received enormous praise and came to be regarded by most Americans as secretary of state in everything but name. The president, too, was grateful.

Kissinger spent most of the rest of 1971 in preparation for the Nixon trip to China. Recalling the cancellation of President Eisenhower's visit to the Soviet Union in 1960 because of the downing of an American spy plane over Russia, Kissinger suspended all overflights of Chinese territory. He also took some tentative first steps toward implementing the main concession that he had made to Chou En-lai: to permit the ultimate reunification of Taiwan with China. Nixon issued orders to reduce the 9,000-man American garrison on Taiwan, and Secretary of State William Rogers declared in August that henceforth the United States would change its China policy in the United Nations. America would support Peking's admission, even its being seated on the Security Council as a veto-wielding permanent member, but would oppose the ouster of Taiwan from the UN's General Assembly or from UN membership.

In September, Lin Piao made a desperate bid for power in China; had he succeeded, he might have nipped the growing rapprochement between China and America in the bud. He failed, however, and died under somewhat mysterious circumstances in a plane crash over the Gobi Desert on his way to Russia. In October, Kissinger announced that he would return to China in order to make concrete arrangements for the Nixon visit. Kissinger was to be in Peking in late October, which was precisely the time for the annual debate on China in the General Assembly of the United Nations.

The China vote in the United Nations took place on October 25. Kissinger was supposed to have left Peking on October 24, but he postponed his departure for two days. Thus, while George Bush, the American ambassador to the United Nations, tried to rally votes to keep Taiwan's seat in the General Assembly, Kissinger was cementing the new relationship with Chiang Kai-shek's bitterest enemy. The signal was obvious to the majority of UN delegates. After twenty-two years of diplomatic warfare, the United States would no longer oppose Peking's admission to the world organization. Despite intensive last-minute lobbying by George Bush to keep Taiwan in, the United Nations decided to make a clear-cut choice. By a vote of seventy-six in favor and thirty-five against, with seventeen abstentions, Peking was voted in and Taiwan was out. Anti-Taiwan delegates danced in the aisles, and Nixon decided to reduce the American contribution to the UN's budget. Privately, of course, he was not surprised by the vote.

One month later, Nixon announced that he would visit China for a week, beginning on February 21, 1972. He also stated that, in his view, "The ultimate relationship of Taiwan to the People's Republic of China would have to be settled by direct negotiations between the two parties concerned." Chiang Kai-shek, in his exile on Taiwan, now felt utterly betrayed by Kissinger and Nixon. The Peking leadership, on the other hand, prepared to welcome the American president. Kissinger hoped that now, at last, he might have the opportunity to meet the aging, legendary leader of China's 800 million people, Chairman Mao Tse-tung.

Not everyone was pleased with America's new China policy. Japan's Prime Minister, Eisaku Sato, felt slighted and began to wonder what these two unpredictable Americans might do next. When the president had devalued the dollar one month after Kissinger's secret trip to China, the Japanese reeled under the impact of "Nixon shock." Sato, shortly afterward, had been eased out of power and replaced by Kakuei Tanaka, who promptly established diplomatic relations with Peking.

The Soviet leadership, too, was of course alarmed. Immediately upon his return from his first trip to Peking, Kissinger had a soothing word for Brezhnev. "Nothing that has been done in our relations with the People's Republic of China," Kissinger declared on July 16, "is in any way directed against any other countries, and especially not against the Soviet Union." The Russians were not convinced. They were expecting Nixon in the Soviet capital in May 1972. Nixon decided to echo Kissinger's reassuring note. "Neither trip is being taken," he asserted, "at the expense of any other nations." The Russians did not believe him, either, and they were essentially correct. Both Kissinger and Nixon hoped that the opening to China would help end the Indochina war by exerting pressure on Moscow to exert pressure on Hanoi. But it took almost an entire year before this strategy finally paid off.

When Kissinger and Nixon arrived in Peking on schedule on February 21, Chou En-lai was on hand to greet the two Americans. To Kissinger's surprise and delight, he and Nixon were invited to meet Mao immediately after their arrival. The two men spent an hour with Mao and Chou, and once again, as on the occasion of Kissinger's first visit, the subjects were philosophy and history.

Almost five years later, I had the opportunity to ask Kissinger what he had thought of Mao Tse-tung. After all, if ever there was a "revolutionary," the chairman certainly was such a man. He had helped to organize the Chinese Communist party half a century before his encounter with Henry Kissinger. He had led the Long March in the 1930s and taken the remnants of the Red Army to a sanctuary more than six thousand miles away. He had led his forces against Chiang Kai-shek, the Japanese, and finally, the Americans in Korea. In 1966, at the age of seventy-four, fearful lest China might emulate the ossified bureaucracy of Soviet Russia, Mao, always the adventurer, had set out to rejuvenate the revolution. I was most curious to hear what the author of *A World Restored* thought of this authentic twentieth-century revolutionary.

Always an admirer of a solitary figure in adversity, Kissinger described Mao Tse-tung in terms bordering upon awe: "Wherever he sat or stood, there was the center of the room. Even though his voice was weak with age and each word was a struggle, he was quite lucid and in absolute command. Chou En-lai fell silent in his presence." Kissinger saw Mao as a modern visionary, a heroic figure, but also a man who could be coopted into a stable international order. "Here was a statesman," Kissinger said, "who combined revolutionary ardor with a sense of pragmatism, a man who had a vision for his people, but who had remained in touch with the practical realities as well." It was clear that Mao, like his prime minister, appealed enormously to Kissinger's sense of romanticism.

The next few days in Peking were devoted to serious deliberations. On the American side, Nixon and Kissinger were the main negotiators on matters of principle, such as Taiwan and Indochina. Their two opponents were Chou En-lai and Chiao Kuan-hua, a deputy foreign minister. Parallel negotiations were being held between Secretary Rogers and China's foreign minister, Chi Peng-fei, on questions of travel, tourism, and trade. The evenings were taken up with banquets, table-tennis exhibitions, and a performance of the ballet *Red Detachment of Women*, hosted by Chiang Ching, Mao Tse-tung's wife. The theme of the ballet was the victory of a young peasant girl over Chiang Kai-shek's troops. Nixon found the performance "excellent theater and superb acting." Kissinger and Chiao worked late into the night in an effort to put together a joint communiqué.

Both sides wanted a positive statement about the visit. Nixon had made the occasion into a television spectacular and needed a successful outcome to impress the voters at home. The Chinese wanted to justify Nixon's presence to their people and also to impress the Russians with proof of tangible Chinese-American cooperation. Yet it became increasingly obvious as the talks progressed that it would not be possible to draft a joint statement to which both sides would be able to subscribe. Some of the differences, especially on the problems of Taiwan and Indochina, could not simply be papered over by a document of studied ambiguity.

Kissinger and Chou came up with an idea that broke the deadlock. Both sides would agree to write separate sections into the communiqué, one expressing the American view of a particular problem and the other setting forth the Chinese position. This technique enabled the negotiators to focus honestly on problems rather than cover them up with diplomatic double-talk. On two occasions, Kissinger and Chou worked until dawn in order to formulate a communiqué that would set forth the differences between the two nations without making them appear to be unbridgeable. In four areas—Indochina, Korea, Japan, and India-Pakistan—the difficulties were manageable. On the matter of Taiwan, however, the two positions were so far apart that even the technique of drafting separate statements ran into virtually insuperable difficulties.

On Indochina, the United States declared its long-range goal of self-determination for the Indochinese people, while the Chinese affirmed their support for the Provisional Revolutionary Government; on Korea, Nixon underlined his support for the South, while Chou supported the North; on Japan, the United States affirmed its alliance with that nation, while the Chinese declared their opposition to a revival of Japanese militarism; and on the Indo-Pakistani war, the United States evenhandedly supported the cease-fire, while the Chinese declared their firm support for Pakistan. In essence, the four statements were little more than agreements to disagree.

Kissinger spent most of his negotiating time and skill on the problem of Taiwan. The Chinese pressed him hard to concede Peking's sovereignty over the island. Implicit in their position was the demand that the United States must abrogate its defense treaty with Chiang Kai-shek, since, the Chinese argued, a province could not legitimately maintain a pact with a foreign country. Kissinger, in turn, refused to annul the Taiwan treaty and insisted that Peking renounce the use of force against the island. Both sides realized that full-fledged diplomatic relations between their two countries would have to be postponed until some mutually acceptable formula could be agreed upon.

Finally, on February 26, Kissinger and Chou reached agreement upon two paragraphs that set forth the two opposing positions with a minimum of rhetoric. In the American paragraph, Kissinger acknowledged that there was "but one China and that Taiwan [was] a part of China," but insisted on "a peaceful settlement of the Taiwan question by the Chinese themselves." He also pledged "the ultimate withdrawal of all U.S. forces and military installations from Taiwan" and a gradual reduction of American forces "as the tension in the area diminish[ed]." The implication was that the United States would gradually withdraw as the Vietnam war drew to a close but would pull out completely only after Peking had renounced force as a way of "liberating" Taiwan. The Chinese paragraph asserted that "the Taiwan question was the crucial question obstructing the normalization of relations between China and the United States" and reasserted the position that the island was a Chinese province. It also implied, however, that Taiwan's ultimate absorption into China would not take place by force. This was about as far as the two sides were able to move toward a compromise.

These were the major problem areas that Kissinger and Nixon covered in a communiqué issued in Shanghai one day before they departed from Chinese soil. Neither side was very happy with the Taiwan statement, but both agreed to rule out a solution by force. Thus, this delicate issue was neatly transformed from a problem to be solved immediately into a process to be managed over a period of time.

In addition, Rogers and Chi Peng-fei had worked out some initial agreements on travel, tourism, and trade. It was also agreed that a "senior U.S. representative" would be stationed in Peking. At the final banquet, Nixon proclaimed that his visit to China had been "a week that [had] changed the world." Kissinger's euphoria was almost greater. "What we are doing now with China is so great, so historic," he stated at a news conference, "that the word 'Vietnam' will be only a footnote when it is written in history."

Kissinger and Nixon returned to Washington to a hero's welcome. In Moscow, the reaction was one of sullen anger and suspicion; in Tokyo, the Sato government collapsed; and on Taiwan, Chiang Kai-shek declared that the United States could no longer be trusted as an ally. One thing was clear to all, however: the bipolar world had definitely come to an end. A triangular constellation now loomed on the horizon.

Nixon and Kissinger had every intention of broadening and deepening the new understanding with China. In March 1972, the Chinese table-tennis team visited the United States, and in April the first American business representatives were invited to visit the Canton spring trade fair. Then, however, the blossoming relationship was temporarily halted because of the Haiphong mining of

May 1972 and the "Christmas bombing" in December. Still, on February 15, 1973, less than a month after the Paris accords on Indochina, Kissinger once again visited Peking. Eager to pursue further normalization of United States-China relations, but frustrated in this quest by the American defense treaty with Taiwan, Kissinger and Chairman Mao settled on a compromise. The United States and China agreed to open liaison offices in Washington and Peking. In addition, each nation made another concession: in exchange for China's release of two captured American pilots and review of the sentence of John Downey, a CIA agent held prisoner in China since the Korean War, the United States agreed to negotiate the settlement of American claims against China and the release of Chinese assets "blocked" in the United States since Korea. In March 1973, David Bruce was appointed to head the United States liaison office in Peking, and Huang Chen, China's former ambassador to France, was named to fill the Washington post. The liasion offices were formally opened in May 1973. In practical terms, they fulfilled most of the functions of regular embassies without stumbling over the divisive issue of Taiwan.

In late 1973, however, a "mini-Cultural Revolution" in China slowed down the process of rapprochement. The ancient sage Confucius came under severe attack for his "bourgeois" philosophy. The music of Beethoven and Schubert was compared unfavorably to *The White-haired Girl*, a Chinese opera that had put Kissinger to sleep during his previous visit. Richard Bach's *Jonathan Livingston Seagull* was denounced for its "reactionary" tendencies, and Michelangelo Antonioni was attacked as a "decadent" film maker. Both Huang Chen and David Bruce went home for about a month before taking up their posts again. The mini-Cultural Revolution, however, was far milder both in scope and content than the upheaval of 1966. It apparently was an expression of bitter disagreements between those forces in the Chinese Politburo led by Chiang Ching, Mao Tse-tung's wife, who considered the United States as the principal threat to China, and those of Premier Chou En-lai, who perceived the Soviet Union as the greater danger. About the only thing the two groups agreed upon was that the philosopher Confucius and Defense Minister Lin Piao—both "unpersons" and dead—were convenient symbols for the enemy.

Kissinger steadily encouraged intellectual exchange and trade, but the Taiwan problem kept these contacts at a fairly modest level. On the issue of academic exchange, for example, China retained virtually exclusive power to decide who would visit, under what circumstances, for how long, to see what, and to meet whom. In fact, the Chinese restrictions upon American contacts were more severe than those imposed by the Soviet Union.

The trade pattern followed an erratic course. Two-way Chinese-American trade approached the $1 billion mark in 1974. During that year, the United States became China's second most important trading partner. In 1975, however, the figure was slashed in half and the Chinese abruptly canceled a large order for American wheat and corn. Taiwan's trade with the United States in 1975 was almost ten times as large, and Hong Kong's was four times as large. The evidence suggests that the Taiwan issue inhibited a more rapid expansion of commercial contacts. Financing problems, the American refusal to grant China most-favored-nation status, and the lack of a formal trade agreement could all be traced back to the absence of full diplomatic relations. Thus, Kissinger's liaison-office solution did not resolve the Taiwan problem, but merely circumvented it. By 1975, rapprochement between China and America had reached a fairly stable plateau. There was little, if any, forward movement. Even a trip to Peking by Kissinger and Gerald Ford in the fall of 1975 did not restore the old momentum.

In February 1976, exactly four years after his first visit as president, Richard Nixon again went to China, this time in the role of tourist. The Chinese government had extended the invitation to the former president, apparently as a signal to Ford and Kissinger that the United States was paying too much attention to détente with the Soviet Union and not enough to China. Chairman Mao hoped that the meaning of an invitation to the architect of the American opening to China would not be lost on his successor. Kissinger, who denied any part in the plans for Nixon's China visit, nevertheless decided to "debrief" his former chief, who had not only been entertained by Chairman Mao personally but also by Chou En-lai's successor, Hua Kuo-feng.

By 1976, a chill wind was blowing out of China in Kissinger's direction. While he was not an unperson in Peking, Chou En-lai's successors regarded him with growing mistrust and ambivalence. They felt that he had overplayed the Soviet card and that the time had come perhaps to turn the tables on the United States. They sensed that Kissinger's triangular policy was vulnerable. In politics, as well as love, triangles are inherently unstable. There was no guarantee that the United States would always remain the "lady."

What had brought Henry Kissinger to Peking for the first time, in 1971, and what brought him back seven more times by the end of 1975 was, first and foremost, the possibility of using this odd Sino-American coupling as leverage on the Soviet Union. Kissinger made sure that he would hold the best position in the triangle, as the only point with lines to the other two. He was careful to keep the United States in a position equidistant from the two Communist powers. Yet, his triangular policy was based upon one fundamental assumption, which was absolutely essential for its success: the permanent hostility between China and the Soviet Union.

After the death of Mao Tse-tung in 1976, a power struggle erupted in China over the succession to the legendary chairman. Chiang Ching, Mao's widow, led a radical group that believed the United States was a greater threat to China than was the Soviet Union. She lost the fight to Hua Kuo-feng and a more moderate faction that believed the Soviet Union posed a greater danger to China than did the United States. Chiang Ching was purged from the Chinese leadership, and the successors of Chou En-lai took over the reigns of power.

The great turning of 1971 was the result of objective changes in the global power constellation. America's withdrawal from Vietnam, the Soviet presence on the Chinese border, and the American decision to balance its relations with China and the Soviet Union but to remain equidistant from them both were primarily responsible. Yet it was also true that both China and America had been fortunate to have as diplomatic leaders men of the caliber of Henry Kissinger and Chou En-lai, both equipped with realistic perceptions of themselves and of each other, a rare knowledge of history, and an even rarer gift for empathy. This personal dimension no doubt accelerated the movement away from fantasy and fiction toward rapprochement and reality. Kissinger and Chou En-lai had recognized the objective conditions necessary for a turn for the better in the relations between China and America. They had seized the crucial moment at one of history's great junctions and helped to make it happen. By this recognition and determined action, Chou En-lai and Kissinger made their claim to historic statesmanship.

China policy under Jimmy Carter was in essence a continuation of the policy of Henry Kissinger. In late 1978, to the intense displeasure of the Soviet leadership, Carter formally recognized the People's Republic of China and "derecognized" the Chinese regime on Taiwan. "Playing the China card" might make the Russians more tractable on a strategic arms limitation treaty was the President's opinion. Besides, American businessmen were clamoring to sell their products to "one billion customers." On the Chinese side, Deng Hsiao-ping, the new Chinese strong man, had abandoned Mao Tse-tung's revolutionary ideology and set China on a course of industrialization and modernization. America, the former enemy, had suddenly become the model. In his visit to the United States in early 1979, Deng emphasized the need for China and America to stand together against the threat of "Soviet hegemony." And shortly afterward, China invaded pro-Soviet Vietnam in order to give a bloody nose to the nation that had tried to dismember China's protégé, Cambodia. China and the Soviet Union thus waged a limited war by proxy while the United States observed a scrupulous neutrality. Clearly, Kissinger's triangular policy was still very much in fashion. The new Sino-American friendship was made in Moscow as much as Soviet-American détente had been made in Peking a decade earlier. And the United States was still the "lady in the triangle."

As Soviet-American relations cooled in the wake of the Soviet invasion of Afghanistan in 1980, Sino-American relations became even more cordial. United States Defense Secretary, Harold Brown, visited China and posed for photographers while standing in a Chinese tank. The United States began to coordinate its containment strategy against the Soviet Union with China, and the Chinese leadership, in turn, began to talk as if China were a de facto member of the Western alliance system. The Chinese gave aid and comfort to Afghan rebels fleeing from the Russians and canceled talks on improving relations with the Soviet Union. They also decided not to renew a thirty-year friendship treaty in Moscow, permitting it to lapse in 1980.

Under the first term of President Ronald Reagan, Sino-American perceptions warmed to the point of friendship. The United States redefined China as a "friendly non-aligned country." The Chinese, in turn, invited the President to visit their country and instituted English as the official second language to be taught in all Chinese schools. The reason for this increasing closeness was not only the obvious negative bond forged by the iciness that prevailed in U.S.-Soviet relations, but the equally important positive bond created by China's decision to modernize and to move toward a mixed economy. To carry out this modernization program, China needed America's help.

The China that Ronald Reagan saw was rapidly moving away from communism. Deng Hsiao-ping, the eighty-year-old leader and survivor of the Long March, had dismantled most Maoist institutions. Most important, the new leadership had virtually decollectivized agriculture. While it was still illegal to buy or sell land, peasants now signed long-term contracts with the government. These obligated them to meet certain production quotas. Beyond these quotas, however, peasants disposed of surpluses in any way they saw fit. Many began to amass considerable wealth by working above and beyond the demands of the state quotas. Deng commented approvingly that it was correct "to make some people rich first so as to lead all the people to wealth."[1] The "supply-side" flavor of this economic philosophy may have appealed to Ronald Reagan. In addition, private plots on rural communes were expanded, and prices of produce from these plots were determined by supply and demand. As a result of this increase in "free enterprise," agricultural output in China rose dramatically during the early 1980s. "It doesn't matter what color the cat is," Deng said, "so long as it catches mice." Under Mao, such a statement might have drawn a prison sentence for treason. Yet, under Mao, millions of peasants did not have enough food to eat, while under his successors, starvation became virtually a thing of the past.

The increase in disposable income sparked a consumer revolution in China. A growing middle class indulged itself in television sets, refrigerators, and washing machines. In towns and cities, individuals could open restaurants and motels. Wealthy families were even permitted to hire cooks and nannies.

In 1984, economic reforms were expanded to cities and the industrial sector. Prices of most consumer items were allowed to fluctuate in response to supply and demand. Competition was encouraged in factories. As one factory manager put it: "The days where those who contribute much and work hard have the same

[1] Donald Zagoria, "China's Quiet Revolution," *Foreign Affairs*, Spring 1984, p. 883.

pay as those who contribute little or even do not work at all should be finished."[2]

In December 1984, in a final irony, *People's Daily* announced that "one cannot expect the works of Marx and Lenin to solve today's problems." A week later, the Communist party corrected itself by declaring that the article should have said "to solve *all* of today's problems."

The fact remained that China's new leaders found Marxism-Leninism too stale to guide a modern state. What the Soviets clung to as history's ultimate revolution, in Chinese eyes, had itself become ripe for revolutionary challenge. Deng Hsiao-ping, in a revealing statement, admitted that China was "perfecting communism through capitalism."[3] And in that quest, the help of the world's leading capitalist nation had become essential.

One scholar, in a perceptive essay, has compared this Chinese modernization to the Soviet system in the 1920s under Lenin's New Economic Policy.[4] While this may be correct, it must not be forgotten that the NEP period in Russia was eclipsed by Joseph Stalin. It is most improbable that a Chinese Stalin will succeed Deng Hsiao-ping. Far too many of his reforms are likely to have become irreversible.

Tens of thousands of Chinese students were studying abroad during the 1980s. In the United States alone, there were more than 50,000. These are almost certain, over time, to constitute a group committed to keep China's door open to the outside world. Dozens of new universities sprang up all over China. In Shanghai alone, there were over fifty institutions of higher learning.[5] In 1984, the Chinese Ministry of Education purchased $4 million worth of scientific books from the United States in order to help China overcome the "dark age" of the Cultural Revolution. Christian churches and Buddhist temples were reopened. Foreign trade with the United States went up from $1 billion in 1978 to $5 billion in 1984. In that year alone, over 1,000 contracts were signed to import advanced Western technology and equipment.[6]

[2] *Time*, December 3, 1984.
[3] *The New York Times*, December 16, 1984.
[4] Zagoria, *op. cit.*, p. 880.
[5] *The New York Times*, July 1, 1984.
[6] Zagoria, *op. cit.*, p. 889.

The political system, too, was somewhat liberalized. While there were no free elections and no civil liberties in the American sense, political controls were loosened and people were less afraid to voice their opinions. *People's Daily* declared that "literary creation must be free" and writers would never again become victims of political persecution. Economic decision-making was decentralized and it became possible for provinces and municipalities to sign contracts with foreign governments without having to get Beijing's approval. Tourist trips to Hong Kong were organized and visits to the United States were no longer an impossible dream.

President Reagan's visit to China in April 1984 was very successful. Even though the Chinese deleted some passages about God, capitalism, and freedom from the President's speeches, the encounter between the two leaders was warm and cordial. A number of agreements were signed, including one pertaining to the development of nuclear reactors in China. Even the Taiwan issue no longer appeared as an insurmountable problem. Reagan left with good feelings about his first trip to a Communist country, especially since it was one in which Russians were no longer popular and millions of little children were busily studying English.

During Ronald Reagan's second term as President, American rapprochement with China continued to accelerate, probably as a result of the Chinese leaders' decision to modernize their country and to move away from orthodox communism to something resembling a mixed economy. By 1984, the aging Deng Hsiao-ping had groomed a younger man as his ultimate successor: Zhao Ziyang, who, like Deng himself, had been humiliated by the Red Guards under Mao in the 1960s and who was equally committed now to sweeping economic reforms. Zhao had been instrumental in introducing the "household responsibility" system in the countryside, which made it possible for peasants to manage their farms as they liked, so long as they met their share of the state quotas. Increased income on the farms sparked greater demand for consumer goods, thus prompting reforms in the urban and industrial sectors along similar lines. Just as it had done with the farms, the government made arrangements to lease or contract the operation of industrial and commercial enterprises. The lessee paid rent for the use of a factory, but as in the West, after payment of a specified amount, the lessee was allowed to keep what he earned. By the time Zhao Ziyang had succeeded Deng to the position of party chief in 1987, about 15,000 such arrangements had been set up and most were operating profitably.

Even more astounding was the reopening of the Shanghai Stock Exchange, which had been closed since 1949. In September 1986, when trading began, 2,000 Shanghai citizens lined up to buy stock. Since then, stock exchanges have been opened in several major cities. One by-product of this initiative was the introduction of joint ventures between Chinese and foreign businesses. By 1988, 10,000 such enterprises had been formed, mostly with Hong Kong, the United States, and overseas Chinese who wanted to help their motherland modernize, as well as help themselves.

As trade continued to flourish, the Chinese leaders began to reduce military expenditures. In 1985, Deng called for the demobilization of one million soldiers. As a survivor of the Long March, Deng enjoyed the authority to make such a far-reaching decision. As a result, more economic resources went into homes, farms, and consumer goods. Signs proclaiming "Time is Money" began to appear in factories all over China.

By the late 1980s, China's economic reforms and her leadership's "new thinking" began to resemble Mikhail Gorbachev's *perestroika* in the Soviet Union. Not only did Communist party slogans begin to disappear, but at Beijing University, the country's most prestigious institution of higher learning, a towering statue of Mao Tse-tung was hauled down in the middle of the night. Many members of the faculty interpreted this event as a symbol of the decline of rigid Communist ideology. Mao in China seemed to be suffering the same posthumous fate under his successors as Stalin had suffered under Gorbachev in Russia.

Not everything went smoothly, of course. During 1988, China's economic growth under the new mixed economy became so rapid that unmistakable signs of overheating, including inflation, began to surface. The cities grew at a faster pace than the countryside, and a good deal of corruption and panic buying of staple commodities finally convinced the leadership that the rate of growth had to be slowed. "We have been bold enough," declared Deng Hsiao-ping. "Now we need to take our steps in a more cautious way." As a result, the central government reined in the free markets in some localities and reimposed central controls. Hotels, restaurants, tour companies, taxi fleets, and commodity trading companies were investigated, and in cases of flagrant corruption and profiteering, severe punishments were meted out. It was not likely, however, that these developments signaled a return to orthodox Marxism. Much more likely, they signified the inevitable birth pains of a new economic system, or perhaps, more accurately put, a partial return to a more traditional, uniquely Chinese, economic way of life. Nor did this slowdown alter the new, much more friendly attitude of the Chinese leaders toward the United States.

What is the explanation for China's amazing about-face under Mao's successors? One clue may be found in the fact that Mao's widow remained in prison under a commuted death sentence. She continued to symbolize the horrors of the Cultural Revolution that almost tore China apart in the 1960s and 1970s. During those years, probably close to a million people were killed or driven to suicide. Millions of others were sent to labor camps or remote rural areas. Science and technology were set back by at least two decades. The Chinese people, embittered and exhausted, began to question the very legitimacy of Communist party rule. Respect for the socialist system was at an all-time low.

Mao's successors realized that only drastic changes could ensure their political survival. They had no desire to return to the repression of the Mao era, and so they began to regard the "Great Helmsman" with the kind of ambivalence with which the Russians regarded Joseph Stalin. Gradually, the Soviet model became associated in Chinese perceptions with the horrors of the Cultural Revolution. The Americans, on the other hand, did not trigger too many bitter memories. The Korean War, after all, was a generation removed by now. Besides, the Americans, too, had mistrusted and despised Stalin's domestic repression and imperialist foreign policy. Hence, the negative experience of Mao's Cultural Revolution served as the catalyst that triggered China's modernization program and the friendship with the United States. The founder of Chinese communism thus unwittingly became the architect of its ultimate undoing. History is a great teacher of irony.

There was more irony to come. Mikhail Gorbachev's political reforms in the Soviet Union ignited a bonfire in Beijing. It suddenly dawned on millions of Chinese that Deng Hsiao-ping's economic reforms had left the political dictatorship of China essentially unchanged.

The Soviet leader had scheduled a visit to the Chinese capital in May 1989 in order to mend a thirty-year rift between China and the Soviet Union. He and Deng Hsiao-ping had planned world-wide publicity for this first visit in thirty years by a Soviet leader to Beijing. History, however, takes no reservations.

Tens of thousands of Chinese students, yearning for freedom and democracy, saw Gorbachev's visit as a catalyst for pressing their demands. The Sino-Soviet summit was almost totally eclipsed by a million protesters who crowded into the one-hundred-acre Tiananmen Square in Beijing. The students were joined by workers, peasants, teachers, soldiers, and ordinary citizens from all over China. "Give us democracy or give us death," thousands of banners screamed, paraphrasing Patrick Henry. "We have rice, but we have no laws," one student exclaimed. "The Russians have Gorbachev, but whom do we have?" asked another. Three thousand students went on a hunger strike to emphasize their determination. Deng Hsiao-ping and his conservative premier, Li Peng, called out the army to quell the uprising, but the troops refused to shoot at the students. On May 30, 1989, the Chinese students placed a replica of the Statue of Liberty in Tiananmen Square, directly across from the portrait of Mao Tse-tung. Thus, China's youth had planted their own version of freedom's most powerful beacon in the middle of the nation's capital.

Three days later, with sudden ferocity, everything changed. On direct orders from the aging Deng Hsiao-ping, the Chinese army forced its way into Tiananmen Square and crushed the uprising with fierce brutality. More than 3,000 students were killed and tens of thousands wounded in a Saturday night massacre on June 3, 1989, as the People's Army turned its guns on its own people. On Sunday morning, the square was occupied by the army and the "goddess of democracy" was crushed by a tank. With one stroke, Deng Hsiao-ping, the economic reformer, had become the butcher of Beijing. China's first popular uprising since the Communist victory of 1949 was drowned in blood.

The old men who ruled China now wasted no time to reassert their power. Zhao Ziyang, who had been sympathetic to the students, was stripped of all his posts and replaced by men loyal to Deng. A Stalinist purge descended on China. Chinese citizens accused of "counterrevolutionary activity" were paraded through the streets, tried publicly, and executed by a pistol shot to the head. Foreigners were told that the student uprising had never happened. Indeed, the government declared students had shot and killed over three hundred innocent soldiers. It was George Orwell's *Nineteen Eighty-Four* all over again, complete with the "Ministry of Truth" telling a pack of lies. For American students, there was a profound lesson in the Beijing uprising and its tragic climax. Students their age were prepared to lay down their lives in order to gain a fraction of the freedom that Americans sometimes take for granted.

Thus, almost overnight, China fell back into darkness. At the very moment when Eastern Europe was ridding itself once and for all of the shackles of Stalinism, China's old leaders, taking a leaf from Mao Tse-tung, resorted to Stalinist-type political oppression. The response of most Americans was one of outrage. President George Bush condemned the Chinese action in strong language, yet resisted the temptation to return to America's earlier policy of trying to isolate China. Nor did the Chinese retreat into their old mode of angry isolation. Instead, what evolved after Tiananmen Square was an effort by Bush and Deng Hsiao-ping to meet each other halfway: China embarked on a policy of encouraging a form of controlled capitalism without Western-style political freedom and the United States, while berating and scolding China's Communist dictators, in fact continued relatively unimpeded diplomatic and economic relations with them. Needless to say, neither leader was doing the other a favor. The policy of continued rapprochement was simply a recognition of reality: the United States could not afford to ignore China as an ascendant economic power in Asia and China could not afford to alienate the United States, now the world's only remaining superpower.

Once again, as so many times in the past, some stubborn myths and misperceptions exacerbated relations. Most Americans perceived Tiananmen Square as a crushing blow to freedom. Yet most Chinese peasants defined freedom primarily in economic, not political, terms. Two modest meals a day were more important to them than casting a vote in a polling booth. Tiananmen Square to a Chinese peasant was a minor event in faraway Beijing. To an American, on the other hand, raised in Western logic, Deng Hsiao-ping's belief that he could insulate economic reform from political reform seemed like outrageous nonsense. To a Chinese, indifferent to Western-style democratic institutions, but yearning for a small measure of improvement in his economic lot, economic reform offered a modest ray of hope.

In the Chinese leaders' view, the Soviet Union and Eastern Europe collapsed because their Communist leaders had failed to meet their peoples' basic economic needs, not because they had failed to give them democracy. Thus, whoever was opposed to economic reform should leave office, Deng Hsiao-ping warned his fellow octogenarians. Deng set up "economic zones" where a controlled form of capitalism could be experimented with. Under no circumstances, however, was this experiment to be contaminated with Western-style democratic ideas. And indeed, large port cities like Shanghai and Canton began to bustle once again with renewed economic activity. Nor did the political crisis triggered by the Tiananmen tragedy interrupt this commitment to economic reform. Despite some economic sanctions imposed by the Bush administration, China's economy continued to grow at the amazing rate of 9 percent a year. By 1992, China's growth rate was the second-largest in Asia, exceeded only by that of South Korea. Its foreign exchange reserves approached $50 billion, it enjoyed a substantial trade surplus with the United States as well as a worldwide trade surplus of almost $10 billion. China was even able to extend substantial food and commercial credits to the former Soviet Union. Beijing also made remarkable headway against inflation, bringing it down from an annual rate of 12 percent in 1988 to less than 5 percent in 1992, even though the scope of market-driven prices was gradually expanded to include coal, rubber, farm machinery, and building materials. In the financial area, stock markets opened in Shanghai and Shenzhen and thirty other cities established short-term free markets. The Chinese currency was devalued to bring it closer to the free-market rate and in 1992 the Beijing regime applied for membership in the General Agreement on Tariffs and Trade (GATT).

Small wonder that, when China's leaders convened their fourteenth Communist Party Congress in October 1992, they decided to perpetuate their policy. Seven men committed to economic reform were promoted to the all-powerful Politburo Standing Committee while two hard-liners were retired. Reform, the "paramount leader" Deng Hsiao-ping made clear, would be limited to economic goods and services, and not extended to political institutions. Deng, who was rumored to be almost totally deaf and extremely feeble, appeared briefly to congratulate the new officials and exhorted them to work hard. His daughter held his arm the entire time.

President Bush responded to the Tiananmen crackdown with pragmatism. Responding to an angry Congress, he did impose some sanctions and did prod the Chinese leaders on its human rights policy, but he consistently opposed legislation that would eliminate or impose conditions on renewal of China's most-favored-nation trading status. In 1992, he vetoed such legislation explaining that it would hurt American companies selling goods in China. The Bush administration, in yet another balancing act in 1992, sold F-16 fighter planes to Taiwan, but shortly thereafter released military equipment that had been paid for by China but had been held back as a protest against the Tiananmen Square massacre.

Bush's pragmatism no doubt stemmed from his realization that he needed China's agreement to, or at least its abstention from, American policy in the United Nations. After all, China had a veto power in the Security Council and without its acquiescence, the United States could not have forged an international military coalition against Iraq nor would UN actions in the Balkans, Cambodia, or Somalia have been possible. Moreoever, China was a consistent seller of weaponry to North Korea, Iran, Syria, and Saudi Arabia, and apparently had sold nuclear missile technology to Pakistan in 1992, even though it was a signatory to the UN's Nuclear Nonproliferation Treaty. Armed conflict with nuclear potential between the two Koreas or between India and Pakistan posed a serious security risk to the United States and neither of these problems could be dealt with effectively without substantial cooperation between China and the United States. Similarly, China's policy of moderation toward Taiwan could be greatly lessened by a worsening of its relations with the United States.

Finally, there was the problem of Hong Kong. The British colony was to revert to China in 1997. In 1992, Britain tested China's resolve by instructing Hong Kong's governor, Christopher Patten, to extract guarantees about democratic government after 1997 from China. China's leaders responded icily that Hong Kong's government was exclusively China's business after the expiration of the British lease in 1997. While it is most unlikely that

China would send its People's Liberation Army into Hong Kong, it was nevertheless true that defusing the ticking time bomb was very much in the United States' interest. In 1992, Hong Kong was America's thirteenth largest trading partner. American investments there exceeded $7 billion and nearly 22,000 Americans lived in the territory. Moreover, about two-thirds of China's exports to the United States passed through Hong Kong. Consequently, if the United States adopted policies that reduced trade with China, it would reduce the incentives for restraint in Beijing toward both Taiwan and Hong Kong. Thus, a punitive policy by the United States against China would create unintended victims in Taiwan and Hong Kong.

In early 1993, the Beijing regime made three decisions that many Western diplomats interpreted as efforts to reduce American criticisms about human rights violations and, possibly, as peace offerings to the new administration of President Bill Clinton. First, in January, several generals who had been promoted in 1989 because of their prominent role in the Tiananmen crackdown were demoted or dismissed while some officials who had disapproved of the killings were rehabilitated. Second, Wang Dan, a prominent Chinese dissident who had come to symbolize the pro-democracy demonstrators in Tiananmen Square, was released in February. "I don't regret a thing," the freed dissident said in an interview with Reuters. "In the future, I have two plans: one is to try to get readmitted to Beijing University. The other is to try to continue working for democratization."[7] Finally, in April, after four decades of bitterness, envoys from Beijing and Taiwan met to clear the way for a historic meeting to be held in Singapore. The intent was to begin a high-level dialogue that would attempt to turn forty years of enmity into a cooperative future. In June, Clinton, continuing in his predecessor's footsteps, renewed China's most-favored-nation status for another year, but made further renewals contingent on an improvement in that country's human rights record.

In overall historical perspective, it is not likely that Deng Hsiao-ping's policy of economic reform and maintenance of the political status quo will succeed in the long run. In the first place, China's Communist octagenarians cannot defy mortality forever. China in

---

[7] *The New York Times*, February 18, 1993.

1993 resembled the Soviet Union ten years earlier when Brezhnev, Andropov, and Chernenko tried desperately to perpetuate the old Soviet system. But Mikhail Gorbachev with his iron broom was already in the wings. It is not unlikely that the growing "commercial communism" in China's southern cities might set the stage for political reform once the old men of China are gone and younger men and women have taken their place. And among those younger leaders there may be former dissidents who survived Tiananmen Square. It would not be the first time in recent history that the political prisoners of yesterday would emerge as the political leaders of tomorrow. And besides, communism is in full retreat the world over. In short, sometime before the year 2000, a Chinese Gorbachev may well make his appearance, a liberator from the ranks of China's youth that almost had its day in 1989. And then, after a century of travail and revolution, Dr. Sun Yatsen's democratic dream, which he had nurtured as a youth, might be fulfilled at last.

Part Two

THE ROLE OF PERCEPTION IN RUSSO-AMERICAN RELATIONS

Chapter Eight

Czarist Russia and the United States

There is a strange sense of paradox about the relations between Russia and America during the eighteenth and nineteenth centuries. The two peoples saw little of one another and their systems of government were radically different; yet the two nations almost always encountered each other with intensity. Relations between them at different times ranged from affection through ambivalence all the way to hostility and hatred. Russians and Americans were rarely indifferent to one another. Most of the time, these intense emotional reactions rested on images, fictions, and legends rather than on facts. Policy decisions with the most serious consequences often flowed from these legends, particularly on the American side.

This chapter will examine four significant Russo-American encounters during the eighteenth and nineteenth centuries: Catherine the Great and the American War of Independence; the role of the Russian fleet during the American Civil War; the purchase of Alaska; and the role of the United States during the Russo-Japanese War. Each of these vignettes illuminates a different side of the multifaceted Russo-American encounter. In addition, each shows the dramatic power of perception in the relations of states.

CATHERINE THE GREAT AND THE AMERICAN WAR OF INDEPENDENCE

Legends about international relationships are usually born in times of stress and danger. They are burned into the national consciousness under the impact of crisis and then live on tenaciously, often developing a life all their own, quite independent of events. Such a legend developed in America during the War of Independence about Catherine the Great. It was to dominate the thinking of most Americans for several generations.

The simple facts were that in 1775 King George III asked Catherine whether he could hire 20,000 Russian soldiers in order to crush his rebellious subjects in the American Colonies. The czarina turned down the request, and no cossacks appeared on American soil during the War of Independence.

The legend that grew out of this episode became the basis of the traditional friendship between czarist Russia and the young American republic. The czarina was perceived as the "Mother of Independence." Americans were brought up to believe that she had spurned the call for help from her fellow sovereign out of love and sympathy for the American revolutionaries.

American historians who were given access to the czarist archives were forced to destroy this myth. The archives revealed that Catherine took an interest in the American Revolution because it affected British and European politics. The empress, from the very beginning, had decided not to interfere on behalf of Britain because a weakened Britain was in Russia's national interest. She had also decided as early as June 1775 that America would become independent in her own lifetime and that "the colonies [had] told England good-bye forever."[1] In her private correspondence, Catherine did not hesitate to say that she believed the colonies to be right and that England had provoked a useless quarrel that was bound to weaken her and, thus, rebound to Russia's advantage. The best course for Russia under the circumstances was neutrality. In her letter to George III, Catherine stated that she had just finished an exhausting war with Turkey and that she deemed it unwise to send 20,000 troops so far from Russian soil.

The conclusion that must be drawn from the above is that the Russian empress dealt with the American question on grounds of pure realpolitik. She neither liked nor disliked the Americans and probably never met an American in her entire life. The only ques-

---

[1] Catherine II, quoted in Frank A. Golder, "Catherine II and the American Revolution," *American Historical Review*, October 1915, p. 92.

tion that concerned her in connection with the American Revolution was the primacy of the Russian national interest.

The American revolutionaries, on the other hand, perceived the Russian empress as a personal friend and explained her refusal to help King George as the high-minded act of an unselfish ruler. In essence, they confused personal motives with political consequences. The traditional friendship between the people of Russia and America was born out of this confusion.

When, in 1780, Catherine II organized the neutral nations of Europe into an alliance called the Armed Neutrality, the young American republic once again hailed her as the Mother of Independence and assumed that, without question, the Russian empress had formed the league out of sympathy for the struggling colonies.

The facts, again, were quite different. By forming the Armed Neutrality, the empress hoped to force Britain to acknowledge the rights of neutral shippers and, thus, to benefit Russian commerce. She also hoped to be a mediator in Britain's war with Spain, France, and the Netherlands and, thus, to establish herself as the arbiter of the destiny of Europe.

The news of the Armed Neutrality reached America just after the disastrous defeats of Charleston and Camden. There is evidence that the good tidings lifted American morale and strengthened the determination of the colonists to fight on to Yorktown and beyond. Another legend now sank roots: the Armed Neutrality won the war for the embattled colonists. As late as 1905, *Harper's Weekly* declared: "The surrender of Cornwallis at Yorktown did not bend the inflexible will of George III; what broke the King's stubborn heart was the adhesion of Catherine II to the League of Neutrals by which British commerce was exposed to a process of strangulation."[2]

The truth was that the Armed Neutrality was not a decisive factor. Catherine ultimately referred to it as the "Armed Nullity." But the American legend about Catherine's role in the American Revolution persisted and became an objective morale factor to be reckoned with in the War of Independence.

American perceptions of Catherine, ironically enough, under-

---

[2] *Harper's Weekly*, September 23, 1905.

went a volte-face in the years from 1793 to 1795, when the Russian empress divided Poland with Austria and Prussia. By that time the American republic had won its independence from Britain and no longer had need of Russian help. American sympathy now went out to the Polish "underdog" fighting for its life. Thaddeus Kosciusko, the Polish patriot, became the "Washington of Poland." Catherine suddenly became a she-wolf and a ravenous she-bear. When she died in 1796, Philip Freneau, "the poet of the American Revolution," wrote a poem completely reversing the legend of the czarina's denial of troops of George III:

> She would have sent her Tartar bands
> To waste and ravage gallic lands,
> She would have sent her legions o'er,
> Columbia! to invade your shore![3]

The early Americans saw what they needed to see and acted on it. But their perceptions bore little resemblance to reality. After the partition of Poland had become a memory, the legend of Catherine the Mother of Independence surfaced again and dominated American thinking for a long time to come. Neither the positive nor the negative view of Catherine had much to do with reality. But both became the basis of policy and outlook for the young American republic.

THE RUSSIAN FLEET AND THE CIVIL WAR

Perhaps the most amazing and yet most durable legend in Russo-American relations was born during the Civil War. The time for such a legend was ripe, for when the guns began to boom at Fort Sumter in 1861, the governments of Czar Alexander II and of President Abraham Lincoln had similar problems and the same European enemies.

First, for more than half a century, czarist Russia had encouraged the growth of the United States as a commercial and naval

---

[3] Fred L. Pattee (ed.), *The Poems of Philip Freneau* (Princeton: Princeton University Press, 1907), III: 136.

counterweight against Britain and France. Hence, on the eve of the Civil War, Alexander II's sympathies clearly were with the cause of the Union. For precisely the opposite reasons, Russia's European enemies, Britain and France, were hoping that the Union would flounder. Britain remained coldly neutral, and France openly supported the South. Second, both governments were fighting insurrections. Lincoln was determined to put down the Southern rebellion; Alexander was facing rebellion by the Poles. Significantly enough, this time the majority of Americans favored the Russian, rather than the Polish, cause. The London *Punch* ran a sardonic cartoon in which Lincoln said the following of Czar Alexander:

> *Imperial son of Nicholas the Great*
> *We are in the same fix, I calculate*
> *You with your Poles, with Southern rebels I,*
> *Who spurn my rule and my revenge defy.*[4]

Lastly, Alexander had freed the serfs, and Lincoln was trying to free the slaves. Thus, it was only natural that "Lincoln the Emancipator" and "Alexander the Liberator" should feel friendly toward one another.

It was against this background that, during the autumn of 1863, two Russian fleets appeared in the United States. Without any explanation, six Russian vessels dropped anchor in New York harbor and another six entered San Francisco Bay. The Russian minister in Washington, when queried about the presence of the vessels, merely stated that they had come for "no unfriendly purpose."

The timing of the arrival of the Russian ships could not have been more dramatic. The battles of Gettysburg and Vicksburg had just been fought, and much terrible fighting still loomed ahead. The rumor immediately swept the North that two "splendid" Russian fleets had "swept" into the ports of New York and San Francisco in order to serve notice to both Britain and France that, should they dare to intervene on the side of the South, they would have to reckon with Russian guns on the side of the North.

The Russian fleet commanders neither confirmed nor denied

---

[4] *Punch*, October 24, 1863.

these rumors, and their enigmatic silence gave further momentum to the growth of a new legend. The fleets had dropped anchor, the legend went, in order to demonstrate that Russia and the United States were about to conclude an alliance against Britain and France. Lincoln and Alexander would unite in order to repel Anglo-French intervention. "God bless the Russians!" exclaimed Secretary of the Navy Gideon Welles, and his sentiment was echoed throughout the entire North.

This legend led to a spontaneous outburst of enthusiasm for the somewhat bewildered Russian visitors. Elaborate balls were held for them in most of the northern cities. Innumerable toasts were drunk to Lincoln the Emancipator and Alexander the Liberator. General Hiram Wallbridge declared in New York that "There shall be two great hemispheres, one the Eastern and the other the Western. The one shall be represented by Russia, and the other by the United States."[5] The Russians tactfully spoke of Russo-American amity but gave no specific reasons for their presence in the two American ports. There was only a single lapse from this pattern. During a disastrous fire in San Francisco, some 200 Russian volunteers helped fight the blaze, and the grateful citizens of the city staged an elaborate ball for the Russian volunteers. Toward morning, the rumor swept the city that two Confederate destroyers were about to sail into San Francisco Bay and bombard the city. The Russian Rear Admiral Popov, probably under the spell of the enthusiastic reception given him and his men, was so carried away that he issued an order to repel the Confederates should the need arise. Upon hearing of this move, the Russian Minister of Foreign Affairs in St. Petersburg, Prince Gorchakov, sternly countermanded Popov's order. This move, however, in no way dampened the enthusiasm of the Americans for their Russian visitors. Before the Russians departed in 1864, they were lavishly entertained in Washington by leading members of the Cabinet and the Congress. They were widely perceived in the United States as the allies of the Northern cause.

The conviction that the presence of the Russian fleet in American waters had helped to save the Union lived on tenaciously for many years. When Alexander II was assassinated in 1881, Secre-

---

[5] General Hiram Wallbridge, quoted in the London *Times*, October 15, 1863.

tary of State James G. Blaine dispatched the following note of condolence to his successor:

> The Emperor [had] sent a large and powerful fleet of war vessels as a proclamation to the world of his sympathy in our struggle and of his readiness to strike a blow on the side of the Union if any foreign power should strike a blow in aid of the insurrection.[6]

Blaine concluded by saying that the United States deeply appreciated the czar's act "even at the risk of plunging his own empire into war."

The truth about the visit of the Russian fleet to America did not come to light until 1915, when an American historian, Dr. Frank A. Golder, was given access to the official czarist records. Drawing on these primary sources, Golder concluded that the Russian visit "had nothing whatever to do with American affairs" and was to be explained solely in terms of the Russian national interest.[7]

In 1863, the French and British threat to Russia was very real. In case of war, the czar reasoned, the Russian fleet would be trapped in the Baltic Sea by the British. Hence, the fleet was given orders to drop anchor in a friendly neutral port. Every available harbor in the Pacific was in the hands of England, Holland, Spain, Portugal, or France, none of whom could be trusted. Taking these factors into consideration, the choice of American ports was logical. The Russians would be sure of a friendly reception there, and when the time came, their ships could leave port to prey on the vulnerable merchant ships of the British. New York and San Francisco were ideally suited as temporary bases for the Russian fleet. Indeed, when the danger of war had passed in 1864, the Russian commanders were ordered home. Upon their arrival in Kronstadt, the czar thanked them for their service and promoted nearly all of the sailors to higher ranks in the navy. He looked at this cruise as "one of the great practical achievements in the history of the Russian navy and one of the noteworthy pages in the history of his reign."[8]

---

[6] U.S. Department of State, *Papers Relating to the Foreign Relations of the United States, 1881* (Washington, 1882), p. 1014.

[7] Frank A. Golder, "The Russian Fleet and the Civil War," *American Historical Review*, July 1915, p. 805.

[8] Czar Alexander, quoted in *ibid.*, p. 811.

Research into the Russian archives also revealed that the Russian fleet hardly swept into New York and San Francisco. The condition of the twelve vessels was far from splendid. All the ships were wooden, and although some of them had engines, the principal propellant was wind. Moreover, the sails did not fit properly, the sailors were inexperienced, and scurvy broke out on board during the long voyage. Two vessels had to be left behind as unseaworthy, and one was wrecked some thirty miles off San Francisco. Both Britain and France had ironclad ships in their navies, and any one of them could have made short shrift of the Russian ships in a hostile encounter. It is quite probable that in case of a naval engagement, the entire Russian fleet would have been annihilated.

Yet the legend of the selfless Russians continued for half a century after the event. Most Americans stubbornly believed that the Russian ships had come to America for the single purpose of helping the Union in its darkest hour. At the time it was born, the legend boosted the morale of the United States when it needed such boosting most, and Secretary of State W. H. Seward was encouraged to deal more boldly with Britain and France than he might have otherwise. For purposes of national policy, the myth of the Russian fleet became as important as if it had been a fact. In the words of a leading diplomatic historian: "The realization that the United States had one firm friend in Europe who was restraining its enemies bolstered faltering Northern morale, and—although this can never be proved—may have spelled the difference between quitting and continuing on to victory."[9]

THE PURCHASE OF ALASKA

In 1867, three years after the Russian fleet left American shores, Russia sold Alaska to the United States for $7,200,000. When Secretary Seward asked the Congress to approve the purchase that he enthusiastically endorsed, the debate was heated and even bitter. What finally secured congressional approval was American gratitude for Russian assistance to the United States during the

[9] Thomas A. Bailey, *America Faces Russia* (Ithaca: Cornell University Press, 1950), p. 80.

Civil War. In short, "Seward's Icebox" or "Walrussia," as Alaska was referred to derisively, was purchased as a debt of gratitude to Czar Alexander II.

As it became apparent over the years that the new American possession was valuable and as its vast natural resources increasingly became an enormous asset to the United States, the legend gradually took hold that the czar had sold his huge possession to his American "ally" for a pittance, out of sentimental regard for the traditional Russo-American friendship. Like the fleet legend, the Alaska purchase legend became the basis of policy, even though it had little to do with the actual facts of the transaction.

The unadorned facts are that Russia decided to dispose of Alaska in her own national interest. First, Russian America, as Alaska was then called, had become a burdensome economic liability to the czar. The Russian-American Company, which had a monopoly over the territory, was bankrupt, and the Russian government was in no mood to act as a receiver in bankruptcy. Second, should Britain wish to annex Alaska, the Russians, with their weak navy, would be in no position to defend the territory. Thus, Alaska was a permanent hostage to Britain. Third, the Russians were aware of the growing spirit of Manifest Destiny then on the upsurge in the United States. The Americans had taken over west Florida and Texas. A gold rush had brought them to British Columbia. The czar was aware of gold deposits in Alaska. In view of the possibility of an American gold rush, this knowledge was an additional incentive to sell. Under such conditions, it might be difficult, if not impossible, to defend the territory. Thus, while many Americans later believed that the Russians had sold Alaska because they had no knowledge of the gold deposits, the opposite was the case.[10] Finally, the friendship of the Americans was of importance to the czar, especially in the light of continuing tensions with Britain. Thus, the decision to sell was reasonable; the alternatives seemed to be the possible loss of both the territory and the friendship of the United States.

When Edouard de Stoeckl, the Russian minister in Washington, hinted that the emperor might be persuaded to sell Alaska, Secretary Seward avidly rose to the bait. Seward was a convinced

[10] A. G. Mazour, "The Prelude to Russia's Departure from America," *Pacific Historical Review*, September 1941, pp. 311–319.

advocate of Manifest Destiny and his eagerness to purchase Alaska made him a poor bargainer. He quickly settled for a purchase price of $7,200,000, even though the Russian archives revealed that the czar would have sold the territory for as little as $5,000,000.[11]

Seward's real battle was not with the Russian negotiators but with the American Congress. Senators and congressmen alike, burdened with the problems of Reconstruction, were shocked at Seward's decision to spend such a large amount of taxpayers' money for what appeared to be an almost worthless piece of real estate. The secretary of state had to launch an educational campaign in order to convince the reluctant legislators. He pointed out the vast economic resources of Alaska, the improvement in America's strategic position, the imperatives of Manifest Destiny, the commercial advantages that Alaska yielded in the competition with Britain, and, finally, the necessity of preserving and strengthening Russo-American amity. He enlisted the enthusiastic support of Charles Sumner, the powerful chairman of the Senate's Committee on Foreign Relations, and one of the leading orators of the time, for his cause. Sumner gave a three-hour speech advocating the Alaska purchase. He cited all the economic and commercial benefits that would accrue to the United States, but the climax of his speech was a reminder to the senators that Russia had been the only real supporter of the North during the Civil War. Czar Alexander, out of his deep regard for the United States, had decided to sell Alaska for very little money. Under the circumstances, it would be shabby behavior indeed to throw it back in his face. Besides, his goodwill might be needed again in the future. Thus, influenced by Sumner's effort, and with the memory of the Russian fleet still fresh in their minds, the senators approved the Alaska purchase on April 9, 1867, by a vote of 37 to 2. Most of the legislators agreed with Senator Cameron of Pennsylvania that the purchase was "an act of recompense to a tried friend."

The House of Representatives presented a much more difficult hurdle than the Senate. Many congressmen dwelt at length on the worthlessness of Alaska. The territory was referred to in the most uncomplimentary terms as "the country of short rations and long twilights." While most congressmen were mindful of the need to

---

[11] F. A. Golder, "The Purchase of Alaska," *American Historical Review*, April 1920, pp. 419–420.

preserve Russo-American friendship and made grateful references to the Russian fleet, doubts were expressed as to whether friendship called for the sacrifice of taking over "Walrussia" for a price of several million dollars. Representative Benjamin F. Butler argued that if it was necessary to pay $7,200,000 to retain the czar's goodwill, then the United States should pay the amount and refuse to take over Alaska.

The prolonged debate in the House so upset Russian Minister de Stoeckl that he suggested at one point that the emperor offer Alaska to the United States as a gift in order to shame the Americans into paying. Alexander II vetoed this suggestion, whereupon de Stoeckl hired prominent lobbyists in Washington to get the House to pass the appropriation. Even some bribery of congressmen seems to have been involved. What finally won the day for Seward was a combination of factors. First, many congressmen were reluctant to "haul down Old Glory" from Alaska. As Congressman William Orth of Indiana stated: "Shall that flag which waves so proudly there now be taken down? Palsied be the hand that would dare remove it! Our flag is there, and there it will remain."[12] Second, Seward's educational campaign about Alaska's potential economic wealth had made a deep impression in the House. And finally, the legend of the Russian fleet still cast a powerful spell. Most congressmen were reluctant to vote against "the only true friend of America." Thus, the appropriation for the Alaska purchase passed the House on July 14, 1868, by a vote of 113 to 43. The deal was consummated, but not without a bitter aftertaste. The Americans believed that they had paid in full their debt of gratitude for the Russian fleet. Minister de Stoeckl, on the other hand, was so unnerved by the congressional debate that he requested the czar for another assignment in order to "breathe for a while a purer atmosphere than that of Washington."

As the years passed, the value of Alaska, of course, became increasingly apparent. Americans began to read back into the past the mood of the moment. A feeling of gratitude for the czar's apparent generosity developed retrospectively. As relations with Russia slowly began to worsen toward the turn of the century, as George Kennan revealed the horrors of the Siberian exile system to

---

[12] Congressman William Orth, quoted in Thomas A. Bailey, A *Diplomatic History of the American People* (New York: Appleton-Century-Crofts, 1950), p. 401.

Americans for the first time, as pogroms and clashing power objectives began to poison the traditional friendship, the memory of Czar Alexander's "selflessness" in ceding Alaska for a pittance still remained a bond in Russo-American relations. As the objective dictates of power and national rivalry drove the two nations ever further apart, as the differences in the two systems of government became more and more dramatically apparent, the legends of the generosity of Czar Alexander, myths though they were, still exercised a remarkable influence, especially on the American side, in delaying for some time the decline of Russo-American relations into suspicion and hostility.

THE DEATH OF A LEGEND: THE RUSSO-JAPANESE WAR AND THE UNITED STATES

Alexander II was killed by an assassin's bomb in 1881, and with his passing the golden age of Russo-American relations came to an end. Under the heavy hand of his successor, Alexander III, ominous events took place that gradually eroded the American legend of Russia like so many drops of corrosive acid. A violent wave of anti-Jewish pogroms that followed the assassination of Alexander II swept across Russia and brought large numbers of immigrants to the United States. The horrible tales of these pogroms outraged many Americans and made them turn away from Russia. When in 1891 the distinguished American publicist George Kennan[13] exposed the truth about the conditions of prisoners in Siberia in his classic *Siberia and the Exile System*, the legend was shattered almost beyond repair. Thus, on the eve of war between Russia and Japan, American sympathies were definitely with Japan, to the incredulous surprise and consternation of Czar Nicholas II and the entire Russian press. Even the able and gifted Russian diplomat Count Sergei Witte, who represented his country at the Portsmouth peace talks, was unable to reverse the anti-Russian tide in America. Theodore Roosevelt had only unkind words for the Russians. They were perceived by him as stupid, insincere, treacherous, and corrupt. Czar Nicholas was seen as "a preposterous little

---

[13] A distant relative of the scholar-diplomat George Frost Kennan.

creature."[14] A legend had died, and another had risen to take its place.

The anti-Jewish pogroms in Russia from Kiev in 1881 to Kishinev in 1903 turned large segments of American public opinion against Russia. In 1882, Representative Samuel S. Cox of New York City in demanding action listed 167 places where there had been riots, burnings, pillagings, rapes, and murders.[15] The number of Jewish families reduced to beggary was estimated at 100,000. The pogroms continued during the 1880s and 1890s and culminated in the frightful orgy of Kishinev, which seemed to many Americans to be condoned by the bureaucracy of Nicholas II.

The outcry of horror in the United States was not limited to the Jews alone. But the State Department was too embarrassed to protest vigorously, primarily because of America's questionable policies regarding the black population. As one Berlin cartoon had President Theodore Roosevelt remark to the czar: "You cut up your Jews, I'll burn my Negroes."[16] Some Americans argued that out of gratitude for past favors, the United States should not now criticize Russia too harshly. But leading American Jews, such as Oscar S. Straus, began to undermine the basis of Russo-American friendship by casting serious doubts on the fleet legend.[17]

Perhaps no one single person did more to bury the American legend of Russia than George Kennan. To most Americans of 1880, Siberia was a frozen wasteland to which convicts were banished by edict of the czar. Kennan was the first American ever to visit Siberian prisons, and his exposé, published in 1891, became a classic of thoroughness and dramatic power. The conditions he found were horrible beyond belief. Victims were banished without trial; torture was commonplace; starvation was the rule of the day; and the callousness of prison officials was barbaric. Kennan, a gifted writer and lecturer, brought countless American audiences to the verge of tears with his forceful and evocative descriptions.

---

[14] H. F. Pringle, *Theodore Roosevelt* (New York: Macmillan, 1931), p. 385.

[15] U.S. Congress, House, *Congressional Record*, 47th Cong., 1st sess. 1882, pp. 651–658.

[16] *Review of Reviews*, September 1903, p. 269.

[17] Oscar S. Straus, "The United States and Russia: Their Historical Relations," *North American Review*, August 1905, pp. 244–245.

And, for the first time, he delineated a distinction that was increasingly perceived by the Americans—between the Russian government and the Russian people. "As for me," Kennan wrote, "my sympathies are with the Russia of the people, not the Russia of the Tsars."[18] This distinction increasingly dominated American perceptions of Russia and exercised a profound influence on American policy toward Russia during the Bolshevik Revolution.

When the Japanese fleet attacked Russian naval units at Port Arthur in a surprise attack and without any declaration of war, most American newspapers praised the clever and courageous Japanese who were not afraid of Russian bully tactics and were resourceful enough to catch the Russians off guard.[19] Kennan, now a distinguished war correspondent, wrote that the Japanese were superior to the Russians and that Russian prisoners of war were better off in Japanese prison camps than they would have been as czarist exiles in Siberia. Even though Japan had fired the first shot, most Americans were on the side of the Japanese "underdog"; it seemed like a contest between David and Goliath. President Roosevelt convinced himself that Japan was "playing our game." If Russia won, she would presumably close the door for the United States in Asia while Japan would keep it open for American commerce. Even though there was little evidence to support this claim, it permeated the thinking of most American government officials and business interests.

The Russian response to this American about-face was one of shock and anger. The Russian press during the Russo-Japanese War was full of references to American ingratitude for past favors. Moreover, Russia was a white Christian nation, and in times of threat from the yellow peril, white Christian nations should stand together. Finally, the Japanese aggressors had clearly struck the first blow, while Nicholas II was a man of peace who had initiated the Hague Peace Conference. The American attitude was both stupid and incomprehensible to most Russian officials.

A new debate began in the United States about the role of the Russian fleet during the Civil War. Serious doubts were cast on the old legend. Especially after the disastrous defeat of the Russian

---

[18] George Kennan, *Century Magazine*, July 1893, p. 472.

[19] The parallels to the attack on Pearl Harbor are remarkable, but few Americans drew them in 1941.

fleet at the Tsushima Strait, many Americans began to question just how useful the fleet would have been to the Americans if it had been engaged in naval battle by Britain or France. So far as Alaska was concerned, cash had been paid and no debt was involved. Pogroms and Siberian prisons had brought into being a far less generous, even a cynical, reaction to Russian claims on American gratitude for favors received in the past.

By 1905, both Russia and Japan were exhausted from the war. Russia's navy was crippled, and she faced the possibility of revolution at home. Japan was near the end of her manpower and economic resources. The story of Theodore Roosevelt's mediation at Portsmouth is well known and will not be recounted here. What is important is that the changed attitudes of the United States and Russia toward each other became painfully clear to both sides during the negotiations.

Czar Nicholas II was badly shaken by the new American hostility. In 1905, near the end of the war, he asked the following of the American ambassador: "Say to your President I certainly hope that the old friendship which has previously existed and united the two nations for so long a period will be renewed."[20] The czar knew that the ancient friendship had been shattered, and he was eager to rebuild it. He sent to Portsmouth the brilliant diplomat Count Witte, who did his best to swing American public opinion away from Japan back to Russia. But a careful analysis of American press attitudes during the Portsmouth negotiations demonstrates that "the great majority of the press remained unswervingly pro-Japanese on the specific issues which divided the Portsmouth delegates."[21]

A new image had taken hold: the Russian government was a group of blundering despots and liars; the Russian army was inept; the navy was beyond hope; and the people were the abject victims of a brutal and mindless tyranny. "It is the system that has failed, not the men," explained the American *Review of Reviews*. While during the reigns of Catherine and Alexander the Russians could do no wrong, under Nicholas they could do little that was right.

---

[20] Czar Nicholas II, quoted in Bailey, *America Faces Russia, op. cit.*, p. 205.

[21] Winston B. Thorson, "American Public Opinion and the Portsmouth Conference," *American Historical Review*, April 1948, p. 454.

THE BIRTH AND DEATH OF LEGENDS

Perhaps the most remarkable conclusion to be drawn about American perceptions of Russia during the pre-Bolshevik period is how violently they swung from one extreme to the other, while Russia, the object of these perceptions, changed relatively little. For an entire century, Russia was America's trusted friend. Catherine's refusal to lend troops to King George, Alexander's dispatch of the Russian fleet to American ports, and Alexander's sale of Alaska, all were perceived as selfless and generous acts and uncritically accepted as such. The legend of Russia, the "trusted ally," was born in these events, and policy decisions of far-reaching importance were based on the assumption that all the legends were true.

Russia, under both Catherine and Alexander, had acted purely in accord with the dictates of her national interest. Though somewhat surprised by the effusive gratitude of the Americans, the czars did little to dispel it. When the pendulum of American perceptions swung to the other extreme, Nicholas II was bewildered and shocked. He tried to appeal to the ancient friendship, but the old American image of Russia, once dead, could not be resurrected. Americans saw prisons and pogroms in Russia, where formerly they had seen only goodwill and benevolence. This perception, equally one-sided as its predecessor, led to policies that helped estrange America from Russia.

One cannot help but note the unevenness of the American attitudes. Russian views of America were fairly accurate, and Russian policy was cold and selfish, but steady and fairly predictable. The young American republic tended to see the Russians either as angels or as monsters. Personal factors such as trust and friendship were read into policy; personal motives were perceived as national objectives; and, finally, romanticism yielded to bitterness and disillusion.

Perhaps legends grow more easily in young nations than in old. Young America had to supplant one legend with another, equally distorted. Czarist Russia, nearing its end, did not indulge in legends. Only with the advent of the Bolshevik Revolution did the new Russian leadership fashion legends of its own.

Chapter Nine

The Bolshevik Revolution and the United States

The shattering events that changed the face of Russia in 1917 also had a profound impact on the United States. The reaction of the American public-at-large to the Russian Revolution and its aftermath was marked by wide swings of emotion. The events of March 1917 were widely perceived as the triumph of democracy in Russia. Most Americans believed that Russia, having thrown off the czarist yoke, would fight even harder on the Allied side against Germany. After all, Russians would now be fighting for themselves, and not for a cruel tyranny that had been imposed on them for centuries.

When Russia signed a separate peace treaty with Germany, however, and left the war in March 1918, the American public was swept by a sense of outrage and betrayal. The Bolsheviks who had been seen as liberators from czarism were now perceived as German agents and as a threat to civilization in general and to American democracy in particular. The attitude of the American public now swung to the opposite extreme. The greatest danger to the human race was no longer the German "Hun," but the Bolshevik "Red." The Bolsheviks, most Americans believed, were not really Russian at all. If Lenin and his clique could only be removed, the true democratic spirit of Russia would at last assert itself.

Little wonder then that there were powerful popular pressures in the United States in 1918 favoring armed intervention in the

Russian civil war. This intervention did indeed take place in the summer of 1918; not until after the end of the war were American troops withdrawn from Russia. Still, the bitterness toward the Bolsheviks remained. It manifested itself in the "Red Scare" that swept the United States in 1919 and resulted in the deportation of many Americans with Communist sympathies. Romanticism had turned to cynicism, disillusionment, and bitter hatred.

President Woodrow Wilson had been deeply affected by the Russian Revolution. Eager to "make the world safe for democracy," he quickly welcomed the new "democratic Russia" as a "fit partner for a league of honor."[1] Wilson retained a favorable disposition toward the Soviet Union even after the new Soviet government left the war. Indeed, he resisted the popular pressures for armed intervention in the civil war until the summer of 1918. What finally prompted him to intervene was not so much the hope of overthrowing the Bolsheviks as the desire to come to the rescue of a contingent of anti-Bolshevik Czechoslovaks who were fighting their way westward through the Russian interior. Wilson did not really perceive the new Soviet government as the "Red Terror" poised to engulf the Western world. But he intervened because the lives of sons and brothers and husbands were at stake. In this sense, American policy was not based on distorted perceptions or unrealistic expectations, but on a relatively sober military calculation in which the cruder perceptions and motivations of the American public appear to have played a fairly minor role. A year later, however, when the popular fury against the Bolsheviks had hardened, America endured the short-lived but intense Red Scare at the instigation of Attorney General A. Mitchell Palmer.

On the Bolshevik side, the two leading figures with sustained interest in the United States were V. I. Lenin and Leon Trotsky. Although their attention was largely focused on Europe, they nevertheless had very definite views of the United States during the turbulent years of world war and revolution. These perceptions were deeply influenced by Marxist ideology. Even before the United States entered the war, America was seen as a nation in which a few self-seeking capitalist monopolists were imposing their control on the large masses of exploited workers. When the United

---

[1] Woodrow Wilson, War Message to Congress, April 2, 1917, *Papers Relating to the Foreign Relations of the United States*, Supplement I: *The World War*, 1918, p. 200.

States joined the struggle against Germany and the Central Powers and thus became an ally of the czarist regime, Lenin pronounced his scorn for both sides in the war. Lenin's triumph in November 1917 brought this loathing to the surface. It was perfectly clear to him that he should take Russia out of the war at the earliest opportunity. Let the imperialists devour each other while Russia maneuvered, bided her time, and slowly grew in strength. Not even President Wilson's Fourteen Points speech of January 1918, with its conciliatory comments about the new Soviet government, changed the Soviet leader's view. Several weeks later and one month before the Brest-Litovsk Treaty of March 1918, which took Russia out of the war, Lenin had the following to say:

> The war with England and America will go on for a long time; the aggressive imperialism of both groups has unmasked itself finally and completely. Under such conditions a socialist Soviet Republic in Russia will be a model for all other peoples and excellent material for propaganda purposes. On the one side there will be the bourgeois system engaged in a strife between two coalitions of confessed plunderers, and on the other side a socialist Soviet Republic living in peace.[2]

While some Bolsheviks flirted briefly with the idea of regarding the United States as the lesser evil, Lenin firmly rejected such an attitude. The Allied military intervention in the summer of 1918 only hardened Lenin's convictions. His perceptions of the United States at that time were set forth with great clarity in his "Letter to American Workingmen from the Socialist Soviet Republic of Russia," written in August 1918. In this remarkable document, the United States was seen as a house divided between a few greedy plutocrats on the one hand, and the mass of destitute workers on the other. Lenin said, "America has become characteristic for the depth of the abyss which divides a handful of brutal millionaires who are stagnating in mires of luxury, and millions of laboring, starving men and women who are always staring want in the face." It was only a question of time, in Lenin's view, until the revolution would come to America. "The American working class will not follow the lead of the bourgeoisie," Lenin predicted confidently; "it will go with us against the bourgeoisie." On August 30, 1918, the day he was shot and seriously wounded, Lenin gave a speech

---

[2] Lenin, quoted in *Pravda*, February 24, 1918.

in Moscow in which he once again revealed his view of the United States: "A handful not of millionaires but of billionaires takes over everything, and the entire population remains in slavery and subjection."[3]

The evidence suggests that Lenin's policy toward the United States was derived directly from this ideological model. While Wilson's policies toward the new Bolshevik government were based on a number of interrelated factors of which the American perception of the Soviet Union was only one—and by no means the most important one—the Bolshevik leader perceived the United States almost completely through the prism of Communist ideology and fashioned his policy accordingly.

The essential thesis of this chapter, then, is that Lenin and, to a lesser extent, Wilson saw what they expected to see. Wilson, before the Allied intervention, saw a Russia that was largely fictitious, and Lenin saw the same in the United States. Thus, the two men often talked past each other and their statements about each other's countries frequently took on an exasperating air of irrelevance. Their policies unfortunately followed suit. George F. Kennan, in describing these early Soviet-American encounters, recounts the hoary anecdote about two cross-eyed men who bumped into each other. The first asked, "Why in hell don't you look where you are going?" To which the other replied, "Why in hell don't you go where you are looking?"[4]

AMERICA VIEWS RUSSIA: 1917–1920

The great majority of Americans, from the president down to the rank-and-file, saw the overthrow of czarist Russia as the triumph of freedom and democracy, American style. The unanimous reaction of statesmen, businessmen, labor leaders, editors, and politicians to the events in Petrograd was truly extraordinary. Elite and public alike shared this view virtually without dissent. George Kennan, then widely regarded as the leading authority on Russia, pro-

---

[3] Lenin, quoted in George F. Kennan, *The Decision to Intervene* (Princeton: Princeton University Press, 1958), p. 462.

[4] George F. Kennan, *Russia and the West Under Lenin and Stalin* (Boston: Little, Brown, 1961), pp. 10–11.

claimed "the complete triumph of democracy" in March 1917.[5] Other commentators were equally enthusiastic. *The New York Times*, referring to the government of Prince Lvov, stated editorially that "democracy [was] the very soul of the Russian revolution, the sustaining principle of the new Government."[6] President Wilson, in his war message to Congress on April 2, 1917, not only pronounced the new Russian government as "a fit partner for a league of honor," but despite Russia's czarist past, continued to describe that nation as "democratic at heart, in all the vital habits of her thought, in all the intimate relationships of her people that spoke their natural instinct, their habitual attitude towards life."[7] Religious groups were lavish in their praise. The reaction of *Zion's Herald*, a Boston Methodist weekly, was typical: "Autocracy has received its death blow; democracy has triumphed. All of America rejoices in the dawn of the new day for Russia."[8] And the Washington *Star* editorialized: "A free people naturally wants all the other peoples of the world to be free."[9] Russia was thus perceived as a Slavic version of the United States and Russian "democracy" as a replica of the American model.

The facts, well known in retrospect, were quite different. Prince Lvov and his government were wealthy landowners with strongly aristocratic tastes. The majority of the population were peasants with little or no experience in self-government, who harbored bitter resentments against the landholding classes. The political situation in Russia in the spring of 1917 was hardly ripe for democratic government.

In most of America, the wish inspired the thought. In March 1917, the United States was about to declare war on Germany and help to "make the world safe for democracy." It would have been embarrassing, to say the least, to be allied with the czarist autocracy in this crusade. The Russian Revolution was nothing less than providential. It removed the embarrassing czar just in time for Wilson's war message and, in the view of most Americans, rein-

---

[5] George Kennan, "The Victory of the Russian People," *Outlook*, March 28, 1917, p. 546.

[6] *The New York Times*, March 16, 1917.

[7] Wilson, *War Message, op. cit.*

[8] *Zion's Herald*, March 21, 1917.

[9] Cited in Leonid I. Strakhovsky, *American Opinion About Russia* (Toronto: University of Toronto Press, 1961), p. 6.

stated the Russian people as fellow belligerents in the democratic cause against the German kaiser and the Central Powers. Russia had not only become a democratic nation, she would now also become a formidable military ally. In the American mind, democracy in Russia and continuing the war were inextricably linked. This misperception of the March Revolution was destined to bear bitter fruit when the real nature of the revolutionary process in Russia began to reveal itself.

The American ambassador to the Provisional Government was a sixty-seven-year-old former grain merchant from Missouri, David R. Francis. Francis, who was almost completely out of touch with the realities in Russia, sent back glowing reports about the prospects of the new government. In June, Wilson dispatched Elihu Root, a conservative and wealthy elder statesman, on a goodwill mission to Russia. Root was to encourage the Russians to keep up the fight against Germany. While walking through a Siberian village in June 1917, however, Root stated: "I am a firm believer in democracy, but I do not like filth."[10] He was not equipped to understand the Russian Revolution; nor were most Americans at the time.

When the Bolsheviks seized power in November 1917, most Americans reacted as if the impossible had happened. And since it was impossible, it would soon cease happening. Again, a distinction was drawn in the American mind between the Russian people and the "usurping gang" of Bolshevik leaders.[11] The American missionary spirit asserted itself in the pages of the influential New York World: "Russia cannot be abandoned, either to Germany or to anarchy."[12] The predominant belief in the United States was that the Bolsheviks were a small minority whose crazy ideas would soon topple them from power, whereupon the democratic instincts of the Russian people would again rise to the surface. The New York Times, according to a study made by Walter Lippmann during the period from November 1917 to November 1919, predicted the fall of the Bolsheviks from power no fewer than ninety-one times.[13] It also reported four times that Lenin and Trotsky were

[10] Elihu Root, quoted in Philip C. Jessup, Elihu Root (New York: Dodd Mead, 1938), II: 361.
[11] Literary Digest, December 8, 1917, p. 15.
[12] Cited in ibid.
[13] Cited in The New Republic, August 4, 1920.

planning flight and three times that they had already fled. Three times it announced Lenin's imprisonment and once even his death.[14]

The separate peace of Brest-Litovsk convinced the United States that the impossible might last a little longer than had been anticipated. The *North American Review* confessed: "We have optimistically—and somewhat credulously—called Russia free, a republic, a democracy. Russia has not, for a single day, been either a republic, a democracy, or free."[15] Most Americans reacted to Brest-Litovsk as an act of Bolshevik perfidy and regarded the Russians as cowardly quitters at best or German agents at worst. Trotsky was awarded the "ignoble peace prize" by several American newspapers, and one paper, the Kansas City *Star*, with a strong suggestion of sour grapes, stated: "Well, if Russia is lost to us, all right. We never did want to make the world safe for the Bolshevik kind of democracy anyway."[16]

The cycle of President Wilson's perceptions of Russia swung within narrower confines than that of the American public-at-large. The president had been critical of the czar but not violently so. The victory of the Bolsheviks disappointed him but did not outrage him. He even made some conciliatory gestures toward the new Soviet government in early 1918, although he decided to withhold formal recognition. Some contemporary American observers of the Russian scene have claimed that this American reluctance to recognize the new regime and the decision not to have any dealings with it precipitated Brest-Litovsk and Lenin's determination to pull Russia out of the war. Raymond Robins, for example, the head of the American Red Cross Mission to Russia in 1918, maintained that "the bitter anti-Bolshevism of his government was to blame for the separate peace."[17] He recounted a dramatic scene according to which Lenin, just before the meeting of the Fourth All-Russian Congress of Soviets on March 16, 1918, asked him whether he had heard from Washington about the possibility of recognition. When Robins replied in the negative,

[14] *Ibid.*

[15] *North American Review*, February 1918, p. 186.

[16] Cited in *Literary Digest*, January 12, 1918.

[17] U.S. Senate, *Hearings Before a Subcommittee of the Committee on the Judiciary*, 65th Cong., 3rd sess. (1919), pp. 800–801.

Lenin mounted the rostrum and convinced the delegates to ratify the Brest-Litovsk Treaty. The inference here is that the United States was responsible for Brest-Litovsk.

The historical evidence does not bear out the Robins thesis. George F. Kennan in his *Russia Leaves the War* has demonstrated conclusively that Lenin was determined to take Russia out of the war regardless of American policy toward the new Soviet government.[18] The Bolshevik slogan of "an end to the war" was an integral plank in the platform that had swept Lenin to power. It was not contingent on what the Americans would or would not do. Nevertheless, Robins testified before the Senate Judiciary Subcommittee in March 1919 and convinced a number of influential opinion shapers of his views, among them, Arthur Bullard, who was Colonel Edward M. House's representative in Russia in 1918, and Professors Edward A. Ross and Samuel N. Harper. President Wilson, significantly enough, ignored the suggestions of Robins and his circle. Wilson's attitude toward the new Bolshevik regime was essentially one of aloofness—one does not engage in commerce with the devil. On the occasion of the Brest- Litovsk Treaty, the American president sent the following statement to the Soviet government: "The whole heart of the people of the United States is with the people of Russia in the attempt to free themselves forever from autocratic government and become the masters of their own life."[19] But he added, regretfully, that the United States would not be able to offer either economic aid or recognition.

The All-Russian Congress replied to Wilson's message in kind, thanking "the toiling and exploited classes of the United States of North America" and expressing

> its warm sympathy and its firm confidence that the happy time is not far distant when the toiling masses of all bourgeois countries will throw off the yoke of capitalism and will establish a socialist order of society, which alone is capable of assuring a firm and just peace as well as the cultural and material well being of all the toilers.[20]

[18] George F. Kennan, *Russia Leaves the War* (Princeton: Princeton University Press, 1956), pp. 487–517.

[19] Acting Secretary of State Polk to Consul-General Summers at Moscow, March 11, 1918, *War Message, op. cit.*, pp. 395–396.

[20] Quoted in Kennan, *Russia Leaves the War, op. cit.* pp. 512–513.

In the words of a leading scholar of the period, "Suddenly, Americans were hearing their own gospel, in Bolshevik translation, returning to them like an ironic and ominous echo. Two missionaries were now competing for the souls of the peoples of the world."[21]

Even after Brest-Litovsk, most Americans still believed that the Russians were democratic at heart and anxious to defeat the German autocrats. The myth of the Bolsheviks as a transient, German-inspired phenomenon died hard. Lenin, after all, had been spirited into Russia in a train provided by the German general staff, and Trotsky's real name was Bronstein. *The Saturday Evening Post* told its two million subscribers that Germany practiced despotism by an elite, but Lenin represented a "despotism by all the lowest."[22] The Bolsheviks were an evil that the Wilson administration boycotted diplomatically and the vast majority of Americans opposed vehemently. Thus, when Japan, Britain, and France prepared for intervention against the Bolsheviks in April 1918, and when the counterattacks of the Whites at the same time had reduced the areas under Soviet control to the size of medieval Muscovy, the demand for American military intervention mounted. Wilson resisted these pressures for several months, even though he had come to believe that "the new dictatorship in Russia was just as selfish, ruthless, and pitiless as that of the Czars, and his heart went out to the ill-starred masses."[23] During May and June, the public clamor grew in vehemence, and numerous high officials, both in the Wilson administration and in elective office, demanded intervention, either for anti-Bolshevik or anti-German reasons or a combination of both. As Senator James Reed of Missouri told the Senate: "If Russia rises against the entering troops, that would prove that Russia is already Germanized."[24] Many of the president's diplomatic advisers joined the interventionist tide. What finally forced Wilson's hand, as we have seen, was a marooned contingent of some 45,000 Czechoslovak soldiers in east-

[21] Peter G. Filene, *Americans and the Soviet Experiment, 1917–1933* (Cambridge: Harvard University Press, 1967), p. 37.

[22] *The Saturday Evenings Post*, July 6, 1918.

[23] R. S. Baker and W. E. Dodd, *The Public Papers of Woodrow Wilson, 1917–1924* (New York: Harcourt, Brace, 1927), II: 70.

[24] U.S. Congress, Senate, *Congressional Record*, 65th Cong., 2nd sess., August 22, 1918, p. 9348.

ern Russia who caught the popular fancy and whose thousands of relatives in America put additional pressure on Congress and the president. A force of 9,000 Americans was sent to Russia, and the resulting loss of lives in battles with Bolshevik contingents embittered both sides even further.

New myths about Bolshevik Russia sprang up in the United States during the interventionist phase. The Bolsheviks now became veritable monsters who had ordered the nationalization of Russian women. In October 1918, *The New York Times* reported that, in certain Russian provinces under Soviet control, every eighteen-year-old girl had to register at a "bureau of free love" and was then given a husband without her consent.[25] Senator Lawrence Sherman of Illinois delivered a lengthy speech on the subject in the Senate in January 1919. Such reports appeared in numerous American papers until late 1919.

After the Allied armistice with Germany in November 1918, American intervention simply no longer made sense. The Czechoslovaks had been evacuated; the war was over; and the parents of the American soldiers in Russia brought great pressure to bear on their representatives in Congress to bring their sons home. Enthusiasm for intervention turned to bitterness that Americans were still suffering and fighting in Russia despite the armistice in Europe. The public clamor against the intervention was now as vociferous as it had been six months earlier in favor of it. But not until June 1919, after hundreds of casualties, were American troops withdrawn from northern Russia, and the last troops did not leave Siberia until April 1920.

During the intervention, the American attitudes toward Russia froze into an almost bizarre hostility. As one observer put it: "Bolshevism means chaos, wholesale murder, the complete destruction of civilization."[26] According to *Current History*, the issue was "Bolshevism Against Civilization." As late as November 1919, Secretary of State Lansing was still in favor of extending diplomatic recognition to the White General Kolchak, and Senator William A. Smith of Michigan asserted that "the Russian people, God bless

[25] *The New York Times*, October 26, 1918.

[26] Lincoln Steffens to Allen H. Suggett, *Letters* (New York: Harcourt, Brace, 1938), I: 466.

them, [were] anxious to overthrow the Bolsheviks and to fulfill a noble destiny."[27] When the Bolsheviks had clearly won the civil war, Americans finally despaired about the "democratic spirit" of Russia. There now developed considerable support for making Russia a trusteeship under the League of Nations and thus to supervise her gradual entry into civilization.[28] William Allen White concluded bitterly in October 1919: "Let the thing fry in its own grease. So far as interior Russia is concerned, the whole trouble with Russia is Russia."[29]

The Red Scare of 1919 exposed the darker side of the missionary spirit. The emotions of the two crusades against Germany and Bolshevism, not yet dissipated, frantically sought new objects. Vindictiveness and xenophobia now took command. Strikes in Seattle and Boston and a Communist coup in Hungary provided additional fuel for the mounting hysteria. In November 1919, Attorney General Palmer arrested 450 supposed Communists in 12 cities and one month later seized 4,000 more suspects in 33 cities. On December 21, 1919, 249 persons were actually deported on the "Soviet Ark" to the Soviet Union. As one supporter of the attorney general put it, "My motto for the Reds is S.O.S.—ship or shoot. I believe we should place them all on a ship of stone, with sails of lead, and their first stopping place should be hell."[30] The Red Scare, in the words of one thoughtful observer, was "Wilsonianism turned inside out, confident messianism become paranoid, intolerant Americanism seeking to purify the nation of alien and disturbing elements."[31]

Thus, most Americans by 1920 perceived a Russia that had merely changed chains. After a few brief glimpses of liberty, she was now enslaved by a despotism far more diabolical and cunning than that of the czars. Czarism, though objectionable, was at least content to oppress its own people. The Bolsheviks, however, were determined to impose their fearful philosophy beyond their own borders on the rest of the world.

[27] U.S. Congress, Senate, *Congressional Record*, 65th Cong., 3rd sess., January 24, 1919, p. 1081.

[28] *The New York Times*, January 12, 1919.

[29] William Allen White, quoted in Filene, *op. cit.*, p. 61.

[30] Quoted in Foster R. Dulles, *The Road to Teheran* (Princeton: Princeton University Press, 1944), p. 164.

[31] Quoted in Filene, *op. cit.*, p. 63.

THE BOLSHEVIKS VIEW
THE UNITED STATES: 1917–1920

Lenin's empirical knowledge of the United States was quite slender. He seemed to have had little interest in it and probably identified it with the England he came to know during his period of exile in London. America seemed to have been just another capitalist country and not a very important one at that. The Decree on Peace, which Lenin drafted personally in the fall of 1917, referred to England, France, and Germany as "the three mightiest states taking part in the present war." The United States was not even mentioned, though it had entered the war in April 1917.

Trotsky had visited the United States from January 13 to March 27, 1917. During this brief stay in New York City he lived in the Bronx on 162nd Street, in what he described as a "working-class district." He spent most of his working day in the editorial offices of the Russian-language socialist newspaper *Novy Mir* near Union Square. In his autobiography, he relates that he studied American economic life in the New York Public Library and adds that his "only profession in New York was the profession of a revolutionary socialist."[32] Before leaving New York, Trotsky urged his followers to keep on organizing in order "to overthrow this damned rotten capitalistic government."[33] The evidence suggests that the rich variety of American life, the "flesh-and-blood America . . . remained for him—fortunately for the peace of his brilliant but dogmatic mind, unfortunately for the course of Soviet-American relations—a closed book."[34]

Hence, even while Lenin and Trotsky were still fugitives from Russia, they regarded the United States as an intrinsic part of the capitalist world, which they hated with every fiber of their deeply political natures. The fact that this hatred was transferred from its primary objects—England, France, and Germany—made it no less real. But what they hated was not the real America of 1917, but a fictitious America, one that had been created half a century earlier by the pen of Karl Marx.

Both Lenin and Trotsky had been taken completely by surprise

[32] Leon Trotsky, *Mein Leben* (Berlin: S. Fischer Verlag, 1930), p. 259.
[33] Leon Trotsky, quoted in Thomas A. Bailey, *America Faces Russia* (Ithaca: Cornell University Press, 1950), p. 238.
[34] Kennan, *Russia Leaves the War, op. cit.*, p. 32.

by the March Revolution. As good Marxists, they had expected the revolution to strike first in Germany or in England. When it occurred in one of the least industrialized countries in Europe, the two Bolshevik leaders happened to be in exile but were galvanized into action at once. As is well known, Lenin was permitted by the German government to traverse Germany in the famous sealed train. He entered Russia in April. A few weeks later, he and Trotsky were hard at work to turn the March Revolution into a full-fledged victory for the Bolshevik cause.

When the Bolshevik Revolution struck in mid-November, the first policy statement, issued on the very day of the revolution, was the Decree on Peace. In this document Lenin proposed an immediate armistice and also called on the class-conscious workers of England, Germany, and France to liberate the toiling masses of the world. The document was aimed at "peoples," rather than governments and, to some extent at least, was meant to encourage social revolution in the three European countries. The United States was not mentioned even once.

The first Soviet policy statement regarding the United States directly was made by Trotsky, at a meeting of the Central Executive Committee of the Soviet of Workers' and Peasants' Deputies, held four days after the promulgation of the Decree on Peace. His statement sums up the view of the early Bolshevik leaders very well:

> The United States began to intervene in the war after three years, under the influence of the sober calculations of the American Stock Exchange. America could not tolerate the victory of one coalition over the other. America is interested in the weakening of both coalitions and in the consolidation of the hegemony of American capital. Apart from that, American war industry is interested in the war. During the war American exports have more than doubled and have reached a figure not reached by any other capitalist state. Exports go almost entirely to the Allied countries. When in January Germany came out for unrestricted U-boat warfare, all railway stations and harbors in the United States were overloaded with the output of the war industries. Transport was disorganized and New York witnessed food riots such as we ourselves have never seen here. Then the finance capitalists sent an ultimatum to Wilson: to secure the sale of the output of the war industries within the country. Wilson accepted the ultimatum, and hence the preparations for war and war itself.[35]

[35] Leon Trotsky, cited in *ibid.*, p. 88.

An analysis of this statement reveals the tragic gaps between perception and reality that dominated Trotsky's thinking on the matter of the United States. First, he dismissed American democracy as a preposterous sham and saw the real rulers of American political life in the monopoly capitalists of Wall Street. Second, he accused the United States of desiring to weaken the Allies in order to profit from the economic disaster of both sides. Third, Wilson's decision to enter the war was seen as a capitulation to monopoly capital. And finally, Trotsky painted a picture of hunger and deprivation far worse than anything that had been seen in Russia. To what extent Trotsky really believed these things and to what extent he consciously used them to advance the Bolshevik cause may never be precisely known. But it is a safe assumption that he believed *some* of the things he said. And his experience in the drab interior of an obscure Russian paper in New York probably did little to correct these stereotypes; perhaps it even reinforced them.

Lenin's writings before the 1917 revolution are replete with references to the United States. In *Imperialism, the Highest Stage of Capitalism,* written in exile in 1916, Lenin first developed the thesis that the war then in progress was "imperialist" on both sides. England, Germany, and Japan had already reached the highest stage of capitalism that made a nation inexorably imperialist. The nation about to reach that stage, according to Lenin, was the United States, whose economic expansion had recently been "even more rapid than in Germany and for this very reason the parasitic features of American capitalism stood out with particular force."[36] Such was the vigor of this new American imperialism that it was "actually beating Great Britain" and would soon clash with the expansionary drives of the other capitalist powers. In Lenin's view, therefore, the United States as a capitalist nation was inescapably committed to the imperialist exploitation of other countries. Its trusts, monopolies, and cartels would make sure of that.

Lenin, like Trotsky and the other Bolshevik leaders, regarded American entry into the war with cynicism. Wilson's assertion that the motive was to "make the world safe for democracy" was dismissed with utter contempt. The United States, in Lenin's view, was "infected with the same flame as Germany" and would go to

[36] V. I. Lenin, *Sochineniya (Complete Works),* 4th ed. (Moscow: State Publishing House for Political Literature, 1950), 27:553.

the "same savage and insensate lengths" to attain its sinister objectives. Only the proletarian revolution could save the United States from ultimate self-destruction.

It is safe to assume that these convictions remained with Lenin until his death. The little contact he had with America and Americans did nothing to shake them. Not even President Wilson's conciliatory gesture toward the new Bolshevik government, made in January 1918 in his Fourteen Points speech, was able to jar the consistency of Lenin's world view. Even though—according to one eyewitness of Lenin's first reaction to the speech—the Bolshevik leader "was as joyous as a boy over the President's humanly understanding words toward Russia and his recognition of the honesty of Bolshevik purpose," Lenin's attitude quickly reverted to the old hostility.[37] Several days later, Lenin gave his first diplomatic reception to the various "bourgeois" ambassadors then residing in Petrograd, including the American ambassador David R. Francis. Lenin's own description of this event is striking:

> After live, real Soviet work, in the midst of workers and peasants who are occupied by real things, by the cutting of the forest and the tearing out of the roots of the landowners' and capitalist exploitation—one was suddenly obliged to be carried into a "strange world," to be brought face to face with some sort of arrivals from a new world, from the camp of the bourgeoisie and its voluntary and involuntary, conscious and unconscious servants, dependents, lackeys, and defenders. . . .
>
> As though history has inadvertently or mistakenly turned the clock back and we had before us, instead of January 1918, May or June 1917! It is a terrible thing! To fall from the midst of living people into the company of corpses, to breathe the smell of corpses . . . this is something unbearable![38]

In light of the above, Lenin's iron determination to take Russia out of the war, even at the price of the harsh peace terms imposed by Germany at Brest-Litovsk, is hardly surprising. It is true that the Bolsheviks, in their quandary, inquired, just before signing the peace treaty, about possible aid from the Allies, including the United States. Lenin, in response to a question posed by the other members of the Central Committee as to whether capitalist aid against Germany was acceptable, penned the following message on

[37] Cited in Kennan, *Russia Leaves the War, op. cit.,* p. 260.
[38] Lenin, *Sochineniya, op. cit.,* 22:182.

a piece of paper: "I request that my vote be added in favor of the acceptance of potatoes and arms from the bandits of Anglo-French imperialism."[39] Thus, Lenin did proclaim that aid could be accepted, but only if the very life of the Bolshevik government were at stake. Actually, nothing ever came of this feeler, since Lenin threw his enormous prestige behind the Brest-Litovsk settlement.

We have referred above to the hypothesis that the Soviet government might have decided to continue the war against Germany in exchange for diplomatic recognition or some tangible evidence of friendliness from the United States. Not only did Raymond Robins defend this view at the time of Brest-Litovsk, but so have some recent historians, claiming that the United States—swayed by the fear and prejudice of American capital—had needlessly estranged the Soviet leaders in the early days of their power. Not only has George F. Kennan's meticulous study of Brest-Litovsk punctured this thesis decisively, but a study of Lenin's role in the October Revolution makes it seem inconceivable that Lenin could have done anything *but* take Russia out of the war after his seizure of power. After all, that was the main reason why he had come to power in the first place. It would have been suicidal for the Bolshevik leaders to do anything else but sue for peace, and it was no accident that the Decree on Peace was Lenin's first official proclamation. With Lenin's accession to power, the departure of Russia from the war was a certainty. It was consistent with the pragmatic political realities of the hour, and it flowed logically from Lenin's profoundly held conviction that both sides in the war were evil. Brest-Litovsk, then, was seen as a precious breathing spell during which Soviet power could be consolidated and strengthened.

It should be noted in passing that the Soviet perceptions of the United States were not limited to Russians alone. A number of Americans who were caught up in the fever of the March and October revolutions shared these views. The most prominent of them, no doubt, was the young Harvard intellectual John Reed, author of the poetic and evocative *Ten Days That Shook the World*. Reed saw his own country so much through Bolshevik eyes that Trotsky, in January 1918, took the incongruous step of appointing "Citizen John Reed" as consul-general of the Soviet government

[39] *Ibid.*, 27:520, n. 13.

in New York. Needless to say, the United States government found Reed's credentials wanting, but the episode illustrates the atmosphere of unreality that dominated relations between the two countries during this period.

With the beginning of the American intervention, first in northern Russia and then in Siberia during the summer of 1918, Lenin's anger at the United States mounted to extreme hatred and fury. Both he and Trotsky believed that the Allies, including the United States, had been responsible for the uprising of the Czechs in Siberia, which in turn had precipitated the Wilsonian intervention. Soviet historians have held to this view down to the present day. In September 1957, for example, *Pravda*, in connection with the fortieth anniversary of the October Revolution, offered the following interpretation of the intervention:

> In the effort to throttle the young republic of the Soviets, the imperialists, led by the leading circles of England, the U.S.A., and France, organized military campaigns against our country. From all sides—from north and south, east and west—the attacking hordes of interventionists and White Guards poured onto our territory. . . . For over three years the Soviet Republic was obliged to fight off the mad armed attack of the combined forces of the imperialist beasts of prey. . . .[40]

Lenin's policy was to fight all the interventionist forces with equal ferocity. On one occasion, this undifferentiated view of all capitalists cost him a measure of power. During May and June 1918, the northern port of Murmansk was occupied by Allied contingents including some American troops. Even though Murmansk was threatened by the Germans, Lenin absolutely refused to strike a bargain with the Americans stationed there. A review of this episode affords a fascinating glimpse into the subtle relationships between ideology and power. The head of the Murmansk Soviet, A. M. Yuryev, was a practical man who favored a Soviet détente with the Allies at Murmansk. As a result, Lenin dispatched a stern warning to him: "If you still refuse to understand Soviet policy—a policy equally hostile to the English and to the Germans—you have yourself to blame."[41] To which Yuryev replied: "It is all very well for you to talk that way, sitting there in Moscow. We our-

---

[40] *Pravda*, September 15, 1957.
[41] V. I. Lenin, cited in Kennan, *The Decision to Intervene, op. cit.*, p. 374.

selves know that the Germans and the Allies are imperialists, but of the two evils we have chosen the lesser."[42] Lenin, in turn, decided to purge Yuryev from the party. But the price that he paid for ideological purity was that Murmansk was turned into what might be called an anti-Soviet Soviet.

If one looks at the American intervention in perspective, the conclusion is inescapable that this ill-starred adventure embittered Soviet-American relations for decades to come. In fact, the leaders of the Soviet Union have never permitted their citizens to forget it. Soviet historians for the last half century have portrayed the intervention as a concerted and major military effort by the Western governments, mustering all the force they could, to bring down the Soviet government.

Lenin, holding fast to his Marxist convictions, composed his "Letter to American Workingmen" in August 1918, at the height of the intervention. He believed, it seems, deeply and sincerely that the working classes in America would oppose the interventionist policies of their capitalist masters and ultimately overthrow their tormentors altogether. As it turned out, the intervention did end, but its aftermath, rather than a Communist uprising, was the Red Scare.

The tragedy of the early Bolshevik-American encounters is that the deepening devil mirror images became more and more one-dimensional as time went on, until virtually all reality was lost.

When the United States entered the war in April 1917, it saw itself as an embattled democracy engaged in the struggle to make the world safe. The problems of Russia were seen in American terms. As George F. Kennan put it:

> There is nothing in nature more egocentrical than the embattled democracy. It soon becomes the victim of its own war propaganda. It then tends to attach to its own cause an absolute value which distorts its own vision on everything else. *Its* enemy becomes the embodiment of all evil. *Its* own side, on the other hand, is the center of all virtue. The contest comes to be viewed as having a final apocalyptic quality.[43]

Similarly, the Bolsheviks regarded the October Revolution as the most important phenomenon on earth. With equally tenacious

[42] A. M. Yuryev, quoted in *ibid.*, p. 374.
[43] Kennan, *Russia and the West Under Lenin and Stalin, op. cit.*, p. 5.

egocentricity, they believed that they were the bearers of all virtue and that it was the sole ambition of the Western European powers and of the United States to crush them. If one studies the accounts of Soviet historians of the period, one sees almost no evidence that a world war was in progress. The Americans regarded this war as a holy crusade; the Bolsheviks regarded it as a squabble among rival imperialists. Each side perceived itself as the sole purveyor of the good life on earth.

These self-images, of course, determined the perceptions of the adversary's character. The Americans came to view the Bolsheviks with gradually deepening horror. At the time of the Red Scare, Bolshevism had become the devil incarnate. Lenin and Trotsky, in turn, regarded the United States with increasing contempt, which, by the time of the intervention, had developed into a bitter and relentless hatred. Most Americans viewed the Bolsheviks as more wicked in their intentions than the old czarist regime. The czar, after all, had harbored no global ambitions. The Bolsheviks, however, preached world revolution and had established the Comintern in order to subvert the non-Communist part of the world. Similarly, Lenin believed that the United States, by virtue of its capitalist nature, would be driven inexorably to expansion and imperialism.

Finally, Wilson and most of his fellow Americans viewed the Bolsheviks as a transitional phenomenon. There was the hope that they would be overthrown and that the intervention might speed the process. Lenin, too, saw the United States as a house divided and its power built on sand, ready to collapse under the determined onslaught of its workers.

This was the way in which two great peoples collided in the cauldron of world war and revolution. And this was how they started on a road that was to lead them to the brink of war. Neither Wilson nor Lenin was able to transcend his experience or to expand his vision. Each remained within his universe, and neither developed a sense of empathy for the other's destiny. Thus, neither could teach his people to reach out across the gulf that was to separate Americans and Russians for generations.

Concrete policy decisions flowed from these perceptions. On the American side, the March Revolution was seen as the triumph of democracy and the birth of a powerful new ally in the war. This linkage between democracy and war proved fatal; it led to the

American insistence that Russia continue the war even though her people were desperately longing for peace. The price that the United States paid for having Russia in the war for one more year was the victory of Bolshevism.

On the Soviet side, Lenin and Trotsky viewed the United States through the lenses of Marxism. The empirical reality of America remained largely inaccessible to them. This peculiar perception led to a policy of a priori rejection of America as a political presence in the world. Any meaningful modus vivendi or partnership was foreclosed by both Lenin and Trotsky. There was simply not enough room for both systems in the world for very long.

Thus, each side came to perceive the other as its mortal enemy. And since both sides believed this with growing intensity and deepening conviction, by 1920 they had come very close to being right.

Chapter Ten

The Establishment of Diplomatic Relations between the United States and the Soviet Union

Perception played a particularly interesting role in United States-Soviet relations during the decade preceding the establishment of diplomatic relations. In a curious and subtle way, each nation used the other as a flattering mirror of itself. At different times, the failure of one became proof of the success of the other.

In the Soviet Union, the turmoil of revolution was soon followed by the ravages of famine. When Lenin introduced the New Economic Policy (NEP) in 1921, however, and defined his new initiative as "state capitalism," most Americans perceived this move as a capitulation to the "natural forces" of capitalism. The prosperity that marked the United States economy during the 1920s made it easy for American capitalists to indulge in self-congratulation.

Ten years later, the tables had turned dramatically. By the early 1930s, the success of the first Soviet Five-Year Plan presented a striking contrast to the withering depression that was holding the American economy in its grip. To the Soviet leadership, this contrast was a convincing demonstration of what it had been claiming all along: capitalism carried within itself the seeds of its own destruction and communism constituted the wave of the future. The horror at the impoverishment of the American masses that was now expressed by many Russians paralleled the sentiments that Americans had expressed about the Soviet Union a decade earlier. As the debates over the need for greater state controls and discipline in the United States began to crystallize with the emergence of Franklin Delano Roosevelt's New Deal, Russians enjoyed pointing out its socialist inadequacies in much the same way that Americans had earlier identified the capitalist shortcomings of Lenin's New Economic Policy. As Americans had used Russia to mirror their own achievements in the 1920s, so did Russians now use America as a yardstick of their successes in the 1930s. And both sides saw in themselves and in each other essentially only what they wanted to see.

These images still prevailed on the eve of diplomatic recognition in 1933. The establishment of diplomatic relations was a response to the dictates of *raison d'état* in both the political and the economic spheres. This chapter will present an analysis of the complex manner in which negative perceptions had to be reconciled with the need, based on realpolitik considerations on both sides, to take positive steps toward rapprochement.

AMERICANS VIEW THE NEW ECONOMIC POLICY AND RUSSIANS VIEW THE DEPRESSION

American views of Soviet Russia between the end of the war and the onset of the Great Depression tended to combine defensive outrage with arrogant self-righteousness. The material values of the prosperous "new era" of the twenties permeated most of American life and also conditioned perceptions of the Soviet Union. The views of most Americans, from the president down to the laborer, were a mixture of prejudices and stereotypes that had been formed during the turbulent years of the Bolshevik Revolution. These attitudes lived on with a remarkable tenacity. Contradictory evidence and even dramatic new developments in the Soviet Union did little to change them. Rather, new facts were arranged into old categories. Only the profound and traumatic effects of the Great Depression forced Americans to look at themselves, and also at Soviet Russia, in a new and somewhat less one-dimensional light.

The election of Warren G. Harding to the presidency in 1920 marked the "return to normalcy" in the United States. In Soviet-American relations, President Harding continued the nonrecognition policy of his predecessor. His secretary of state, Charles Evans Hughes, insisted that he would have nothing to do with the Bolsheviks who had repudiated their lawful debts, refused to make reparations for confiscated American property, and fomented revolution abroad.

Most American public officials in the twenties praised themselves and attacked the Soviet system with equal vigor. Henry Ford was known at home and abroad as the spokesman for the new era's efficiency, innovation, and prosperity. The president of the National Association of Manufacturers stated in 1922: "Ours is a land of undreamed of opportunity such as none but a Christian civilization and the genius of democratic institutions could create."[1] Economic pride became synonymous with patriotism, and the United States was frequently referred to interchangeably with civilization. The American businessman ruled the new era with supreme confidence. His values guided government, defined success, and even affected religion. They were intensely material values, but with powerful Messianic overtones.

Bolshevik Russia was perceived as the antithesis of civilization. Senator Henry L. Myers of Montana, in a speech to the Senate on April 28, 1920, expressed quite accurately the views most of his countrymen held of the Bolsheviks:

> They have utterly destroyed marriage, the home, the fireside, the family, the cornerstones of all civilization, all society. They have undertaken to destroy what God created and ordained. They defy alike the will of God, the precepts of Christianity, the decrees of civilization, the customs of society. It is hard to realize that such things exist and are tolerated by the civilized world.[2]

Civilization, in the American view, had become a verbal basket into which all good things were thrown, while Bolshevism had

[1] National Association of Manufacturers, *Proceedings of NAM*, Twenty-Seventh Annual Convention, May 8–10, 1922, p. 115.

[2] U.S. Congress, Senate, *Congressional Record*, 66th Cong., 2nd sess., April 28, 1920, p. 6208.

come to connote the incarnation of all evil. Most Americans wanted to have nothing to do with such a brutal government, but many continued to hope, as they had done in Wilson's day, that the Russian people would get rid of their Bolshevik masters. As the Baltimore *Sun* editorialized in 1920: "The less we meddle, the sooner Russia will throw her pirates overboard." A small minority entertained the hope that capitalism would succeed where intervention had failed. Thus, the *Review of Reviews* suggested that "With outside pressures removed, and with opportunities restored for selling Russian wheat, flax, and other products and buying manufactured goods, Russia may become a sane country within a few years."[3] The dollar, it was hoped, would convert those who had been impervious to words and armies.

In March 1921, the Soviet Union abruptly changed direction. Confronted with the threat of total economic breakdown, Lenin adopted the New Economic Policy, confessedly a "strategic retreat" from the radical economic programs of war communism. The Soviet premier instituted some capitalist incentives in order to rescue the economy from disaster. Among these were a measure of private trade, private property, and the abandonment of wage fixing. Lenin described the NEP in the famous formula "one step backward in order to take two steps forward."

Americans immediately saw in NEP the death of communism. As Senator Joseph I. France told *The New York Times* after a four-week tour through the Soviet Union: "Russia is reverting to capitalism inevitably, by the play of relentless natural forces."[4] Walter Duranty, the correspondent for *The New York Times*, reported the end of communism in the fall of 1921.[5] The *World's Work* declared that "Lenin has an astonishingly open mind for a fanatic and so he may learn the necessity for production by capitalistic methods."[6] Typical of this volte-face in American perceptions was the reaction of William H. King, Democratic senator from Utah. In 1919, he had told the Senate that "any man who support[ed] Bolshevism [was] an enemy of civilization." After returning from Russia in 1923, he informed the Senate that the

[3] "The Menace of Russian Propaganda," *Review of Reviews*, 61 (February 1920), 121.

[4] Joseph I. France, quoted in *The New York Times*, August 1, 1921.

[5] Walter Duranty, *The New York Times*, October 5, 1921.

[6] "For a Talk with Lenin," *World's Work*, February 1922, pp. 348–349.

Communists were firmly in power, but were rehabilitating the stricken nation with extraordinary success by resorting to good capitalist methods.[7] On the whole, Americans suddenly saw the birth of a new capitalist Russia. The Soviet leaders were succeeding because they had surrendered to capitalism and to American methods and values.

Shortly after the launching of the NEP, a terrible famine descended on Russia which threatened more than 30 million people with a lingering death. Conditions became so desperate that Maxim Gorky, the world-renowned Russian writer, appealed to "all honest people" in Europe and America for aid. Encouraged by the NEP experiment and eager to help the new Soviet version of capitalism, the American people responded with enthusiasm. Secretary of Commerce Herbert Hoover was authorized to organize a massive relief program under the auspices of the American Relief Administration (ARA). Thus, in mid-1921, Hoover, a leading spokesman for individualism and capitalism and a severe critic of the Bolsheviks, was directing a relief mission to the Soviet Union. The paradox resolves itself when one takes note of Hoover's statement made in 1921 that "American charity had planted the American flag in the hearts of all those little ones and it is a greater protection to the United States than any battleship."[8] In Hoover's opinion, the American dollar would succeed where Allied armies had failed in rescuing Russia from the Bolsheviks. Toward the end of the massive American relief effort, Colonel William N. Haskell, reporting to Hoover, said the following: "To the mind of the Russian common people, the American Relief Administration was a miracle of God which came to them in their darkest hour, under the Stars and Stripes. It turned the corner for civilization in Russia."[9] The American missionaries brought bread together with their creed. It was Manifest Destiny with a dollar sign.

Not surprisingly, the Bolshevik leaders regarded American charity with extreme ambivalence. The foreign loaf was feared almost as much as the foreign sword. Lenin had difficulty understanding why the United States would dispense charity to the Russian peo-

[7] U.S. Congress, Senate, *Congressional Record*, 68th Cong., 1st sess., December 13, 1923, pp. 256–276.

[8] Herbert Hoover, in *The Saturday Evening Post*, April 30, 1921.

[9] Haskell to Hoover, August 28, 1923, cited in ARA, *Bulletin*, No. 41 (October 1923), 2–3.

ple while refusing to recognize their government. At frequent intervals during the relief program, Lenin accused the Americans of giving food to anti-Communist elements. The suspicion that the United States might have ulterior motives never left the Soviet leader's mind.

When Lenin died in 1924, America exulted. American editors described him as "another scourge of God," "the Judas of the real Russian revolution," and "one of the great wreckers of history." The *United Presbyterian* exclaimed: "The great beast has gone down into the pit! Glory be to God!"[10] Communism was dead. Capitalism and civilization had triumphed.

Americans were utterly unprepared for the eventuality that one day the tables might be turned, that the Soviet Union might be an economic success and that the United States might come close to economic disaster. The business spokesmen of the new era of the twenties overlooked the dangers in their basically economic definition of American success and Soviet failure. Julius H. Barnes, president of the Chamber of Commerce in 1925, found it incredible that "a nation living just above the verge of utter barbarism attempts to instruct orderly America, busy with its expanded economic life and social opportunities typified by its eighteen million automobiles and its towering skyscrapers."[11] The assumption was, of course, that until the Soviet Union had an equal number of automobiles and skyscrapers, it had no right to criticize the United States. But what if the Soviet Union should begin to approximate American material standards? What if the skyscrapers housed empty offices and no customers could be found for the automobiles? What if the boom of the twenties should become a bust? And what if the Soviet planned economy should boom?

By 1930, this was exactly what had happened. Herbert Hoover, then president, tried desperately to pull the United States out of the quicksands of depression. Unemployment was rampant. American government officials and business leaders began to look at the Soviet Union with fear. Russia was driving ahead to complete her first Five-Year Plan. The United States had no plan, but it had millions of unemployed. The United States-Soviet relationship, as

[10] Quoted in Peter G. Filene, *Americans and the Soviet Experiment, 1917–1933* (Cambridge: Harvard University Press, 1967), p. 87.

[11] Julius H. Barnes, quoted in *Nation's Bussiness*, November 1925, p. 20.

if by some cruel trick of fate, had been turned upside down. America, the "New World," had suddenly become old and decadent, and the "new civilization" of the Soviet Union, inspired by Marxism-Leninism, was bestriding the world like a colossus. Many Americans began to demand economic planning and looked with envy at the Soviet Five-Year Plan. Others felt that the Soviet Union might be able to rescue American industry by placing large orders in the United States. The irony of the new situation was not lost on anyone.

The Soviet leadership now viewed the United States with new contempt. The Soviet press mocked Hoover's efforts to salvage the corpse of capitalism with traditional capitalist methods. Stalin referred to the 3 million unemployed in the United States as "the first swallows of an impending spring." In a speech to representatives of the American Communist party, he declared that the moment was not far off when a revolutionary crisis would develop in America and would be the beginning of the end of world capitalism. In an interview with Walter Duranty of *The New York Times* in late 1930, he predicted that the economic crisis in America would become much more severe. The Depression had finally and fatally exposed capitalism's great weaknesses and inherent contradictions. Capitalism could not exist without markets. The mutual rivalry among capitalist states had created a situation in which each country endeavored to exclude all others from its own markets while gaining access to theirs. Militarization and war were bound to arise from this rivalry and finally bring about the self-destruction of the entire system.

Only one power, according to Stalin, stood aloof from this frenzied and violent competition for world markets. The Soviet Union did not have to resort to devious stratagems or armed force to maintain the growth of its economy, since it was independent of the contradictions of capitalism. By virtue of its example, the Soviet Union was showing the world that socialism was not only possible, but was the only way in which orderly progress could be achieved. As Stalin declared in his interview with *The New York Times:* "We will show the foreigners and the whole world that socialist production is possible and is growing and will succeed."[12]

Other Communist leaders echoed Stalin and showered the

---

[12] Joseph Stalin, quoted in *The New York Times*, December 1, 1930.

United States with their disdain. Politbureau member Lazar Kaganovich, in an address to the Ninth Congress of the Communist Youth League in 1931, reviewed the Depression in America and compared it with progress in the Soviet Union. Bringing his audience "to the verge of hysterical laughter," he illustrated the capitalist contradictions of American life with the following words:

> Even rich America, which thought it had found perpetual prosperity, is now so embarrassed by unemployment that a certain town recently decided to clear snow from its streets by men with shovels instead of with big machinery—to provide work for the unemployed. Whereupon one of the newspapers suggested that if providing work was what mattered, why not remove the snow with teaspoons and employ thousands more?[13]

One year later, Vyacheslav Molotov, in a speech delivered before the Seventeenth Party Congress, described as a "pillar of bourgeois society the famous American capitalist Al Capone." It was a mistake, Molotov insisted, to regard the Chicago gangster merely as a renegade and a criminal within a peaceful and law-abiding society. Capone was, rather, a major capitalist in his own right and a powerful figure in the American establishment. He was a criminal only by Communist, not by capitalist standards:

> Al Capone is a big capitalist, one of the pillars of bourgeois society, possessing numerous enterprises, and drawing huge revenues. From the American and European press, we learn that despite his relative youth—32 years—Al Capone has already made more than $700 million. In a word, this Chicago bandit is not one of the small fry of the capitalist world but one of the biggest capitalist sharks in the United States.[14]

Molotov concluded with the conviction that capitalism, with its Al Capones, was doomed, while the Soviet Union, with its shock brigades of socialism, was marching to complete victory.

The Soviet leadership did not confine its contempt to the American economy. No less emphatically, it held that American capitalism engendered a spiritual and cultural decay, of which the

---

[13] Lazar Kaganovich, quoted in *The New York Times*, January 17, 1931.

[14] V. Molotov, *The Second Five-Year Plan*, Speech to the Seventeenth Party Congress of the Communist Party of the Soviet Union (Moscow: Moscow Publishing House, 1932), p. 6.

alleged toleration of criminals like Al Capone was only a symptom. Perhaps the most scathing indictment of the United States came in 1932 from Maxim Gorky, who a decade earlier had appealed for American charity. In an open letter "to American intellectuals," Gorky described the "bourgeois intelligentsia" as "the nurse of the capitalist class." "The philosophical and ecclesiastical vestments of the bourgeoisie," Gorky declared, "that old and filthy fabric [was] thickly besmirched with the blood of the toiling masses. The intelligentsia has patched up with white stitches the soiled garment of capitalism." The doctrines of Marx and Lenin, in Gorky's view, were the only salutary antidotes against the poison of selfish Philistine American thought.

Gorky went on to criticize general American values with equal savagery. Americans, he pointed out, were fond of collecting "postage stamps and tramway tickets" rather than serious art. Science existed only insofar as it was able to serve the objectives of crass self-enrichment or to increase the sexual energies of bourgeois libertines. "Rotten bourgeois society, mad with hatred and panic [was] undermining culture in order to produce a rich crop of idiots who [would] be too stupid to recognize the monstrosity of the capitalist system."[15] In conclusion, the Soviet writer invited American intellectuals to join in the great task of creating a new proletarian way of life.

As can be seen from the above, there was little that was tentative about Russian perceptions of the United States in the early 1930s. At the core, there was a profound contempt for decadent American values coupled with an orgy of self-congratulation on the occasion of the success of the Five-Year Plan. America, for most Russians, remained during her period of adversity a symbol for all that was evil and hostile to the advance of civilization. Similarly, the Soviet Union served as a mirror for the prejudices and fears of American capitalists. On both sides, the mirror was terribly distorted, reflecting only selected facts. The business leaders of the new era and the "social engineers" of the early thirties refused to see anything in it that they did not wish to see. The same was true of their Soviet counterparts. Thus, two missionaries

---

[15] Maxim Gorky, quoted in Alexander Kaun, *Maxim Gorky and His Russia* (New York: Macmillan, 1931), *passim*.

with two mutually exclusive visions competed for the hearts and minds of their peoples. Little room for accommodation remained where two Manifest Destinies collided.

THE DECISION TO ESTABLISH DIPLOMATIC RELATIONS

"In the long run facts will control," said Henry Ford in June 1930.[16] These were prophetic words. Despite bitterly hostile perceptions on both sides, the United States and the Soviet Union decided to establish diplomatic relations in 1933. On each side, negative perceptions had to contend with hard, objective political and economic facts that clearly pointed in the direction of diplomatic recognition. Finally, after agonizing debate and self-examination, both sides decided to be on speaking terms with one another. Realpolitik had won.

In the United States of the early thirties, a vigorous debate raged over the issue of recognition. In almost every case, those who argued against recognition rested their case on distorted perceptions of the kind that we have described. Those who favored recognition, on the other hand, generally permitted new empirical evidence to influence their views.

First, there was the issue of the Bolshevik repudiation of debts amounting to approximately $650 million and the Bolshevik seizure of private properties amounting to $300 million, owned by American corporations and other business interests. Many Americans felt that recognition would place the seal of approval on Soviet flouting of contracts that were recognized under international law. "Soviet lies have made Russia's word as good as her bonds," observed the New York *Herald Tribune*. The Communists should recognize their financial obligations to the United States and begin to make some payments. If they showed no such evidence of good faith, the argument ran, continuation of the policy of nonrecognition was fully justified.

By 1933, however, the image of the Soviet Union as a "deadbeat debtor" nation no longer tallied with the facts. Actually, the

[16] Henry Ford, "Why Am I Helping Russian Industry?" *Nation's Business*, June 1930, p. 22.

Soviet government had recognized its legal obligations to the United States at a conference held in Genoa in 1922 but had made a counterclaim based on the damages caused by American troops during the military interventions in Siberia and northern Russia. The Genoa conference broke down because no agreement could be reached. By 1933, the Depression had forced several nations, including France, to default on their debt payments to the United States, while Italy and Great Britain were making only token payments. There was the further problem that, if the Soviet Union would agree to reimburse the United States in full, it would then be haunted by other creditors to pay sums far beyond its capacity. Most important, during the twenties the Soviet government had established an excellent reputation for honoring its financial obligations, and a number of American corporations, in negotiating new contracts for exports, had privately worked out reasonably satisfactory adjustments of their confiscation claims.

Second, there was the problem of Communist propaganda and subversion. The Communist party in the United States was viewed with extreme fear by many Americans. To extend formal recognition to the Soviet Union would enable it to open embassies and consulates from which to disseminate its subversive ideology. Supporters of recognition admitted that the presence of Communist propaganda in the United States was undesirable, but pointed out that nonrecognition would not stop such propaganda. The Communist party in the United States was in fact weak and torn by internal dissension. Moreover, even though a wide chasm of differences continued to persist in the political systems of the two societies, a degree of convergence had taken place between them in their economic forms of organization. After all, Russia had moved toward state capitalism under the NEP, and even under Stalin some private property and quasi-capitalist incentives continued to exist. In the meantime, under the New Deal, the United States had begun to move away from laissez-faire capitalism toward planning and a larger measure of government controls. Moreover, advocates of realpolitik pointed out that the rising danger of Nazism in Germany and of militarism in Japan were in themselves potent arguments for recognition. Russia and America might have to learn to live together in order to defend themselves against Germany and Japan.

Third, the image of the "godless" Bolshevik persisted. The

official atheism of the Soviet government continued to shock millions of religious Americans. The *Literary Digest*, for example, reported in 1923 that, during atheistic celebrations in Moscow, young men dressed as devils danced around burning effigies of Jesus, Moses, and Mohammed.[17] Related to the image of the godless Bolshevik was that of the "free-loving" Bolshevik who had abolished the sacrament of marriage and nationalized Russian womanhood to satisfy his degraded lust.

The facts again were quite different. While it was true that atheism was the official dogma of the Soviet Union, this dogma had lost much of its militancy by the thirties. The Russian Orthodox Church was not persecuted by the government. Rather, it was used by it as an additional vehicle of political control. While there were still considerable outcroppings of anti-Semitism, there was little evidence of persecution of Christians and Moslems who chose to practice their faiths. So far as the government's attitude toward the family was concerned, the days of free love were definitely over by Stalin's time. If anything, Russia of the thirties had become almost Victorian in its sexual mores and laws governing marriage and divorce. Few Americans of the "jazz age" of the twenties would have felt comfortable in the Soviet Union at the time of the first Five-Year Plan.

Fourth, the distinction between the Russian people and their Communist masters persisted with remarkable tenacity in the minds of many Americans. The point was frequently made that the Soviets had established not a dictatorship *of* the proletariat, but a dictatorship *over* the proletariat. The Bolsheviks had never permitted a free election, and to recognize them would blast the hopes of Russian liberals who might be the torchbearers of true democracy. The assumption here was that the Communist regime was transient and unstable; to establish diplomatic relations with it would bestow a legitimacy on it that might well give it a permanence it did not deserve.

The facts again presented a different picture by 1933. The Soviet government, despite intervention, famine, and catastrophe, had nevertheless been able to maintain itself in power. Not only had it weathered terrible storms but it was well on the way toward making Russia into one of the leading industrial powers of the

---

[17] *Literary Digest,* April 14, 1923.

world. While it was true that the Soviet Union was a dictatorship that had used extremely oppressive methods, especially during the years of forced collectivization, by the early thirties many Soviet citizens exhibited great national pride and a measure of genuine loyalty to their government. In 1930, approximately 10,000 Americans visited the Soviet Union.[18] Most of them, upon their return, talked about the vigor of the Soviet state and the impressive advances made under the Five-Year Plan. As the *Ohio State Journal* put it rather plaintively: "One of the most annoying things about Soviet Russia is that she is still managing to get along."

Finally, there was the question of trade. Many leading Americans accused the Soviets of using forced and convict labor in their production system and of then dumping their products on the American market in order to destroy the economy. In July 1930, for example, Assistant Secretary of the Treasury Seymour Lowman prohibited the entry of a shipment of Soviet paper pulpwood, claiming that it had been made by convict labor. To protect the American economy, the assistant secretary banned the pulpwood and proposed an investigation of Soviet manganese ore, coal, and timber on similar grounds.[19] In September 1930, Secretary of Agriculture Arthur M. Hyde accused the Soviets of selling short 7.5 million bushels of wheat in Chicago in order to depress American wheat prices and thereby sabotage the market. Hyde's announcement provoked a near panic. The charge turned out to be completely false. In a Senate bill proposing an embargo on all Soviet goods produced by convict labor, the following phrase appeared: "We see the beautiful structure of our civilization built so lovingly by those who made our great nation blasted, torn apart, and consumed by the collective labor of the USSR."[20]

On the other hand, trade was a powerful argument in favor of recognition for those who looked at the facts. The Soviet Union offered a huge potential for American markets. In 1933, the Soviet foreign minister talked of placing orders abroad for $1 billion. Obviously Britain and France, who had extended recognition, would receive the major share of these orders unless the United

---

[18] *Fortune*, March 1932.

[19] *The New York Times*, July 26, 1930.

[20] U.S. Congress, Senate, *Congressional Record*, 71st Cong., 3rd sess., February 27, 1931, p. 6231.

States followed suit. Not only would manufacturers and merchants benefit from such increased trade, but new jobs would be created for tens of thousands of unemployed Americans languishing on government relief rolls. As the El Paso *Herald* quipped in 1931: "A dangerous Red is any Russian who appears in America without placing an order for machinery." In short, recognition would be mutually profitable: the United States needed the Russian market, and Soviet Russia needed American goods.

A survey of opinion polls in the United States during the early thirties showed a sharp trend toward recognition. A State Department analysis of editorials in 183 newspapers undertaken in March 1931 revealed only 13 percent in favor of recognition and 63 percent against any change in diplomatic policy. In October 1933, just before recognition, the Committee on Russian-American Relations of the American Foundation published the results of a questionnaire that had been sent to more than 1,100 newspapers. In this questionnaire 63 percent of the editors favored, and only 27 percent opposed, recognition. The evidence suggests that, during the two-and-a-half-year interval between the two surveys, a drastic change in American opinion had occurred.

Any analysis of this dramatic shift must remain impressionistic. It is highly probable, however, that the bitter opening years of the thirties made most Americans more receptive to new facts and more critical of old prejudices and misperceptions. Men do not abandon stereotypes through rational analysis but through trauma and catastrophe. The Great Depression was such a catastrophe.

On the Soviet side, old cliché-ridden perceptions of the United States also vied with the dictates of realpolitik, but in their own peculiar way. Few of the official statements that emanated from the Soviet Union failed to invoke the usual epithets when referring to the United States. The American "ruling classes" were variously described as imperialists, Wall Street sharks, oppressors, plunderers, and criminals. On the other hand, the Soviets wanted American capital, provided they could get it on favorable terms. They wanted trade in order to import those goods that Russia desperately needed. They wanted diplomatic recognition in order to facilitate the extension of credits and the development of Soviet-American trade and—amazingly and paradoxically enough—for prestige in the community of capitalist states.

This curious ambivalence had been typical of the Soviet government's attitude since 1917. Neither Lenin nor Stalin ever had anything good to say about the United States, but both consistently worked toward, in fact demanded, diplomatic recognition from a regime they had vowed utterly to destroy. Both the negative perceptions as well as the objective needs for diplomatic relations persisted over the years. The resulting schizoid attitude of the Soviet government on the matter of recognition has been captured by George F. Kennan in his own paraphrase of Soviet policy toward the United States:

> We despise you. We consider that you should be swept from the earth as a government and physically destroyed as individuals. We reserve the right, in our private if not in our official capacities, to do what we can to bring this about: to revile you publicly, to do everything within our power to detach your own people from their loyalty to you and their confidence in you, to subvert your armed forces, and to work for your downfall in favor of a Communist dictatorship. But since we are not strong enough to destroy you today—since an interval must unfortunately elapse before we can give you the *coup de grace*—we want you during this interval to trade with us; we want you to finance us; we want you to give us the advantages of full-fledged diplomatic recognition. . . . An outrageous demand? Perhaps. But you will accept it nevertheless. You will accept it because you are not free agents, because you are slaves to your capitalistic appetites, because where profit is involved, you have no pride, no principles, no honor. In the blindness that characterizes declining and perishing classes, you will wink at our efforts to destroy you. . . . Driven by this competition which you cannot escape, you will do what we want you to do until such time as we are ready to make an end of you. It is in fact *you* who will, through your own cupidity, give *us* the means wherewith to destroy you.[21]

In addition to the economic facts, some hard political facts convinced Stalin that rapprochement with the United States had become a necessity by the early thirties. The Japanese seizure of Manchuria in 1931 threatened Soviet Russia on her eastern flank. The memory of Japanese intervention during the civil war made the Soviet leadership doubly apprehensive. In addition, the rise of Hitler in Germany and his repeated anti-Bolshevik utterances posed an ever more menacing threat from the West. Russia had to de-emphasize, perhaps even postpone, the export of revolution

---

[21] George F. Kennan, *Russia and the West Under Lenin and Stalin* (Boston: Little, Brown, 1961), pp. 184–185.

and, like any other national state, had to seek allies. In the emerging power balance of the thirties, America seemed a logical nation with which a partial détente might be both desirable and profitable.

Thus, by 1933 the stage was set for mutual recognition, even though negative perceptions persisted on both sides and continued to live on in a twilight world of their own. Most Americans continued to hate the Soviets for what they thought they *did*; and most Russians continued to hate Americans for what they thought they *were*.

While reality thus triumphed over misperception, distorted images continued to have a residual effect. They made it very difficult for a genuine modus vivendi to develop between America and Russia during the thirties. Had one been achieved, it might have made possible a common front against the Axis powers *before* the cataclysm of World War II forced the two superpowers to become close—though temporary—allies.

One cannot help but wonder how different the world might have been if the Soviet Union and the United States had been able to work together effectively during the 1930s to stem the rise of the Axis powers and thereby to prevent the calamities that followed. Undoubtedly, the residual spillover of the old cliché worked to prevent such genuine collaboration. Even during the "grand alliance" of World War II, there never was complete trust between Americans and Russians. There never emerged a supreme command as under Marshal Foch in 1918. The Soviet Union and the United States essentially waged two separate wars against the Axis. Each fought the common enemy in its own way. They were quasi-allies, rather than full-fledged allies. Thus, the old misperceptions still took their toll. They compounded the difficulties besetting the grand alliance and contributed to its eventual disintegration. No doubt they hastened the coming of the cold war and the tragic confrontations of the postwar world.

Chapter Eleven

The Cold War Spiral: Germany and the Division of Europe

The victory of the Allies over Nazi Germany also marked the beginning of a new conflict: the cold war. Much has been written about this tragic development and of the manner in which the positions of the two superpowers gradually hardened and ultimately congealed into a posture of relentless hostility. But little has been done to ascertain how much of this process was determined by the power realities of the times and how much by the images that the two superpowers held of themselves and of each other. These perceptions had powerful operational consequences in the policies that led directly to the cold war.

In order to analyze Soviet perceptions of the United States at the end of the war, we must first ascertain the role played by ideology in the overall Soviet cognitive view of itself and of the United States. Then we must determine the degree to which these ideological "lenses" yielded a distorted picture.

There is no doubt that Stalin's perception of the United States at the end of the war was colored, to some extent, by Marxist-Leninist ideology. But a perusal of his policies suggests that ideology alone did not prompt him to join or break any alliance that he would not have joined or broken on the grounds of pragmatic considerations of national interest. There are indications, however, that in some cases ideology retarded or speeded up the change. Certainly Marxism-Leninism compounded the difficulties besetting the grand alliance during World War II and contributed to its disintegration; no Communist nation could conceive of a permanent alliance with the leading capitalist power. This residual quality of ideology no doubt hastened the coming of the cold war. One leading scholar of Soviet foreign policy has expressed this well:

> The Marxist-Leninist tradition has made it very difficult to reach a *modus vivendi* with the Soviets which the Americans have been genuinely anxious to do. A belief in the inherently aggressive tendencies of modern capitalism obviously excludes any agreement except an armed truce of undetermined duration. Likewise, the acceptance of the Leninist theory makes it almost impossible to believe in the friendly intentions of American leaders.[1]

To Stalin, then, Marxism-Leninism was an instrument for ordering and comprehending reality, but it was not the only instrument. There were also considerations of realpolitik. After all,

> In the Second World War the Soviets could scarcely have permitted their Anglo-American partners to extend Western influence into all sections of the power vacuum created by the Axis defeat. American expansion in both Europe and Asia has often been hesitant and reluctant. Nevertheless the war ended with an American general in Berlin and another in Tokyo. This the Soviets could hardly afford to neglect.[2]

On balance, it is likely that the residual effect of Communist ideology was powerful enough to preclude in Stalin's mind more than a transitory alliance with the United States.

It is tempting to explain American policy toward the Soviet Union during and after World War II purely in terms of reaction to the ideologically conditioned expansionary moves of the Soviet Union. Yet here again we must beware of the pitfall of the single-factor analysis. No doubt there is much truth in such an interpretation of American policies, but it explains only part of the picture. It is quite clear, for example, that World War II had broadened the United States' definition of its strategic interests. Soon after hostilities had ended in Europe, the entire North Atlantic, from the Azores to Iceland and Greenland, had come within the sphere of American influence. And as a result of the occupation of Japan,

[1] Barrington Moore, Jr., *Soviet Politics—The Dilemma of Power* (Cambridge: Harvard University Press, 1950), p. 392.
[2] *Ibid.*

the Pacific was transformed into what was virtually an American strategic lake. Indeed, World War II had created several power vacuums that the United States had decided to fill long before the cold war actually crystallized.

However, it is nevertheless clear that the United States' reaction to Stalin's perception of America as a predatory capitalist power contributed to the coming of the cold war. President Roosevelt had remarked at Yalta that two years would be the limit for keeping American troops in Europe. But shortly before his death, on March 24, 1945, when handed a cable from Stalin, he banged his fists on the arms of his wheelchair and said: "Averell [Harriman] is right; we can't do business with Stalin. He has broken every one of the promises he made at Yalta."[3] Roosevelt, and Truman after him, were quite bewildered by the Soviet portrayal of the United States as an inherently aggressive nation. So deep was the disparity between the image and reality that the American leaders could only conclude that Soviet ideology could not possibly represent a truly held conviction. It must be a screen for political cynicism and a deliberate distortion of reality by men who lusted for world domination. In short, ideology, which for the Soviet leaders served as an instrument for comprehending reality, was perceived by the Americans as a deliberate smokescreen for Soviet imperialist ambitions. As President Truman put it at the signing of the North Atlantic Treaty in 1949:

> We are like a group of householders . . . who decide to express their community of interests by entering into a formal association for their mutual self protection. . . . We have no purpose of aggression against others. To suggest the contrary is to slander our institutions and defame our ideals.[4]

Thus, the impasse had become complete. By 1949, the cold war had begun to assume the proportions of a struggle between two competing theologies. It had passed out of the realm of ambiguity into a period of moral clichés based on absolute definitions of good and evil that were to blight relations between the superpowers for over a decade. Out of the syndrome of forces respon-

---

[3] Franklin D. Roosevelt, quoted in Arthur Schlesinger, Jr., "Origins of the Cold War," *Foreign Affairs*, October 1967, p. 24.

[4] Harry S Truman, White House Press Release, April 4, 1949.

sible for the origins of the cold war, perception played a major role. Stalin no doubt perceived the United States as more hostile toward the Soviet Union than it actually was, and the United States, failing to grasp this fact, reacted to Soviet actions first with misgivings, then with anxiety, and finally with outright hostility. Thus, perception and counterperception clearly had operational consequences on policy. The effects of these perceptions on policy, however, were different in the Soviet Union and the United States. President Roosevelt believed, at least until early 1945, that a long-range accommodation with the Soviet Union was possible. Stalin, on the other hand, partially conditioned by his ideological views, believed in no more than an armed truce of fairly short duration.

The impact of perception on policy became particularly pronounced, of course, after the reciprocal cold war images of mutually hostile intent had become firmly embedded in the minds of American and Soviet leaders. This had occurred by the late 1940s. Hence, to highlight the perception factor, our case study is drawn from the cold war period itself: United States-Soviet interaction over the rearmament of Germany between 1949 and 1955.

In 1949, both superpowers were still apprehensive about their former enemy. For both, Germany had been a formidable antagonist, defeated only recently and at great cost; and at Potsdam, both had solemnly agreed that under no circumstances was Germany to be rearmed.

The original American commitment to the North Atlantic Treaty Organization (NATO) called for no German participation, nor did it envisage a major commitment of American resources. NATO only "formally registered a widespread belief . . . which had crystallized during the Berlin blockade, that Soviet encroachment could be prevented only if the United States associated herself . . . *before* the outbreak of war, with the efforts of Western European nations to defend themselves."[5] Official United States policy held that the Western European nations in NATO, given a moderate degree of additional American aid, had time to create the necessary defensive forces on their own. German participation was considered neither necessary nor desirable.

[5] Robert Osgood, NATO: The Entangling Alliance (Chicago: University of Chicago Press, 1962), p. 28.

Within American policy circles, however, this stance was viewed with serious misgivings. By 1949, the Soviet threat already appeared great in the eyes of many American leaders. Secretary of State Dean Acheson, for example, was privately convinced that German military participation in NATO would ultimately be necessary. So, too, were key American military leaders. The Army Joint War Plans Branch had already drawn up a plan for Western defense in which the incorporation of several German divisions in NATO was regarded as essential.[6] Not until late in 1950, however, was the United States government able to act publicly upon its private convictions, for to have done so earlier would have been to risk wrecking the NATO alliance itself.

In 1950, the Western European nations still perceived the Soviet threat quite differently from the United States. Germany still ranked high, or even higher, on the scale of perceived threats than did the Soviet Union. For the United States, however, the Soviet threat had well outdistanced that of Germany. This "perceptual deadlock" was only broken by the outbreak of the Korean War. Korea united the alliance in its collective assessment of the Soviet threat, for the United States was not alone in its belief that the North Korean invasion had been Soviet-inspired or in its fears that Korea might be a herald of Soviet aggression in Europe. Most NATO allies agreed. Korea thus "precipitated the first—and only—serious attempt to create the forces . . . for withstanding a Soviet attack in Europe."[7]

The United States seized the opportunity to press the other NATO nations to agree to a new policy toward Germany. At the Three-Power Foreign Ministers' Conference in New York in September 1950, the United States offered to comply with two of the Europeans' most pressing demands: to assign an American as the Supreme Commander of an integrated NATO command, and to increase substantially its troop commitment to Europe. In return, the Europeans were to consent to the incorporation into the NATO command of some ten or twelve armed German divisions.

This proposal was greeted with considerable ambivalence by the European NATO members, now caught in a painful conflict

[6] Lawrence W. Martin, "The American Decision to Rearm Germany," in Harold Stein (ed.), *American Civil-Military Decisions* (Birmingham: University of Alabama Press, 1963), pp. 648–649.

[7] Osgood, *op. cit.*, p. 68.

between old fears of Germany and newly enhanced fears of the Soviet Union. The effort to resolve this conflict gave rise to the ill-fated plans for a European Defense Community (EDC). While the long debate over the EDC delayed the rearmament of Germany for five years, the Allies did agree in 1950 to the principle of German military participation in NATO and to the relaxation of restrictions on German industrial production.

If, from the American point of view, the new policy on Germany was dictated by the necessities of self-defense, the Soviets saw the proposal in a radically different light. By ending the state of war with Germany without Soviet consent, the United States had clearly violated the Potsdam agreement, and by proposing the rearmament of Germany, it had shown its true intent: to "use Western Germany, its manpower and material resources . . . behind which are the aspirations of the USA ruling circles for world supremacy."[8] The decision to lift the limits on German steel production only proved the point in the Soviet view: "The true meaning of the New York communiqué is that now the heavy industry of the Ruhr is openly being adjusted to meet the Western Powers' military strategic war tasks."[9] So obvious was this motivation, the Soviets concluded, that NATO statements of purely defensive objectives were an insult to their intelligence. If the United States really sought to demonstrate good faith, it ought to return to the German policy decided upon in 1945 at Potsdam. The USSR then proposed a new Four-Power Conference to discuss such a return, but the United States, convinced of Soviet bad faith, opposed it unless the agenda also included the problem of East-West tensions in general. The Soviets took the rejection as the expected endorsement of their original conviction. Both sides were thus entrenched in their belief of the other's insincerity.

It is fruitless to ask at this point whether either side was sincere in its offers, either before or after 1950. The tragedy of the cold war lay precisely in the fact that its defining characteristic was so total an attitude of distrust that any serious diplomatic effort at a

[8] Statement by the foreign ministers of the USSR, German Democratic Republic, Poland, Czechoslovakia, Hungary, Romania, Bulgaria, and Albania in Prague, October 21, 1950, in Beate Ruhn von Oppen (ed.), *Documents on Germany Under Occupation 1945–1954* (London, New York, Toronto: Oxford University Press, Royal Institute of International Affairs, 1955), p. 523.

[9] *Ibid.*

compromise was rendered impossible. The attitude itself, to be sure, was intangible and subjective. Out of it, however, grew the concrete reality of a divided Germany.

The hardening process took some five years from beginning to end. In December 1950, the NATO Council agreed to the principle of German participation in an integrated European military force. On July 9, 1951, the United States, Britain, and France formally ended the state of war with Germany. In May 1952, the Bonn Convention was signed between the three Western Powers and the Federal Republic of Germany, revoking the Occupation Statute and abolishing the High Commission. Simultaneously, the Pleven Plan for the European Defense Community was inching forward to ratification. EDC's inception, it was hoped, would create a European army of mixed nationalities, including German officers and troops.

Each of these steps was seen from the Soviet side as a confirmation of the USSR's worst expectations. The "imperialist warmongers" were proceeding on schedule, increasing the "aggressive" North Atlantic Treaty's military capability, absorbing Western Germany into their sphere of influence, and re-creating a German army—all in the name of "defense." The Soviet Union tried several times to stop these developments. Its diplomatic overtures, however, were unable to satisfy what the United States regarded as the basic requirements for European security. In American eyes, these efforts appeared cynical plays for time by the Soviets and were accordingly rejected.

On the issue of German reunification, the United States insisted on free all-German elections as a prerequisite. The Soviet Union rejected this proposal for fear of losing East Germany. Its counteroffer, embodied in the Grotewohl Proposal of November 1950, called for the establishment of an all-German Constituent Council with equal representation from East and West Germany. This council was then to prepare for the formation of a provisional all-German government to consult with the four powers on a peace treaty. Only then was it to organize all-German elections.[10]

The United States in turn rejected the equal representation proviso in the Soviet proposal, for should only a few of the West-

---

[10] Heinrich Siegler, *The Reunification and Security of Germany* (Bonn: Siegler and Company, 1957), p. 83.

ern representatives vote with those of East Germany, the East would have been able to control the entire council. In September 1951, the Soviet Union dropped this proviso and offered to give free elections priority over a peace treaty in the council's tasks. The new Soviet conditions stipulated that "all democratic parties and organizations" were to have the right to submit lists of candidates and to form election blocs.[11] The United States, fearing that the Soviet definition of democratic parties and organizations would differ irreconcilably from its own, also rejected this proposal.

At the base of this diplomatic impasse lay the superpowers' utter distrust of each other's *intent*. There is a certain irony in the Soviet Union's repeated demand that the Allies return to the German policy decided upon at Potsdam, for objectively speaking, the Potsdam agreements had constituted a satisfactory settlement in 1945. Their viability five years later, however, depended upon one vital subjective factor: each superpower had to have confidence that the other would not attempt the absorption into its own orbit of the whole of a reunified Germany. By 1950, that confidence was precisely what was lacking. Hence, no diplomatic formulas, however ingenious, could be devised.

Meanwhile, the fate of Germany was being decisively altered by the development of the Pleven Plan. It was hoped that by the creation of an international army and the mixing of officers and troops of different nationalities under a unified command, German armed power might be so effectively interwoven with that of the other members that its disturbing implications would be minimized. In February 1952, Bonn approved the EDC proposal, with the condition, however, that Germany would have to be accepted within the community as a sovereign and equal partner. Since the EDC idea not only satisfied the United States' sense of urgency over strengthening NATO, but also went far to allay its fear of an independent German army, the quid pro quo demanded by Bonn seemed acceptable in American eyes. Thus, the seeds of a separate West Germany were sown by America's fear of the Soviet Union.

To the USSR, the EDC looked ominous, for it foreshadowed the incorporation of West Germany into the NATO alliance. In an effort to forestall this development, the Soviet Union in 1952

[11] *Ibid.*

offered to consider several new concessions on the issue of German reunification. On March 10, it accepted the American demand for the guarantee of democratic rights to all Germans. In a dramatic reversal of its earlier stand, the Soviet Union even offered to allow Germany an independent armed force sufficient for the requirements of national defense.[12] In a subsequent note on April 9, it also accepted for the first time the principle of free all-German elections, subject to supervision by a commission made up of representatives of the four powers.[13] As a vital part of this settlement, however, Germany was to pledge not to join any alliance directed against any member of the anti-Hitler coalition.[14] This, of course, meant NATO, which the Soviets maintained was directed solely against them.

American distrust, however, was by now too firmly entrenched. Given the conviction of hostile Soviet intent, the new proposal seemed fraught with dangers. Compared with the proposed EDC, the United States declared, the Soviet proposal for limited German national forces was a "step backward" in the search for peaceful cooperation.[15] Nor was the abstention of a reunified Germany from all military coalitions acceptable. In American eyes, the USSR would attempt to absorb all of Germany, and without German resources, NATO would be seriously weakened. Hence, the United States responded that any all-German government must be free to join any alliance whose objectives were compatible with the principles of the United Nations.[16]

Stalin's death in March 1953 was followed by some Soviet gestures of accommodation, but these were seen merely as a cunning new tactic. In the words of General Alfred M. Gruenther, then Supreme Allied Commander, they were no more than "a confidence game."[17]

Subsequent diplomatic efforts foundered upon this rock of mutual suspicion. The Berlin Conference of Foreign Ministers in

[12] *Ibid.*, pp. 84–85.
[13] Werner Feld, *Reunification and West Germany-Soviet Relations* (The Hague: Martinus Nijhoff, 1963), p. 106.
[14] Siegler, *op. cit.*
[15] Feld, *op. cit.*, pp. 132–133.
[16] *Ibid.*
[17] Alfred M. Gruenther, quoted in *The New York Times*, September 1, 1953.

1954 failed to break the deadlock over Germany despite certain modifications of the Western stand included in the new Eden Plan. Shortly thereafter, the Soviet Union amazed the Western powers with a startling proposal. On March 31, 1954, the USSR announced that it intended to apply for membership in NATO. The Soviets argued that if NATO were indeed a true collective security pact, and not a closed alliance directed specifically against the Soviet Union, the Western powers could have no excuse for excluding the USSR. If, on the other hand, they did in fact deny the Soviet application, their real intentions would be unmasked.

The American reaction was one of stunned disbelief, although among Western diplomats in Moscow there were some who held that the Soviets were actually serious. A new realization among the Soviet leaders of the perils of atomic warfare, these observers maintained, had caused a genuine reassessment of the world situation, a clearer grasp of the dangers of war in a world of nuclear weapons, and a determination to avoid such a holocaust.[18]

The State Department, however, declared that it had "no evidence" that Moscow was "sincere" in seeking an end to the cold war. The Soviet Union, it said, was trying instead to recover from its failure at the Berlin Conference to "undermine Western security."[19]

The United States thus rejected the Soviet bid out of hand. When criticized by other NATO nations for acting precipitously and without consulting its allies, the United States defended its behavior by stating that it had "wanted to avoid any impression that the proposals were getting the slightest consideration."[20]

Sincere or not, the USSR came out ahead in the episode. Those Soviet policy makers who believed their own statements about the United States could now draw psychological support from the fact that NATO had "proved" its true intentions. Those who were more cynical could use the rejection as excellent propaganda. At any rate, the Soviet Union charged that the State Department "was so fearful of a possible positive reaction by Western Europe to the Soviet's NATO proposal that [it] did not wait to

[18] *The New York Times*, April 2, 1954.
[19] Quoted in *The New York Times*, April 3, 1954.
[20] Quoted in *The New York Times*, April 4, 1954.

get a full text before issuing a negative commentary."[21] The harsh tone of this statement, of course, only hardened the United States' conviction of Soviet hostility.

The USSR then presented yet another proposal for a European settlement. Declaring that the EDC project was leading to a threat to European security in the form of a revival of German militarism, the Soviets proposed a new and wider conference toward an all-European security pact along the lines of Locarno. Pending a final reunification settlement, *both* Germanies were to be included in the agreement, while all parties were to renounce the use of force as a means for resolving disputes.

This new initiative was rejected by the United States as another Soviet effort to undermine the Western defense system.[22] The American press characterized the Soviet offer as a ruse, as a transparent maneuver, or as a baited trap. Instead of dissuading the United States from its policy of German rearmament, the Soviet proposal produced the opposite effect. The United States took it as a signal to intensify the pressure for the ratification of the EDC.

At this point, however, the four-year agony of the EDC proposal was drawing to a close. In August 1954, after one of the most tumultuous sessions in French parliamentary history, it went down to defeat. The State Department was dismayed, for the defeat of the EDC also destroyed four years of American policy toward Germany. After four years of delicate diplomacy, the death of the EDC appeared to put NATO right back in its vulnerable state of 1950. Since the USSR appeared as menacing as ever, it now seemed preferable to embark upon a possibly more dangerous course with respect to Germany than to allow the situation to drift further:

> The real answer lies in the immediate admission of West Germany to the North Atlantic Treaty Organization. . . . Either the Germans are to be trusted or the Communists will rule Central Europe. . . . Germany can be trusted as long as she retains a republican form of government . . . with the E.D.C. out of the way, the decks have been cleared for action on an alternative—returning Germany to an independent posi-

---

[21] *Ibid.*

[22] *The New York Times*, November 15, 1954.

tion in Europe. It's a chance to take, but not nearly as dangerous a chance as leaving Europe at the mercy of Soviet Russia today.[23]

The admission of West Germany to NATO was, of course, precisely what the Soviets wanted above all to prevent. The defeat of the EDC was greeted in the Soviet Union with pleasure and relief. On October 6, Molotov declared that the USSR stood ready to discuss any new proposals. Its only condition was that the EDC was not to be replaced by an alternative project for remilitarizing Germany.[24] In American eyes, however, this condition was unacceptable, for if a sovereign Germany were *not* armed and brought into the Western defense system, it was regarded as far too likely to be attracted to the East.[25]

This made the vicious circle complete, for if the American goal were in fact attained, the Soviet Union could only regard this as clear-cut confirmation of its longstanding conviction that the United States would stop at nothing to implement its hostility toward the USSR.

An alternative plan for German rearmament was indeed advanced by the United States. By October 23, 1954, barely two months after the defeat of the EDC, the Paris Agreements, providing for the revision and expansion of the Western European Union (WEU) to include Germany, were drawn up and signed. The Three-Power Occupation of Western Germany was formally ended, and the Bonn republic became a fully sovereign state in all matters save those pertaining to Berlin and the final peace treaty. West Germany was to proceed to equip twelve conventional divisions that were to be incorporated into the structure of the Western European Union. The WEU in turn was accepted by the NATO Council as part of the North Atlantic Treaty system.

The Soviets reacted strongly: "These decisions . . . have been dictated by the aggressive circles of power striving for world dominion on the basis of pursuing the notorious policy of strength."[26] They warned that the ratification of the Paris Agreements would create an entirely new situation in Europe, perhaps postponing indefinitely the final reunification of Germany. In its

[23] Quoted in the New York *Herald Tribune*, August 31, 1954.
[24] Siegler, *op. cit.*, p. 87.
[25] *The New York Times*, August 31, 1954.
[26] Quoted in *The New York Times*, October 24, 1954.

effort to prevent such ratification, the Soviet Union, in October 1954, strongly intimated that the all-German free elections, so long demanded by the United States, might in fact be held in 1955 if plans to remilitarize Germany were abandoned.[27] This offer was repeated in January and again in February 1955.[28]

It was too late, however. German reunification was now relegated to second place in American priorities. Overriding all else was the imperative of NATO defense. First, the Soviets' urging that a conference to discuss their proposal be convened in the fall of 1954 was taken not as a sign of anxiety but as proof of insincerity, for as Secretary of State Dulles remarked, "the Soviets knew very well that such high-level conferences could not be prepared on such short notice."[29] Molotov accordingly proposed a delay—on the condition that the Paris Agreements not be ratified until the conference had taken place. The United States saw this condition as the real objective: to paralyze Western defense.

The USSR, for its part, saw the United States' rejection as its real objective—to let nothing prevent the Americans from reviving a Wehrmacht

> intended to serve imperialist circles not only as an instrument in their plans of aggression but also as the gendarme of Western Europe.... The adherents of so-called negotiations from a position of strength base their arguments on mental acrobatics.... They assert that they want negotiations in order to ensure peace and security. And with this aim in view they intend to revive the Wehrmacht which undermines peace.... They assert that they wish to settle the German problem. And with this aim in view they intend to revive the Wehrmacht which will prevent a peaceful settlement of the German problem.[30]

Events now moved steadily to a denouement. On May 5, 1955, the Western powers ratified the Bonn Convention, granting sovereignty to the Federal Republic and recognizing Bonn as the sole legal representative of the German people. On May 9, Germany was officially admitted to NATO. The Soviet reaction was to call the Warsaw East Block Conference in May 1955, which concluded

[27] Siegler, *op. cit.*, pp. 87–88.

[28] *Ibid.*, p. 88.

[29] U.S. State Department, Press Release, No. 648, November 16, 1954.

[30] Statement by Polish Premier Cyrankiewicz at the first session of Moscow Conference, November 29, 1954, Polish Embassy, Press Release, No. 87, December 6, 1954.

a multilateral alliance forging the military capacities of the Eastern bloc into the structure of a "Soviet NATO."

The United States had maintained from the beginning that NATO had been created to meet a clear-cut menace. The USSR now maintained just as stoutly that the Warsaw Pact had been dictated by the threat to its security. "The Warsaw Treaty was forced upon us," declared Nikolai Bulganin in November 1955. "It was the result of the position of the Western states, and we are ready to renounce it when a system of European security is created and the Western powers will part with the North Atlantic Treaty and Paris Agreements."[31] No other course was possible any longer. "When military blocs are set up against us, when our countries are surrounded by military bases and when atomic war threats are made, we cannot remain idle."[32] A leading American newspaper retorted that "it cannot be too firmly driven home that Russian conquest of neighboring states preceded and provoked NATO; that the Russian advanced bases in Central Europe preceded and necessitated NATO's base system."[33]

The Warsaw Pact was not the innovation in the military relations of the Soviet bloc that NATO had been in those of the West. The Soviet Union had long had bilateral treaties of mutual assistance with Czechoslovakia, Poland, Romania, Hungary, and Bulgaria; and other bilateral treaties had been in existence among the Eastern European states.[34] The 1955 pact thus only formalized what had been a reality for several years. It did, however, add one new element. The original pact excluded East Germany; but after one more inconclusive conference on Germany at Geneva in 1955, an East Bloc conference was held at Prague in January 1956, which provided for the establishment of an East German army and its subsequent inclusion in the structure of the Warsaw alliance.

Thus, the division of Germany was sealed by policies that had their roots in the superpowers' fear of one another's hostile intent. While fears and divergent perceptions are intangible, they tend to

[31] Nikolai Bulganin quoted in Kazimierz Grzybowski, *The Socialist Commonwealth of Nations—Organizations and Institutions* (New Haven and London: Yale University Press, 1964), p. 183.

[32] Speech by Bulganin at Warsaw Treaty Conference, *The New York Times*, May 12, 1955.

[33] The New York *Herald Tribune*, May 14, 1955.

[34] Grzybowski, *op. cit.*, p. 173.

set limits to the range of policy alternatives. In the case of Germany, genuine compromise and accommodation were beyond those limits.

In retrospect, the tragic element in this development is plain. But the question remains, as Arthur Schlesinger, Jr., has put it, whether it was an example of Greek tragedy, "the tragedy of necessity," where the feeling aroused in the spectator is "what a pity it had to be this way" or of Christian tragedy, "the tragedy of possibility," where the feeling aroused is "what a pity it was this way when it might have been otherwise."[35] It seems that in the case of the superpowers and Germany, perception helped to transform a tragedy of possibility into a tragedy of necessity.

[35] Schlesinger, *op. cit.*, p. 52.

Chapter Twelve

Perception and Policy during the Cuban Missile Crisis of 1962

President John F. Kennedy, reviewing the thirteen days of the Cuban missile crisis of 1962, estimated that the probability of disaster at the crucial point of the confrontation had been "between one out of three and even."[1] In the light of this estimate, humankind's escape from the nuclear abyss seems awesome. A slight shift of the pendulum might have doomed more human lives to sudden extinction than ever before in history. Previous calamities, whether of human or natural origin, would have been dwarfed by comparison. The fact that two mortal men should have held such terrible power demands that we study the event with every tool at our command in order to prevent its recurrence. Humankind might not be so fortunate a second time.

A great deal has been written about the missile crisis, particularly in the United States. Virtually every member of the small group of men who participated in the deliberations of those crucial thirteen days has expressed his thoughts in print. Numerous writers on both sides of the Atlantic have subjected the event to careful scrutiny. No analysis exists, however, that focuses on the role that perception played in the interaction of the Soviet and American leadership and how this perception affected the

[1] John F. Kennedy, quoted in Theodore Sorensen, *Kennedy* (New York: Harper & Row, 1965), p. 705.

decision-making process. This chapter will address itself to this task. An effort will be made to determine President Kennedy's and his advisers' perceptions of Premier Nikita Khrushchev and the Soviet leadership before and during the crisis. The linkages between these perceptions and the policy decisions by President Kennedy will be examined. And the relationship between Soviet perceptions and policy will be analyzed. The circumstantial nature of the evidence may necessitate considerable speculation. A short factual review of the events precedes the presentation of the main hypothesis.

The missile crisis was the climax to rising tensions between the superpowers during 1961. The Soviet Union's action in testing nuclear weapons of unprecedented explosive force had triggered off a major debate over fallout shelters in the United States; the erection of the Berlin Wall had made the tension almost palpable; and the memory of the abortive American-sponsored invasion of Cuba was still fresh. But as yet there had been no direct confrontation.

In mid-October 1962 hard evidence that the Soviet Union was secretly building offensive missile bases in Cuba with headlong speed had been gathered by United States intelligence services. High-altitude photographs had disclosed a medium-range ballistic missile site near San Cristóbal and one near San Diego de los Baños. Tanker trucks, power and instrument installations, missile guidance stations, and erector launchers were clearly visible. And pictures of cylindrical shapes on incoming Soviet freighters confirmed the worst.

The American leadership, which had had evidence of the missile sites by October 15, now weighed its decision silently. For one week the president and his closest associates constituted themselves as an executive committee of the National Security Council and pondered the alternatives. The deliberations were intense, but no word leaked out to the public. The president continued his preparations for the forthcoming political campaign and, as late as October 18, met with Soviet Foreign Secretary Andrei Gromyko, who professed ignorance of the offensive nature of the missile sites in Cuba.

Inside the White House and Pentagon, the War Council considered the alternatives along a kind of "escalation ladder." Six possible responses developed in ascending order of severity: first, do nothing; second, submit an American appeal to the United Nations Security Council; third, make a secret approach to Castro; fourth, conduct a naval blockade of Cuba; fifth, conduct a "surgical air strike" to eliminate the bases; and sixth, launch an invasion of Cuba. The War Council eliminated the first three alternatives as ineffective and the last as unwarranted. The discussion centered around the alternatives in the middle range. The problem confronting the American planners was the classic one of deterrence strategy: how to combine both capability and credibility so that the Soviet leader would be checked by the actual and potential display of American power. Too little power could be interpreted as surrender, too much power as a bluff. Only controlled and flexible use of power at every step would make deterrence effective in the mind of the opponent.

An immediate invasion of Cuba was ruled out because it might have provoked the war which deterrence was designed to prevent. An air strike at the missile bases was also rejected, since Soviet personnel would be killed at the sites and such an action would have been difficult to justify by the nation that had made Pearl Harbor a symbol of infamy. A quarantine seemed to hold out the best hope for a solution. It would entail the requisite show of strength by throwing a naval ring around Cuba, especially if it were coupled with a demand that the Soviet Union dismantle its bases there. Yet it offered the Soviet Union a way out: Khrushchev could avoid a direct confrontation by ordering his ships to change their course. Furthermore, a quarantine would entail no violence, at least not immediately. Thus, on the evening of October 22, President Kennedy announced the American decision to impose a quarantine and added that "any nuclear missile launched from Cuba against any nation in the Western Hemisphere" would be regarded "as an attack by the Soviet Union on the United States requiring a full retaliatory response on the Soviet Union."[2] The issue was now squarely joined between the superpowers in the most dramatic military confrontation of the cold war. It was clear to participants and onlookers alike that Castro's Cuba was only a pawn. The United States had announced a check to the king.

The announcement was accompanied by an unprecedented peacetime mobilization of military power in the United States.

[2] *Department of State Bulletin*, 47 (November 12, 1962), 715–720.

The Polaris fleet was moved within striking range of the Soviet Union, and for the first time Strategic Air Command (SAC) bombers were dispersed to civilian airfields. Half of the SAC force was on airborne alert. If necessary, the United States was ready to deliver an equivalent of 30 billion tons of TNT upon the Soviet Union. An atmosphere of impending showdown also pervaded the Soviet Union, where all military leaves were cancelled. The next seven days took the world to the brink of war.

On October 23, Secretary of State Dean Rusk obtained the unanimous support of the Organization of American States (OAS) for the quarantine. The NATO allies came to the support of the United States, though with misgivings, and not without reminding the United States of its behavior during the Suez crisis. The United Nations Security Council met in the afternoon: the United States demanded the immediate withdrawal of the offensive weapons under international inspection; the Soviet Union condemned the blockade as piracy and asked for its immediate termination. Neither resolution was voted on and the Security Council presented a spectacle of complete helplessness. October 24, United Nations Day, took the world a step closer to the brink. Acting Secretary General U Thant advanced a plan for a two-week cooling-off period to explore the issues. Khrushchev accepted the proposal, but Kennedy rejected it on the ground that the issue of removing the missiles was not negotiable. An appeal by Khrushchev to the British pacifist leader Bertrand Russell to use his influence to effect a general lowering of temperatures was also rejected as irrelevant by the United States. On October 25, Ambassador Adlai Stevenson challenged Soviet Ambassador Valerian Zorin to admit the existence of the missiles, stating that he was prepared to wait for his answer "until hell freezes over." Toward evening, the Russian tanker *Bucharest* approached the blockade zone, and the American destroyer U.S.S. *Gearing* steamed to meet it. Since the Russian vessel carried no contraband, it was allowed to proceed. Khrushchev claimed that the ship had not stopped; the United States claimed that the captain had acknowledged inspection. Neither side backed down.

On October 26 it was learned that several Soviet ships bound for Cuba were changing their course. But, on the other hand, continued photo scrutiny of the missile bases indicated a speed-up in their construction since the announcement of the quarantine. The American offensive had to gather speed before the sites were ready and the missiles operational. President Kennedy spoke of possible "further measures" and did not rule out an air strike at the bases. He also pointed out the numerous possibilities for accidental war if the Soviet Union would not comply. That evening a letter from Premier Khrushchev arrived that looked like a conditional surrender. In it, the premier indicated his willingness to withdraw the missiles, provided Cuba was guaranteed against invasion. This seemed like a fair offer.

On the morning of the following day, however, the White House received a second letter from the Soviet leader that was much tougher in tone and more demanding in content. This time a deal was suggested: the United States was to dismantle its missile bases in Turkey, and the Soviet Union would withdraw its missiles from Cuba.

The War Council now had to make a crucial decision. Superficially, the Soviet proposal seemed reasonable. It expressed a widespread feeling among neutralists that both sides should compromise and sacrifice something. It was generally approved in the United Nations, and several distinguished Western commentators, such as Walter Lippmann, supported it. Nevertheless, the War Council turned down the proposal. First, President Kennedy felt that the first Soviet letter reflected more clearly than the second the Soviet leader's real feelings. And second, to bargain away NATO bases under pressure would be to undermine the entire alliance and engender a Munich psychology. Each time the Soviet Union would gain a strategic advantage in the cold war, it might offer to give it up in exchange for an existing NATO base, until the alliance would be totally dismantled. Thus, by turning down the barter offer, the United States in effect presented the Soviet Union with an ultimatum: remove the bases or further measures would be taken. The brink had been reached.

On Sunday morning, October 28, the confrontation came to an end. Kennedy's gamble on the first Soviet letter had paid off. The Soviet leader reiterated his offer of withdrawing the missiles in return for an American "no-invasion" pledge. The American president accepted immediately and welcomed Khrushchev's "constructive contribution to peace." Other differences were settled in short order. Castro refused to admit on-site inspection by the United Nations to survey the dismantling of the bases, but the

United States decided to forgo such inspection and continued to rely upon its own aerial surveillance. The missile sites were completely stripped within a few weeks and outgoing Soviet ships laden with shrouded shapes that everyone took to be missiles brought the crisis to an end. The world had gone to the brink of nuclear hell and come back.

THE HYPOTHESIS

The basic thesis of this chapter is threefold: first, the proposition that, before the crisis entered its acute phase on October 15, the leadership of each superpower had lost hold of the reality of the other. Thus, President Kennedy was convinced that the Soviet Union would never attempt to place offensive missiles in Cuba; and Premier Khrushchev was convinced that he could do so and the United States would take no forceful action. In other words, both leaders permitted their desires to control their perceptions: Kennedy perceived the Soviet leader as prudent, rational, and respectful of the status quo, and Khrushchev perceived the American president as weak, irresolute, and lacking in determination.

Second, and equally important, both leaders managed to gain a much clearer and more realistic perception of each other during the heat of the thirteen days. Thus, Kennedy learned that Khrushchev, though far from irrational, was still capable of taking dangerous risks and of holding invalid assumptions of America's vital interests; Khrushchev learned that Kennedy, though apparently lacking resolve in the Berlin Wall and Bay of Pigs episodes a year earlier, was nevertheless capable of taking a forceful and determined stand in Cuba in October 1962.

Third, and most important, both leaders corrected their perceptions to conform more closely to reality and based their policy decisions on this more realistic appraisal. This ability on both sides may well have saved humanity from nuclear destruction.

PERCEPTION AND POLICY BEFORE THE CRISIS: KENNEDY AND KHRUSHCHEV

The evidence indicates that neither President Kennedy nor his top aides were prepared for the possibility of Soviet offensive missiles in Cuba. Robert Kennedy described the reaction of the group of men assembled by the president on October 15, shortly after the missiles were discovered: "The dominant feeling at the meeting was stunned surprise. No one had expected or anticipated that the Russians would deploy surface-to-surface ballistic missiles in Cuba."[3] The president, in Theodore Sorensen's words, "had not expected the Soviets to attempt so reckless and risky an action in a place like Cuba."[4]

Prior to October, the president and his advisers were thus predisposed to disregard clues that otherwise might have been examined much more closely. During September, for example, numerous Soviet ships on their way to Cuba were noticed to be riding "high in the water." These ships were later identified as those that had carried the offensive missiles, but at the time intelligence sources largely dismissed them as innocuous lumber ships. A large increase in Soviet personnel in Cuba was detected as early as August, and a U-2 flight over Cuba on August 29 revealed evidence of the construction of surface-to-air missile (SAM) sites. At the same time, however, Soviet Ambassador Anatoly Dobrynin assured both Robert Kennedy and Sorensen that Soviet intentions in Cuba were peaceful. He apparently succeeded in dispelling any doubts that might have lingered in the minds of the two men or in the president's.

President Kennedy's perception of Premier Khrushchev before the crisis as a rational statesman too prudent to risk anything so dangerous as a direct threat to the security of the Western Hemisphere thus led directly to a policy of nonaction with regard to Cuba. If the president or his advisers had perceived the Soviet leader differently, surveillance of the Soviet vessels and of the island would probably have been much more thorough. The clues that were ignored would have led to far more careful analysis, and, in all probability, the missile bases would have been detected earlier. Thus, the "selective inattention" that characterized the American leadership led to the discovery of the missiles only when it was almost too late. "Psychologic," the tendency to ignore or explain away evidence that

[3] Robert F. Kennedy, *Thirteen Days* (New York: Norton, 1969), p. 24.
[4] Sorensen, *op. cit.* p. 673.

conflicts with needs and wishes, was also at work. Not only did Kennedy perceive Khrushchev as prudent and rational, but he also desired a détente with the Soviet Union. To admit the possibility of Khrushchev's plan to place offensive missiles in Cuba would have jarred the American president's mental picture most severely. Kennedy did not want an offensive Soviet missile base in Cuba in the same way in which Zermatt, the famous Swiss ski resort, did not want typhoid fever and refused to acknowledge its existence until epidemic proportions had actually been reached.[5]

On the Soviet side, some speculative reconstruction is necessary. The critical determinants of Khrushchev's perception of Kennedy as weak probably were three events that had taken place during the first year of the Kennedy administration: the Bay of Pigs invasion, the Vienna conference, and the Berlin Wall. In all cases, Kennedy did not perform according to Khrushchev's criteria of firmness and strength. In April 1961, Kennedy initiated an invasion of Cuba, but then failed to complete it and allowed more than 1,000 Cuban refugees to be taken prisoner by Castro. Khrushchev no doubt studied the events of the Bay of Pigs. He would have understood it if Kennedy had left Castro alone or if he had completely destroyed him. But when Kennedy was rash enough to strike at Cuba but not bold enough to finish the job, Khrushchev probably decided that he was dealing with an inexperienced young man who could be intimidated and blackmailed. Khrushchev's decision to place offensive missiles in Cuba was the final gamble of this assumption. In Vienna, in June 1961, while Kennedy talked of the dangers of miscalculation that lead to war, Khrushchev threatened him with a separate Soviet peace treaty with East Germany. And when, in August 1961, Khrushchev built his wall between East and West Berlin, Kennedy did nothing to remove it.

Khrushchev did not announce publicly that he saw Kennedy as weak, but there are strong indications that this was so. In September 1962, the Soviet premier had a meeting with Robert Frost who was visiting the Soviet Union. The aged American poet reported Khrushchev as saying that democracies were "too liberal to

[5] Roberta Wohlstetter, "Cuba and Pearl Harbor: Hindsight and Foresight," *Foreign Affairs*, July 1965, p. 699.

fight."[6] In the course of a conversation with the American businessman William Knox on October 24, 1962, Khrushchev reportedly said about Kennedy: "How can I deal with a man who is younger than my own son?"[7] An immature man, almost a boy in the Soviet premier's eyes, might not stand up under the pressure of a powerful and determined adversary. Henry Pachter, in his analysis of the missile crisis, stated that "Kennedy seemed open to blackmail. Ever since the confrontation at Vienna, Khrushchev professed to doubt that Americans would stand up in a test of will power."[8] And Edward Crankshaw, in his biography of Khrushchev, wrote that "Kennedy's fumbling at the Bay of Pigs affair and his acceptance of the Berlin Wall suggested that he might be the President most amenable to such a lesson."[9]

In addition to perceiving Kennedy as weak, Khrushchev also perceived Cuba to be of less than vital importance to the United States. Roger Hilsman has suggested that "American attitudes toward Latin America, particularly Cuba, derive from an intimate history, which the Soviets seem not to have fully understood."[10] Another observer described the Soviet premier's perception of the American interest in Cuba in the following terms:

> He [Khrushchev] ridiculed the Monroe Doctrine, perhaps the most revered political text in American diplomatic history. Historically, the Monroe Doctrine has encompassed vital national interest. Yet Khrushchev claimed it to be totally outmoded and irrelevant to the current era of international politics.[11]

In 1961, Khrushchev had seen Kennedy act with greater firmness with regard to Berlin than with regard to Cuba. Kennedy might go to war over Berlin, but not over Cuba. With the missiles installed in Cuba, greater pressure could later be placed on Berlin. The place to strike first, then, was Cuba.

[6] Cited in Arthur M. Schlesinger, Jr., *A Thousand Days* (Boston: Houghton Mifflin, 1965), p. 821.

[7] Cited in Elie Abel, *The Missile Crisis* (New York: Bantam Books, 1966), p. 133.

[8] Henry M. Pachter, *Collision Course* (New York: Praeger, 1963), p. 25.

[9] Edward Crankshaw, *Khrushchev* (New York: Viking, 1966), p. 281.

[10] Roger Hilsman, *To Move a Nation* (Garden City, N.Y.: Doubleday, 1967), p. 182.

[11] Joseph G. Whelan, "Khrushchev and the Balance of World Powers," *The Review of Politics*, April 1961, p. 149.

On balance, it is most doubtful whether Khrushchev would have placed offensive missiles in Cuba had he not perceived Kennedy as weak and Cuba as relatively unimportant to the United States.

It should be pointed out here that Khrushchev, like his American counterplayer, seemed also to have been the victim of psycho-logic. He saw what he wanted to see and minimized discordant evidence, thus arriving at the clear picture that allowed him to act. Kennedy may have talked about miscalculation and the need for conciliation at Vienna, but he did nothing to accede to Khrushchev's demands. He may have let the wall go up in Berlin, but he gave no indication of giving up Western interests in the city itself. And even though the Bay of Pigs may have been a fiasco, the American president made numerous policy pronouncements underlining the continuing special concern of the United States for Cuba and the nation's determination to oppose any further Soviet initiatives in the Western Hemisphere.

In sum, then, before the crisis entered its acute phase both leaders saw what they wanted to see. In Kennedy's case, this led to inaction, in Khrushchev's to swift and determined action.

PERCEPTION AND POLICY DURING THE CRISIS: THE AMERICAN SIDE

The thirteen days of the missile crisis can be divided into two distinct phases: the first, or secret, phase, which began with the discovery of the missiles on October 14 and ended with President Kennedy's speech on October 22; and the second, or public phase, which came to an end on October 28.

On the American side, President Kennedy made three crucial decisions during the first phase and three more during the second. Each of these decisions flowed directly from his image of himself or of his opponent. Kennedy's perception of Khrushchev had changed significantly since the discovery of the missiles. While Kennedy still perceived the Soviet leader as a rational man who would not risk a nuclear war once convinced of the American determination to get the missiles out of Cuba, he now saw another dimension in the Soviet leader's personality: volatility and the capacity for dangerous, even reckless, action. This dual perception was responsible for the fine sense of balance that dominated Kennedy's subsequent decisions; his sensitively calibrated crisis management; and his adroit use of power, without erring in applying too much or too little. Let us examine the three decisions President Kennedy made during the secret phase of the crisis.

First, the president decided to seek advice from a group of men with different political outlooks. The most prominent members of this executive committee were the president, Robert Kennedy, Lyndon Johnson, Dean Rusk, Robert McNamara, Maxwell Taylor, John McCone, Adlai Stevenson, McGeorge Bundy, and Theodore Sorensen. Others participated in some of the deliberations, notably Dean Acheson, George Ball, Douglas Dillon, and Arthur Schlesinger, Jr.

Kennedy had learned from the Bay of Pigs disaster about the danger of one-sided, uncontested viewpoints guiding the decision-making process in foreign policy. On that occasion, most of the new president's advisers had perceived a Cuba ripe for an anti-Castro uprising that could be sparked by a handful of Cuban refugees. Almost everyone close to the president had seen what he wanted to see, not what the reality actually was. Kennedy had also learned from Barbara Tuchman's *The Guns of August* how miscalculations can lead to war. In order to minimize this possibility he wanted to avail himself of the widest possible range of opinion to assist him in reaching a decision. As he put it to his brother, "I am not going to follow a course which would allow anyone to write a comparable book about this time, *The Missiles of October*."[12] And in order "not to be dragged along in the wake of events, but to control them," Kennedy was determined to keep the committee deliberations secret. "If our deliberations had been publicized, if we had had to make a decision in twenty-four hours," Robert Kennedy wrote after the conclusion of the crisis, "I believe the course that we ultimately would have taken would have been quite different and filled with far greater risks."[13] In essence, the president's decision to be seriously responsive to a group of advisers with a wide variety of viewpoints and to encourage frank and uninhibited discussion in that small group, removed from all publicity, was a decision to reject psycho-logic, to make sure that

[12] John F. Kennedy, quoted by Robert Kennedy, *op. cit.*, p. 127.
[13] *Ibid.*, p. 111.

opinions with which the president might be out of phase emotionally would nevertheless be weighed on their objective merits. Most important, perhaps, the decision to assemble the executive committee was the alternative to an immediate military strike; Kennedy rejected the latter because he perceived Khrushchev as not only a dangerous but also a "rational, intelligent man, who, if given sufficient time and shown our determination, would alter his position."[14] In short, the president's perception of the Soviet leader provided guidance not only for what to do but, perhaps more important, for what not to do.

The naval blockade of Cuba was by far the most important decision the president took during the secret phase of the crisis. An analysis of the discussion of the six alternatives reveals significant linkages between the perceptions held by the participants and the decisions that were actually made. Kennedy ruled out nonaction from the very beginning, even though he realized that the emplacement of Soviet missiles in Cuba would not have substantially altered the strategic balance in fact. But he was convinced that the balance would have been substantially altered in *appearance*; and in matters of national will and world leadership, as the president was to say later, "such appearances contribute to reality."[15] "If we did nothing, we would be dead,"[16] Schlesinger quotes him as saying, and "the worst course would be to do nothing" he said to Sorensen.[17] Douglas Dillon, commenting on the first meeting of the committee, observed that "the first reaction of the President, with the others in full agreement, was that we simply could not accept the fact of Soviet missiles in Cuba, trained on the United States."[18] Defense Secretary McNamara who argued at first that "a missile was a missile," regardless from where it was fired, soon changed his mind, apparently persuaded by the president's distinction between reality and appearances.

To bring the crisis to the United Nations was dismissed as a dilatory tactic and to make a secret *démarche* to Castro was seen as futile. The first three levels of response were thus considered to be

---

[14] *Ibid.*, p. 126.
[15] John F. Kennedy, quoted in Sorensen, *op. cit.*, p. 678.
[16] John F. Kennedy, quoted in Schlesinger, *op. cit.*, p. 811.
[17] John F. Kennedy, quoted in Sorensen, *op. cit.*, p. 694.
[18] Douglas Dillon, quoted in Abel, *op. cit.*, p. 35.

too weak, even though no one on the executive committee seriously argued that the missiles posed an objective military threat. The president, in the last analysis, "was concerned less about the missiles' military implications than with their effect on the global balance of power."[19] Given this definition of the situation, there was little alternative but to initiate a forceful remedy.

Perception of self and of the adversary also played a crucial role in the discussion of the higher levels of escalation. An invasion of Cuba was rejected almost immediately since Kennedy did not wish to make it appear that his primary aim was the overthrow of Castro. The possibility of an air strike against the missile bases, however, was considered most seriously and for several days was deemed to be the only real alternative to the naval blockade. Several committee members argued that an air strike was the quickest and safest way to eliminate the missiles. A blockade, they argued, might well be irrelevant since the missiles were already on the island. Robert Kennedy, however, found such a course to be incompatible with his perception of the American heritage. "Sunday morning surprise attacks on small nations are simply not in the American tradition," he said; and he added, "My brother is not going to be the Tojo of the 1960's."[20] Schlesinger suggests that most of the members of the committee turned away from the air strike route as a result of Robert Kennedy's statement.[21] The president displayed a keen sense of empathy with his Soviet counterplayer. "They cannot permit us to kill a lot of Russians and then do nothing,"[22] he said, adding: "It isn't the first step that concerns me but both sides escalating to the fourth and fifth steps."[23] Reflecting on the crisis in a speech at American University, in the summer of 1963, he put it most succinctly: "Nuclear powers must avert those confrontations which bring an adversary to a choice of either a humiliating retreat or a nuclear war."[24] An air strike would have done that, a blockade did not. In his book on the missile

---

[19] Sorensen, op. cit., p. 683.

[20] Robert Kennedy, quoted in Abel, op. cit., p. 51, and in Schlesinger, op. cit., p. 807.

[21] Schlesinger, op. cit., p. 807.

[22] John F. Kennedy, quoted in Robert Kennedy, op. cit., p. 36.

[23] Ibid., p. 98.

[24] John F. Kennedy, quoted in Abel, op. cit., p. 193.

crisis, Robert Kennedy stressed his brother's empathy with Khrushchev's position:

> Always he asked himself: Can we be sure that Khrushchev understands what we feel to be our vital national interests? Has the Soviet Union had sufficient time to react soberly to a particular step we have taken? All actions were judged against that standard.[25]

The evidence suggests that, in the last analysis, Robert Kennedy's argument against a "Pearl Harbor in reverse" and John Kennedy's empathy with and multifaceted perception of Khrushchev led away from the physical violence of an air strike to the more limited and nonviolent course of the quarantine. Specifically, the placement of Soviet missiles in Cuba was perceived as a challenge to the American will. A low-level response would have made America *appear* weak, even though little would have actually changed. An air strike, on the other hand, would have made America appear immoral. Thus, the course that was the most compatible with the executive committee's perceptions of the United States was the quarantine.

The third decision during the secret phase of the crisis involved Kennedy's perception of his adversary's intention. Khrushchev, in Kennedy's view, was intent on presenting the United States with a *fait accompli* when the missiles were in place. In the president's words: "They thought they had us either way. If we did nothing, we would be dead. If we reacted, they hoped to put us in an exposed position with regard to Berlin, Turkey, or the UN."[26] Hence, Kennedy decided to keep the committee deliberations secret and to announce the quarantine decision to friend and foe alike in a surprise speech, thus presenting Khrushchev with his own *fait accompli*.

The quarantine speech of October 22 ushered in the public, or direct, phase of the crisis. During the next six days, President Kennedy made three more crucial decisions, each based on his perception of himself or of Premier Khrushchev. After obtaining the unanimous support of the Organization of American States for the quarantine on October 23, he drew the blockade line on the

---

[25] Kennedy, *op. cit.*, p. 125.

[26] John F. Kennedy, quoted in Schlesinger, *op. cit.*, p. 811.

morning of October 24. The first two decisions pertained to the enforcement of this line.

On October 24, Acting Secretary General of the United Nations U Thant sent identical letters to Kennedy and Khrushchev urging suspension of both the blockade and of further arms shipments to Cuba for two weeks. While Khrushchev accepted U Thant's suggestions almost immediately, Kennedy decided to put off a reply until the following day. To accept the suggestions, would, in Kennedy's view, have relieved the diplomatic and military pressure on Khrushchev that the quarantine had set in motion, and that was precisely what the president did not want to do. Kennedy wanted to impress on Khrushchev his determination to stand fast. Thus, he decided to refuse negotiations until Khrushchev showed some willingness to dismantle the missile bases. Once again, Kennedy acted on his perception of Khrushchev as a rational man who, if shown determination without violence and given sufficient time, would alter his position. Accordingly, on October 25, the president rejected U Thant's proposal in the following words: "The existing threat was created by the secret introduction of offensive weapons into Cuba, and the answer lies in the removal of such weapons."[27]

The second decision concerned the first actual encounter between Soviet and American ships on the high seas. "The greatest danger of war as we saw it then," Assistant Defense Secretary Paul Nitze recalls, "was that we would sink a Russian ship trying to run the blockade. If that happened, it seemed highly doubtful that Khrushchev would hold still without further action."[28] In the afternoon of October 25, several Soviet ships approached the quarantine line, with the tanker *Bucharest* in the lead. Even though the ship was thought to carry only oil, which was not on the contraband list, "there were those on the ExCom," Robert Kennedy recalls in his memoir, "who felt strongly that the *Bucharest* should be stopped and boarded so that Khrushchev would make no mistake of our intent and will."[29] The president, however, permitted the ship to pass through the blockade line with only a signal from an American destroyer. This move clearly was based on Kennedy's

[27] John F. Kennedy, quoted by Abel, *op. cit.*, p. 148.
[28] Paul Nitze, quoted in *ibid*, p. 134.
[29] Kennedy, *op. cit.* p. 73.

perception of Khrushchev as a man who, if pushed too hard, might initiate violence. In the president's words, "We don't want to push him to a precipitous action—give him time to consider. I don't want to push him into a corner from which he cannot escape."[30]

The most crucial decision that Kennedy made, however, involved the two fateful letters sent to him by Khrushchev on October 26 and October 27, respectively. When, on October 26, Kennedy received Khrushchev's first letter hinting at his willingness to remove the missiles in exchange for a pledge from the American president not to invade Cuba, the president and his advisers were inclined to respond favorably. Only Dean Acheson, who felt that Khrushchev, when writing the letter, must have been "either tight or scared," thought that "so long as the President had the thumbscrew on Khrushchev, he should give it another turn every day."[31] On October 27, however, just as the president was about to draft an affirmative reply, the second letter arrived in which the Soviet leader raised the price for the removal of the missiles. In this letter, which had been released simultaneously to all the news media, Khrushchev asserted that if Kennedy wanted him to remove the Soviet missiles from Cuba, he would have to remove the American missile base in Turkey. On the same morning, there occurred the only casualty of the missile crisis: Major Rudolf Anderson, Jr., a U-2 pilot, was shot down by Soviet surface-to-air missiles over Cuba. Under this pressure, the consensus against an air strike in the executive committee almost broke down. In Sorensen's words, "Our little group seated around the Cabinet table . . . felt nuclear war to be closer on that day than at any time in the nuclear age."[32] Schlesinger reports that

> We had no choice, it was argued, but a military response, and our tactical analysis had already shown that strikes at the bases would be of little use without strikes at the airfields, and strikes at the airfields of little use without further supporting action, so once the process began, it could hardly stop short of invasion.[33]

Nevertheless, Kennedy refused to bomb the bases. He still believed that a determined, but nonviolent, posture by the United

---

[30] John F. Kennedy, quoted by Robert Kennedy, *op. cit.*, p. 76.

[31] Dean Acheson, quoted in Abel, *op. cit.*, p. 162.

[32] Sorensen, *op. cit.*, p. 714.

[33] Schlesinger, *op. cit.*, p. 827.

States would persuade Khrushchev to retreat, and that an air strike might well push the Soviet leader over the thermonuclear brink.

Most difficult of all, of course, was the specific problem of responding to Khrushchev's two contradictory messages. "No one knew which letter superseded the other; no one knew whether Khrushchev was still in power."[34] Robert Kennedy made the suggestion that the president should respond to the first letter. After all, it had arrived first and probably indicated more accurately than the second the Soviet leader's real perception of the crisis. The president, apparently reluctant to bargain away the Turkish bases under Soviet pressure and fearful of threatening the unity of NATO, agreed to gamble on the first letter, thus rejecting the Cuba-Turkey exchange proposal. This decision was so crucial that it deserves careful analysis.

Robert Kennedy wrote the following account of his brother's rejection of the Cuba-Turkey deal:

> He obviously did not wish to order the withdrawal of the missiles from Turkey under threat of the Soviet Union. On the other hand, he did not want to involve the United States and mankind in a catastrophic war over missile sites in Turkey that were antiquated and useless.[35]

The fact remains, nevertheless, that President Kennedy risked precisely such a catastrophic war. The rejection of the Cuba-Turkey swap was in effect an ultimatum to Khrushchev. Kennedy let Khrushchev know that, unless he dismantled the bases within the next day or two, military action would follow. "The expectation was a military confrontation by Tuesday and possibly tomorrow,"[36] the president's brother said of that Saturday. And the president said on Saturday night, "Now it can go either way."[37]

To argue, as Sorensen does, that "the President had no intention of destroying the Alliance by backing down"[38] seems superficial. The evidence suggests that the answer must be sought at a deeper level and that Kennedy's perception of himself and of the United States played a crucial role in the decision. "We cannot tell

[34] *Ibid.*, p. 829.

[35] Kennedy, *op. cit.*, p. 95.

[36] *Ibid.*, p. 109

[37] John F. Kennedy, quoted by Abel, *op. cit.*, p. 179.

[38] Sorensen, *op. cit.*, p. 714.

anyone to keep out of our hemisphere," young Jack Kennedy had written twenty-two years earlier in *Why England Slept*, "unless our armaments and the people behind these armaments are prepared to back up the command, even to the ultimate point of going to war." In his speech of October 22, 1962, he had said, "One path we shall never choose, and that is the path of surrender and submission," adding, with specific reference to the missiles, "It is difficult to settle or even discuss the problem in an atmosphere of intimidation."

It seems that President Kennedy, in his eagerness to impress his determination upon Khrushchev, may have confused weakness with compromise. In his desire not to appear weak, he apparently never fully distinguished between the danger of the missiles remaining in Cuba and the danger resulting from a removal of the missiles through compromise. Certainly the latter danger was much smaller, but the president seems to have perceived both as equally unacceptable challenges to the American will. A deeply ingrained reaction against the "Munich syndrome" and the determination not to appear weak—stemming perhaps from his encounter with Khrushchev in Vienna—made him risk nuclear war over missile bases in Turkey, which, by his own admission, were obsolete and useless and which, by his own order, should have been dismantled two months earlier. Thus, after twelve days of almost incredible balance and restraint, he risked nuclear Armageddon on the thirteenth day over what appeared to be a side issue. Fortunately for humanity, his luck held and he won his gamble. But by turning down the barter deal, Kennedy relinquished the ultimate choice between peace and war to Nikita Khrushchev.

PERCEPTION AND POLICY DURING THE CRISIS: THE SOVIET SIDE

We have seen that Khrushchev probably perceived Kennedy as lacking determination and that this perception was probably responsible for his conviction that Soviet missiles could be placed in Cuba without eliciting a forceful American response. I shall now attempt to demonstrate that, in the course of the public phase of the crisis, Khrushchev gradually learned to perceive the American president differently and that this changed perception led directly to the decision to withdraw the missiles. Naturally, since there is hardly any access to the Soviet decision-making process, this analysis must be based largely on circumstantial evidence, but even the bits and pieces that can be assembled add up to an impressive case.

Khrushchev's perception of Kennedy as weak seems to have been so firmly embedded that the Soviet leader pursued his course without hesitation and despite some telltale signs in September and early October that Kennedy might not be soft to further Soviet initiatives in Cuba. When, on September 4, Kennedy publicly warned the Soviet Union that if Cuba were ever to become an offensive missile base, the United States would take action to protect itself, Khrushchev responded with a tough public statement: "Today one cannot attack Cuba and expect the aggressor to go unpunished for the attack. If such an attack is made, it will be the start of the unleashing of war."[39] Khrushchev probably regarded Kennedy's warning as political oratory and felt that a threat of war would be sufficient to deter the United States from responding forcefully. Because of this perception, the Soviet leader was unable to see that Kennedy was "drawing a line, and making it extremely unlikely that he would back down if that line was crossed."[40] Even when Kennedy activated the reserves, Khrushchev seemed to remain unaffected. Arnold Horelick suggests some other reasons that might have prompted Khrushchev to continue the missile program. These reasons included the expectation that the United States would respond with diplomatic action, namely, that Kennedy would consult with NATO allies and be persuaded to adopt a nonviolent approach and that the OAS would probably oppose any military action by the United States.[41] These expectations were all based on the assumption of a fictitious Kennedy, one that Khrushchev needed in order to implement his missile program.

The first decision that confronted the Soviet leader during the public phase of the crisis was how to respond to Kennedy's quar-

[39] Nikita Khrushchev, cited in *Digest of the Soviet Press*, October 10, 1962, p. 14.

[40] Wohlstetter, *op. cit.*, p. 701.

[41] Arnold L. Horelick, "The Cuban Missile Crisis: An Analysis of Soviet Calculations and Behavior," *World Politics*, April 1964, p. 381.

antine speech of October 22. It seems that the Soviet leadership was as stunned by the American response as the executive committee had been when it first learned of the Soviet move on October 15. There was no immediate reaction from the Kremlin. Dean Rusk said to George Ball on the morning after the speech, "We have won a considerable victory. You and I are still alive."[42] Neither in Berlin nor anywhere else did a Soviet move materialize. A front-page editorial in *Pravda* on October 24 condemned the United States for a "crude form of blackmail that is bringing down catastrophe upon all mankind" but concluded by declaring that "in the situation that has arisen, a special responsibility falls on the United Nations."[43] This reaction suggested that the Soviet leadership had been thrown off guard by the blockade and now adopted a policy of "wait and see." Though Khrushchev was probably confused by the American move, his precrisis perception of Kennedy had yet to be shaken. After all, Kennedy had thus far only called for a blockade. He had not yet proved his determination to enforce it.

The blockade line was drawn on October 24. Khrushchev now had to make the crucial decision of what to do about it. In the morning of that day, the Soviet leader issued a stern warning: "If the United States Government carries out the program of piratical actions outlined by it, we shall have to resort to means of defense against the aggressors to defend our rights."[44] In the afternoon, he summoned to the Kremlin the American businessman William Knox who happened to be in Moscow on behalf of Westinghouse International. Elie Abel renders a vivid account of this meeting, which deserves to be quoted in full:

> Knox arrived fifteen minutes late to find Khrushchev in a state of near-exhaustion. He looked like a man who had not slept all night. For three hours he treated Knox to a succession of threats, complaints and peasant jokes. It was true, he said, the Soviet Union had missiles and attack planes in Cuba; moreover he would use them if need be.
>
> He wanted the President and the American people to know, Khrushchev added, that if the United States Navy tried to stop Soviet ships at sea, his submarines would start sinking American ships. And that would

[42] Dean Rusk, quoted in Abel, *op. cit.*, p. 110.

[43] Cited in *Digest of the Soviet Press*, November 12, 1962, p. 4.

[44] Nikita Khrushchev, quoted in Abel, *op. cit.*, p. 126.

mean a third world war. Khrushchev complained that he could not understand Kennedy. Eisenhower had been troublesome enough, but Eisenhower was a man of his own generation. "How can I deal with a man who is younger than my son?" he asked the astonished Westinghouse man. Then, extending a stubby index finger across the table in Knox's direction, he talked of weapons, offensive and defensive. "If I point a pistol at you like this in order to attack you," Khrushchev said, "the pistol is an offensive weapon. But if I am to keep you from shooting me, it is defensive, no?"[45]

This exchange suggests that Khrushchev's perception of Kennedy was shaken by October 24 but not yet undermined. This ambivalence was reflected in Soviet policy decisions on that day. Khrushchev issued orders to some of his ships to change course. The ship that was ordered to test the blockade was a freighter that carried no contraband. On the other hand, Khrushchev ordered a speed-up in the construction of the missile sites. His ready acceptance of U Thant's proposal for a cooling-off period suggests that such a period would have given him the necessary time to render the missiles fully operational.

Khrushchev probably changed his perception of Kennedy sometime during Thursday, October 25. Kennedy's rejection of U Thant's proposal, his insistence that the missiles be removed, his warning that "further action will be justified should these offensive military preparations continue," and the continuing massive arms build-up in the United States probably persuaded Khrushchev that Kennedy was not bluffing. What Khrushchev now began to perceive was that Kennedy was determined to get the missiles out of Cuba, that he was planning to bomb Cuba if necessary to attain this objective, and that such an attack could precipitate a nuclear war. The note of desperation that permeated his personal letter to Kennedy suggests this sudden recognition. He wrote:

> Mr. President, we and you ought not now to pull on the ends of the rope in which you have tied the knot of war, because the more we pull, the tighter the knot will be tied. . . . Only lunatics or suicides who themselves want to perish and destroy the whole world before they did, could do this.[46]

---

[45] *Ibid.*, pp. 132–133.
[46] Nikita Khrushchev, quoted in *ibid.*, p. 152.

The perception of acute danger was reinforced by the strategic realities of the situation. Khrushchev had known that the American military machine was exceedingly powerful. But so long as he felt that Kennedy was unwilling to use this power, he had felt relatively safe. As soon as this assumption became questionable, however, the terrible consequences became obvious. If war came, Khrushchev had the choice of either being overwhelmed in a limited air or naval engagement in the Caribbean or of having his country devastated by a nuclear attack. Neither alternative was acceptable. Hence, Khrushchev's new perception of Kennedy as having "tied the knot of war" and willing to commit "suicide," if necessary, to get the missiles out of Cuba probably led him to write his personal letter to the American president.

There has been considerable speculation about the sequence of the two Khrushchev letters. The actual timing of the notes and the reasons for their contradictory content may never be fully known. Michel Tatu suggests that the Cuba-Turkey letter was prompted by the reaction of other Presidium members that Khrushchev had backed down too quickly. He advances the hypothesis that the Cuba-Turkey swap proposal constituted a middle approach between the offer contained in Khrushchev's personal letter and the demands of Soviet hard-liners who insisted on an American withdrawal from all foreign bases.[47] Henry Pachter, in his *Collision Course*, suggests that the second letter, proposing the Cuba-Turkey exchange, had actually been drafted and sent first, but through the regular diplomatic channels of the foreign ministry. The personal letter, Pachter contends, was actually written and sent later, but directly by Khrushchev without clearance with the foreign ministry. Hence, it overtook the other, more formal and demanding, communication.[48] The evidence seems to support Pachter's thesis. The Cuba-Turkey letter mentions Kennedy's rejection of U Thant's proposal but does not make reference to Kennedy's warning about a possible air strike nor does it make reference to the military arms build-up. This seems to suggest that the slow letter, proceeding through channels, had been overtaken by events. Khrushchev's new perception of Kennedy, now reinforced by the ominous events of October 26, probably prompted

---

[47] Michel Tatu, *Power in the Kremlin* (New York: Viking, 1969), p. 263.
[48] Pachter, *op. cit.*, p. 68.

him to write the personal letter indicating his desire to avoid a showdown and his willingness to remove the missiles in exchange for a pledge from President Kennedy not to invade Cuba. When Kennedy did indeed respond to the personal letter rather than to the barter proposal, Khrushchev did not press the matter; he had become convinced that Kennedy would bomb Cuba if he did. In a revealing speech before the Supreme Soviet on December 12, 1962, Khrushchev related how the crisis appeared to him on that day. "Immediate action was necessary," he said "to prevent the attack on Cuba and to preserve peace."[49] He added that "In these circumstances, if one or the other side had failed to show restraint, failed to do all that was necessary to prevent the outbreak of war, an explosion would have followed with irreparable consequences."[50] He also gave the Supreme Soviet a detailed and vivid account of the military preparations that President Kennedy had made:

> Several paratrooper, infantry, and armored divisions, numbering some 100,000 men were allocated for the attack on Cuba. In addition, 183 warships with 85,000 sailors on board were moved toward the shores of Cuba. Several thousand war planes were to cover the landing in Cuba. About 20 percent of the U.S. Strategic Air Command planes, carrying atomic and hydrogen bombs, were kept aloft around the clock.[51]

Hence, when Kennedy pledged not to invade Cuba, Khrushchev was ready to withdraw the missiles and thus to terminate the crisis. "We are interested that there should be no war in the world," he wrote Kennedy on October 28.[52] He now firmly believed that Kennedy had been ready to risk war over the missiles in Cuba and perhaps even over obsolete missiles in Turkey.

We shall never know whether President Kennedy would have thrown the Turkish missiles into the bargain if Khrushchev had not backed down. But we do know that Attorney General Robert F. Kennedy, in a conversation with Soviet Ambassador Anatoly Dobrynin, promised that the missiles would eventually be taken out of Turkey. For political reasons, however, this pledge could not

[49] Nikita Khrushchev, cited in *Digest of the Soviet Press*, January 16, 1963, p. 5.

[50] *Ibid.*

[51] *Ibid.*

[52] Nikita Khrushchev, quoted in Kennedy, *op. cit.*, p. 210.

become part of the agreement. Yet, the missiles were in fact removed from Turkey in mid-1963.

A word should be said abut Khrushchev's self-image during the crisis. First, it was possible for Khrushchev to withdraw the missiles without severe damage to his self-esteem. In December, he told the Supreme Soviet: "Our purpose was only the defense of Cuba."[53] With a pledge from Kennedy not to invade Cuba, Khrushchev could claim that he terminated the crisis with the main Soviet objective accomplished. Second, Marxism-Leninism does not equate retreat with the stigma of defeat. Lenin's concept of "one step backward, two steps forward" could be made to apply to the Cuba encounter. Indeed, anything other than withdrawal might have seemed like reckless adventurism under the circumstances, a shortcoming that Lenin had once condemned as an "infantile disorder."

With all this said, however, the fact remains that retreat for Khrushchev probably was not easy. It takes an honest man to admit that his perception of an adversary might have been wrong all along. It takes a flexible and resourceful man to change his policy upon such recognition. And it takes a strong and courageous man not to place the preservation of his ego before the preservation of the peace.

President Kennedy's and Premier Khrushchev's perceptions of themselves and of each other deeply influenced the course of the Cuban missile crisis. Both saw what they wanted to see before the crisis. As a result, Kennedy lowered his guard in Cuba, and Khrushchev shipped his missiles.

Kennedy viewed the missiles basically as a challenge to the American will. They had to be removed, not because they made America weak, but because they made her *appear* weak. And in order to get them out, Kennedy went to the brink of war. Khrushchev was able to withdraw the missiles with his ego and self-esteem substantially intact. Had he not been able to do so, had he been forced to *appear* weak, nuclear disaster might well have been the consequence.

Each leader showed empathy with the other's perception of the crisis. Robert Kennedy wrote that

---

[53] Nikita Khrushchev, cited in *Digest of Soviet Press*, January 16, 1963, p. 5.

The final lesson of the Cuban missile crisis is the importance of placing ourselves in the other country's shoes. During the crisis, President Kennedy spent more time trying to determine the effect of a particular course of action on Khrushchev or the Russians than on any other phase of what he was doing.[54]

Khrushchev's ultimate recognition of Kennedy's determination and his flexibility at the brink showed similar empathy and self-restraint.

There is one final sense in which perception was perhaps decisive. Neither leader could say to the other, "Do as I say or I shall kill you"; but each was reduced to saying, "Do as I say or I shall kill us both." Force, in the crude physical sense, was no longer a predictable instrument of national policy. Each superpower could have annihilated the other, but by so doing, would have destroyed itself. To put it crassly: since everybody was somebody, nobody was anybody. Since physical force on each side was equally devastating and thus virtually canceled out, subjective perceptions and appearances of power loomed particularly large. Psychology thus superseded hardware, and a state of mind became decisive. The missile crisis was in essence a nuclear war, but one that was fought in the minds of two men and their perceptions of themselves and of each other. Fortunately for all of us, these were good men with political wisdom, moral courage, and a gift of empathy. They grasped not only with their minds but also felt deeply in their hearts both the burden and the terror of the human condition in the nuclear age.

I am forced to add a terrifying postscript to this chapter.

In October 1992, a year after the demise of the Soviet Union, it was revealed by a former adviser to Nikita Krushchev that Fidel Castro, in the midst of the Cuban missile crisis, had sent the following telegram to Khrushchev:

> I propose the immediate launching of a nuclear strike on the United States. The Cuban people are prepared to sacrifice themselves for the cause of the destruction of imperialism and the victory of world revolution.[55]

---

[54] Kennedy, op. cit., p. 124.
[55] Fedor Burlatsky, "Castro Wanted a Nuclear Strike," The New York Times, October 23, 1992.

Fortunately for future generations, Khrushchev turned down Castro's proposition. Perhaps, we owe our lives not only to the brilliance of Kennedy's crisis management, but even more to Khrushchev's courageous decision not to put his ego before the survival of the human race. Yet it is a sobering thought that Castro, thirty years later, remains master of his Communist theme-park in Cuba.

Chapter Thirteen

The Birth and Death of Détente

DÉTENTE AND STRATEGIC ARMS CONTROL

The Cuban missile crisis of 1962 represented a great turning point in Soviet-American relations. Both superpowers had gone to the edge of the nuclear abyss and turned back just in time. The narrow escape from atomic holocaust left its mark on the Soviet and American leaderships alike. Slowly, the frozen hostility of the cold war thawed and gave way to a less abrasive relationship characterized by greater realism and a more businesslike approach. Shopworn slogans and polemics were replaced by more objective assessments of each other's character, intent, and power. An atmosphere of confrontation slowly yielded to an attitude conducive to productive negotiations.

The first concrete result was the partial Nuclear Test Ban Treaty, concluded in Moscow in 1963. During the remainder of the decade, despite the rapid escalation of the Vietnamese war, Soviet-American relations gradually improved. Agreements were hammered out to prevent the spread of nuclear weapons and to insulate outer space and the ocean floors from the atomic arms race. But it was not until 1969 that the new policy was openly articulated. President Richard Nixon, newly elected, declared that an "era of negotiation" would begin, and the Soviet leadership, with a wary eye on China, decided to cooperate with its great capitalist adversary. The gradual process of détente that followed was largely orchestrated by Henry Kissinger. It marked the beginning of a new pattern of "adversary partnership" relations between the superpowers. This fundamental change deserves careful and systematic scrutiny.

While Henry Kissinger was deeply shaken by the Cuban missile crisis, he also saw in it an element of hope. He had always believed that America, unlike Europe, was rather innocent of tragedy and therefore incapable of truly understanding that states, like men, could die. Now at last, America had gazed into the abyss and seen that nuclear death was indeed possible. The Soviet leader, too, had been chastened by the brush with nuclear catastrophe and had shipped his missiles back to Russia. What heartened Kissinger was that both superpowers had apparently learned a lesson. The narrowness of their escape had left a mark.

Henry Kissinger's perception of the Soviet Union was deeply altered by these events. Before the Cuban missile crisis, he had viewed the Soviet Union as the world's leading "revolutionary" power, insatiably bent on global conquest. By the time he joined the government in 1969, Kissinger had changed his mind. A realistic hope now existed, in his view, for creating a Soviet-American community of interests, based upon the common need to avoid a nuclear catastrophe. If this basic premise were admitted, perhaps further bonds could then be forged between the two great powers, deepening their perception of a common destiny. Once this process was set in motion, Soviet Russia and the United States might ultimately form a kind of partnership in the quest for a stable world order, without which there was no real hope for peace.

For Henry Kissinger, America's relationship with Russia was absolutely basic to any policy that sought stability. Détente would depend, at least to some extent, on the ability of the United States to convert the Soviet Union from a "revolutionary" power with unlimited ambition to a "legitimate" state with more circumspect objectives. A legitimate state, in Kissinger's view, could still remain a dictatorship vis-à-vis its own people. This was not his main concern. What mattered enormously to him was adjusting the *external* goals of Soviet Russia to the overall imperatives of a stable world order. If he succeeded in this task, all else, he hoped, would fall into place. Of Kissinger's numerous pronouncements on détente with Soviet Russia, the following statement, made in April 1974, conveyed this central message with the greatest clarity:

Détente is not rooted in agreement on values; it becomes above all necessary because each side recognizes that the other is a potential adversary in a nuclear war. To us, détente is a process of managing relations with a potentially hostile country in order to preserve peace while maintaining our vital interests. In a nuclear age, this is in itself an objective not without moral validity—it may indeed be the most profound imperative of all.

Without stability, no peace was possible. Without the Soviet Union's participation in this quest, there could be no stability and there might not be any survival. These were the twin premises on which Kissinger set out to build détente with Soviet Russia.

When Henry Kissinger assumed office in 1969, nearly a quarter of a century had elapsed since the end of World War II. This twenty-four-year span had witnessed the most relentless arms race in the history of man. By 1969, the money devoted each year by the Soviet Union and the United States to military expenditures amounted to nearly three times what all the world's governments were spending on health and nearly twice what they spent on education. The record of disarmament negotiations was one of total failure. Despite endless conferences, both bilateral and multilateral, not a single weapon, either conventional or nuclear, had been scrapped as a result of a Soviet-American agreement. Mutual mistrust simply was too profound.

By the 1960s, the frustrations over disarmament had led some thinkers to approach the problem in a somewhat different way: in terms of arms *control* rather than disarmament. While the disarmer was primarily concerned with the actual scrapping of existing weapons, the arms controller was more interested in stabilizing the climate in which these weapons existed and in preventing additional arms build-ups. The emphasis here was less on hardware and more on psychology. The hope was that progress on disarmament-related issues might build confidence and ultimately lead to actual disarmament agreements. The partial Nuclear Test Ban Treaty of 1963 was an example of this approach; the Nuclear Nonproliferation Treaty of 1968 was another. The only breakthroughs between the superpowers had taken place in arms control rather than disarmament.

Kissinger, too, was impressed by the arms control approach. Its emphasis on stability appealed to him. But there was a more fundamental reason for his preference. He had always shunned the technical formula approach to problems that he considered basically political in nature. He simply did not believe that nations went to war because they had arms; rather, he felt, they had arms because they deemed it necessary to fight. Hence, he was convinced that efforts at disarmament were bound to fail unless they were preceded by more fundamental, political accommodation. The way to begin, in his view, was not to seek the magic disarmament formula but to concentrate instead on the acceptance, and possible settlement, of political differences.

To put it somewhat differently, Kissinger believed that the problem of disarmament was not disarmament at all, but rather forging détente between the Soviet Union and the United States. Moreover, it was his conviction that even the more modest search for arms control could not take place in a political vacuum; it would first be necessary to narrow the distances between American and Soviet positions in other areas, as well. Kissinger saw a vital connection, for example, between progress in arms control and simultaneous progress on the defusing of the Indochina war. This linkage approach was absolutely basic to his conception of détente. Every problem between the United States and the Soviet Union was linked with every other problem; progress on one would affect progress on all. Kissinger was determined to move on as broad a front as possible. Détente, like peace, was seen by him as indivisible.

When Richard Nixon, in his inaugural address on January 20, 1969, declared that the United States was prepared to enter "an era of negotiation," the Soviet Union responded within hours that it was ready to "start a serious exchange of views" on the problem of arms control bertween the two superpowers. There were several reasons for Brezhnev's eagerness. In the first place, the tensions between China and the Soviet Union had reached a level of potentially explosive danger; second, Eastern Europe was showing signs of increasing turbulence. Only a few months earlier Brezhnev had sent Soviet tanks into Czechoslovakia to crush the Dubček heresy; and finally, the Soviet Union needed American technology and credits in order to infuse new life into the sluggish Russian economy. The Soviet leader seemed to have staked his entire reputation on détente with the United States. He had even been responsive to overtures from West Germany's Chancellor Willy Brandt and had shown increasing willingness to settle the vexing German problem through a diplomacy of compromise. A "serious exchange" about the two superpowers' nuclear arsenals, in Brezhnev's view, was therefore both timely and desirable.

Kissinger was aware of Brezhnev's urgency. While he was equally eager for détente, he wanted to link the beginning of strategic arms limitations talks (SALT) to progress on other issues that divided the two countries. Specifically, he believed that the Soviet Union held the key to peace in Indochina and in the Middle East. Kissinger hoped for a kind of diplomatic barter whereby he could make Brezhnev pay for American concessions on SALT and trade by helping him defuse Vietnam and restore tranquility to the Middle East.

To Kissinger, the linkage concept was a good test of Soviet sincerity on détente. If the Soviet Union was now willing to engage in the "give and take" of diplomatic barter, which linkage diplomacy implied, then this would indeed be evidence that Soviet Russia had at last accepted the legitimacy of the existing international order and abandoned its goal of global conquest.

Nixon, by Inauguration Day, was a respectful student of Kissinger's philosophy. He had read most of Kissinger's books and had even scanned, at Kissinger's request, Spengler's *Decline of the West*. The linkage concept appealed to the president.

During 1969, Kissinger found increasing evidence that the Soviet Union was serious about détente. As a result of Brandt's *Ostpolitik* policy of rapprochement with Soviet Russia, the two Germanies were finally beginning to move toward compromise with each other. The vexing German problem, for so long at the center of the cold war in the heart of Europe, finally seemed to be amenable to reasonable settlement. Kissinger watched these developments with keen interest. While he felt encouraged and was inclined to go ahead with SALT by late 1969, he wanted to make sure that the United States entered these negotiations impeccably prepared. He assembled a staff of first-rate experts, yet made sure that control was concentrated in his own hands. Next to Vietnam, no other issue absorbed his time and energy so much as SALT during 1969. Dobrynin soon realized that it was Kissinger, not Rogers, who set the date on which the negotiations would begin. When the first session of SALT finally convened in Helsinki, on November 17, 1969, Kissinger was ready.

Kissinger's overall philosophical approach to SALT was consistent with his quest for a stable world order. He had never believed that American nuclear superiority over the Soviet Union would be helpful. In his judgment, a rough equilibrium in nuclear arsenals was most desirable. Superiority would be destabilizing and exact parity might be impossible to attain because of the differences in American and Soviet weapons systems. The term he preferred was "sufficiency." Nixon, who in earlier years had been an ardent advocate of American superiority, now echoed Kissinger's opinion. "I think *sufficiency* is a better term," the president declared shortly after he took office, "than either *superiority* or *parity*."

The American and Soviet negotiators both knew from the start that it would probably be hopeless to aim for actual physical disarmament. There was simply not enough trust or good faith between the superpowers to justify such an ambitious goal. Thus, Kissinger's more modest objective of stabilizing the existing balance of terror was preferred by both sides as more realistically feasible. Kissinger assumed, and the Russians agreed, that the balance would have to be stabilized with each side retaining invulnerable retaliatory power. This meant that neither side—even if it struck first—could destroy the other's ability to strike back. The logic of Kissinger's position was the somewhat Machiavellian assumption that the safety of weapons would increase the safety of people. If each side knew that no blow, however massive, could destroy the other's capacity to return the blow, stability would prevail. Mutual deterrence, therefore, rested on the awareness by each side of the other's retaliatory—or second-strike—capacity. The common recognition of this basic premise became the point of departure for the SALT negotiations.

The talks focused on weapons that approached the outer limits of the human propensity for self-destruction. Both sides had offensive weapons of such stupendous destructive power that, in comparison, the Hiroshima bomb virtually paled into insignificance. These intercontinental ballistic missiles (ICBMs) could be launched from a base on land or sea and guided with a fair degree of accuracy to an enemy target an entire continent away. As if this were not enough, the United States had developed a new technology whereby each missile was able to release individual warheads at varying times and angles. Thus, each individual missile could be assigned multiple targets. For a while, this multiple independent reentry vehicle (MIRV) was regarded as the ultimate weapon, against which no defense was possible. It seemed like the Hydra-headed monster of Greek mythology come back in modern form to haunt humanity.

By 1969, however, both the Soviet Union and the United States were experimenting with a possible defense against the MIRV—an antiballistic missile (ABM)—which would function like a bullet aimed to shoot down another bullet. Each side believed that the perfection of an ABM system would give it a decisive edge in the power balance, since it could then risk a first strike against the enemy without having to fear the consequences of retaliation. Needless to say, the cost of an effective ABM system was prohibitive, and its dependability was considered far from certain. Nevertheless, by 1969, both superpowers were already spending billions of dollars on the research and development of the ABM.

When the SALT talks opened in the fall of 1969, the Soviet Union had ICBMs with bigger "throw-weight," or as Pentagon jargon put it, "more bang for a buck." The American ICBMs, however, were purported to have greater accuracy. Besides, the United States had "MIRV'd" a considerable number of its ICBMs and was also working on the ABM. The Soviet Union was striving feverishly to catch up with the United States in MIRV technology.

Kissinger perceived MIRV and ABM as two sides of a single coin, each justifying the existence of the other. He believed that, if the nuclear balance were truly to be stabilized, the talks would have to be addressed simultaneously to both offensive and defensive missiles. Agreement on one but not the other was unacceptable to him.

Kissinger's approach to SALT was quite imaginative. Rather than tie himself down to a specific proposal or even to a number of proposals, he was prepared to accept, as a basis for negotiations, any proposal put forward by the Russians, *provided* it would ultimately yield a balance that was roughly even. It did not matter to him whether an agreement would permit a hundred or a thousand missile launchers; his goal was symmetry. Nor did he care whether an ABM would be limited to the defense of only a single city or of ten; equilibrium was what counted. This emphasis on flexibility saved much valuable time, since it avoided bickering over specific proposals advanced by one side or the other. Kissinger's flexibility, however, never extended to the principle of equilibrium itself. He believed that any nuclear imbalance would be a threat to the stable world order that he was pursuing. "Flexibility," as he had written long before, "[was] a virtue only in the purposeful."

Despite Kissinger's profound knowledge of the subject and

extraordinary negotiating skill, the initial phase of the SALT process of achieving equilibrium was a long and arduous one. SALT I, as it was later designated, went through eight stages (SALT I to SALT VIII) and lasted almost three years. John Newhouse in *Cold Dawn*, his authoritative study of SALT, described the process as "probably the most fascinating episodic negotiation since the Congress of Vienna."

Kissinger was clearly in command of the negotiating process, though he delegated many of its technical aspects to a group of specialists headed by Gerard C. Smith, an official with extensive experience in the field of arms control. At crucial moments, when deadlock threatened, Kissinger would move the negotiations forward, usually by persuading the president to make numerical concessions without impairing the objective of overall balance. For example, he permitted the Russians to keep a larger number of missile launchers because he knew that the United States had more individual warheads.

Finally, on May 26, 1972, in Moscow, Nixon and Brezhnev signed two historic arms control documents, which signified the end of the first phase of SALT. On that day the United States and the Soviet Union renounced the defense of most of their territory and people against the other's nuclear weapons. This was the historic essence of SALT I.

The first document was an ABM treaty of unlimited duration, which placed limits on the growth of Soviet and American strategic nuclear arsenals. The treaty established a ceiling of 200 launchers for each side's defensive missile system and committed both sides to refrain from building nationwide antimissile defenses. Each country was limited to two ABM sites, one for the national capital and the other to protect one field of ICBMs. Each site would consist of 100 ABMs. The United States already had a protected ICBM field in North Dakota and thus, under the terms of the treaty, could add an ABM site around Washington, D.C. The Soviet Union already had an ABM site for the defense of Moscow and thus was permitted to add an ABM site to protect an ICBM field. At the time of the agreement, the Soviet Union had a total of 2,328 missiles: 1,618 land-based ICBMs and 710 on submarines. The United States had a total of 1,710 missiles: 1,054 land-based ICBMs and 656 on submarines.

The second document was an interim agreement limiting

ICBMs to those under construction or deployed at the time of the signing of the agreement. Kissinger and Soviet Foreign Minister Gromyko had held a number of nocturnal meetings in order to define what was meant by "under construction." They finally managed to agree that a missile was deemed to be "under construction" after its parts had been riveted to the hull. This meant the retention of 1,618 ICBMs for the Soviet Union, and 1,054 for the United States. The agreement also froze at existing levels the construction of submarine-launched ICBM missiles on all submarines—656 for the United States and 710 for the Soviet Union. However, each side could build additional submarine missiles if an equal number of older land-based ICBMs or submarine-based missile launchers were dismantled. This "trade-in" provision had been a major stumbling block because the Soviet and American nuclear arsenals were so asymmetrical. How many old missiles were worth one new missile? Once again, Kissinger recommended a numerical concession to Nixon, and this finally broke the deadlock.

SALT I placed no limitations whatever on the qualitative improvement of offensive or defensive missiles; nor did it impose ceilings on the number of warheads that could be carried by offensive missiles or on the number of strategic bombers permitted to each side. Modernization of missiles, including the emplacement of new missiles in new silos, was permitted. Both sides pledged "not to interfere with the national technical means of verification of the other party," and each side retained the right to withdraw from either agreement if it felt that its supreme national interest was in jeopardy.

SALT I thus managed to freeze a rough balance into the nuclear arsenals of the two superpowers. There remained "missile gaps," of course, in specific weapons. The United States, for example, retained the lead in MIRV technology, while the Soviet Union possessed a larger quantity of missile launchers. Nevertheless, the overall effect was the achievement of a rough equilibrium—Kissinger's main objective in the first place.

Kissinger's skill and flexibility were indispensable qualities in bringing SALT I to a successful conclusion. But fortunately, he could be flexible without endangering his goal of overall stability. The higher degree of accuracy of the American missiles and the generally more advanced development of American MIRV technology made it possible to concede an advantage in overall missile numbers to the Russians. It is most unlikely that the Soviet Union would have agreed to SALT I without this numerical advantage. They pursued it with single-minded tenacity. It provided an illusion of superiority for the hard-line members of the Soviet Politburo, who had challenged Brezhnev's commitment to détente with the United States.

Kissinger was ecstatic about the success of SALT I. He thought of it as a great historic step toward a saner world. To his delight, less than a week after the Moscow summit had ended, the United States, together with the Soviet Union, Britain, and France, signed the final protocol of an agreement on the status of Berlin. In addition, the final instruments of a peace treaty between West Germany and the Soviet Union were exchanged.

Détente was sinking roots at last. In the summer of 1973, the two Germanies were admitted, as separate sovereign states, to the United Nations. In June 1973, a second Nixon-Brezhnev summit was arranged by Kissinger, this time in Washington. On that occasion, the two leaders agreed to continue negotiations on the limitation of strategic offensive arms. They also reached an accord on the avoidance of nuclear conflict with each other or with a third nation, pledging restraint on the use of force or the threat of force and agreeing to consult with each other if potentially dangerous situations should arise. Nixon visited Moscow once more in July 1974, only one month before his resignation, but by then his position had been eroded too much by Watergate to permit any further substantive progress.

SALT I placed no restrictions of any kind on the qualitative improvement of missiles. During 1973, the Soviet Union made rapid strides in the evolution of MIRV technology and threatened to catch up with the United States. As a result, Kissinger began to feel that it was a matter of great urgency for the United States to reach a second SALT accord, which would include offensive weapons. He and Secretary of Defense James R. Schlesinger, however, developed profound differences over the most effective way to approach this all-important negotiation.

Schlesinger favored either a dramatic mutual reduction in offensive missiles or, if the Russians did not agree, an all-out arms race. Kissinger maintained that the Soviets would not agree to drastic cutbacks, since they were still behind the United States. Hence, the Schlesinger proposal would result in an unchecked arms race, which the United States would be unable to win. Kissinger thus argued for an agreement that would establish an equilibrium at high force levels, to be followed by step-by-step reductions over a period of time. The Joint Chiefs of Staff agreed with Kissinger, since high force levels would permit them to complete their missile modernization programs. They also contended that Schlesinger's alternative of an all-out arms race was not politically feasible, since Congress would be reluctant to appropriate the necessary funds.

When, in October 1974, President Gerald Ford met with Leonid Brezhnev on the Soviet Pacific coast in Vladivostok in order to discuss the possibilities of a SALT II agreement on offensive missiles, he was accompanied by Secretary of State Kissinger as his main adviser. Once again, the bargaining was tough. Kissinger, after a marathon negotiating session with the Soviet leader, got Brezhnev to drop his demand for numerical superiority. In exchange, Kissinger agreed to a higher ceiling for all kinds of missiles for both countries. This overall ceiling was set at 2,400 missiles for each side, with 1,320 of these permitted to be MIRV'd. No restrictions were set on further qualitative improvements, such as missile flight tests to increase accuracy, or on the development of land-mobile and air-mobile intercontinental ballistic missiles. Nor were any restrictions placed on the development of cruise missiles launched from submarines.

Ford and Brezhnev did not sign a final accord, but reached agreement only in principle. Kissinger, however, expressed the hope that SALT II, once signed, would "put a cap on the arms race" for ten years, "between 1975 and 1985." In terms of permanent achievements, Kissinger said in December 1974, "I would rank the outline for SALT II near the top."

Actually, Vladivostok was a rather modest achievement. The "cap" on the arms race did not signify a reduction of existing weapons stockpiles, but merely a quantitative limitation on the development of further weapons. The United States would have fairly good assurances of the maximum number of Soviet missiles over the next decade. On the crucial matter of verification, however, a major asymmetry prevailed. Since the United States was an open society, with weapons systems subject to constant public scrutiny from their research and development phase to their actual deployment, the Soviet Union could have a high degree of confidence in American compliance with any limitation agreement. The United States, of course, could have no such proof of Soviet honesty. The verification problem was now particularly crucial, since it was important to know, under the Vladivostok accord, whether a missile was MIRV'd or not.

The verification issue began to haunt Kissinger in 1975 and placed in serious question further progress toward SALT II. Admiral Elmo R. Zumwalt, retired chief of naval operations, declared in December 1975 that the Soviet Union had committed "gross violations" of the SALT I accord of 1972 and that Kissinger had not properly informed President Ford. He charged that the Soviets were constructing launch silos for additional missiles and thus were surreptitiously upgrading their ABM defensive potential. He also accused the Soviets of converting "light" ABM missiles into "heavy" ones and thus violating the spirit of SALT I. Kissinger heatedly denied the charges and was supported in his defense by the CIA. By this time, however, the ire of the Soviets was aroused. *Pravda* not only denied any violations of the 1972 accord, but in turn voiced serious doubts about American compliance. It now blamed the United States for the delay in reaching a final SALT II agreement, which, Brezhnev had hoped, would be sealed by the time the Twenty-fifth Communist Party Congress was to convene, in February 1976.

Progress toward SALT II was also stalled over two new weapons, which the United States and the Soviet Union wanted to add to their respective arsenals. The Pentagon had developed a "cruise missile," which was a long-range, jet-propelled, extremely accurate guided nuclear bomb that could be launched from a bomber, a ship, or a submarine. Pentagon spokesmen declared that, since the cruise missile traveled through the atmosphere, it should not be included in the SALT II ceiling of 2,400 ICBMs, which traveled through space. The Soviet Union insisted that the "cruise missile" be included in the ceiling. At the same time, the Soviets had developed a new "Backfire" bomber, which, they declared, should be excluded from SALT II because of its limited range. The Pentagon, insisting that air-to-air refueling could enable it to reach the United States and return, demanded its inclusion in the ceiling.

Kissinger, convinced that "ninety percent of SALT II had been completed" and that an agreement was essential in order to maintain the momentum of détente, clashed more and more with Schlesinger. The defense secretary, in turn, accused Kissinger of making disadvantageous agreements with the Soviets in order to preserve a dubious illusion of détente. While Ford's dismissal of Schlesinger in late 1975 left Kissinger in primary control of foreign policy, the position of assistant for national security affairs was taken away from him. Thus, by early 1976, the future of SALT II was very much in doubt. The allegations of cheating by the Soviet Union, the dispute over the inclusion of newly developed weapons in the overall ceiling, and a deepening suspicion of Soviet behavior in Angola and in the Middle East made Kissinger's position on SALT II extremely vulnerable. It seemed that despite the breakthrough of SALT I, the safety of the superpowers still depended, first and foremost, on their capacity for mutually assured destruction. SALT had made a dent in the balance of terror, but it was little more than a beginning.

President Jimmy Carter and Secretary of State Cyrus Vance continued to pursue the limitation of strategic arms. In a far-ranging speech on foreign policy, delivered at the United Nations two months after his inauguration, the new president called for sweeping reductions in nuclear arms and for a freeze on new kinds of weapons. In the same speech, however, Carter placed great emphasis on human rights and asserted that "no member of the United Nations [could] claim that mistreatment of its citizens [was] solely its own business."

This new emphasis on human rights, which included statements of support on behalf of Russian dissidents, irritated the Soviet leaders, who accused the United States of hypocrisy and "selective morality." The president, the Soviet leaders claimed, ignored violations of human rights in fascist dictatorships, such as South Korea, Chile, and Iran, which the United States considered to be of vital strategic value. The United States declared that SALT II would not be made contingent upon internal changes in the Soviet Union. Evidently, the new administration was convinced that it could pursue *both* détente and a greater emphasis on human rights in its relations with the Soviet Union. The Russian response was skeptical. The United States, the Soviet leadership declared, had no right to play the role of moral world police. Brezhnev stated that it was "unthinkable" that Soviet-American relations could develop normally on such a basis. When Secretary Vance visited Moscow in 1977 in order to pursue SALT II, the

Soviet leadership flatly rejected two American plans to limit strategic weapons, without offering any new proposals of its own. President Carter, however, remained "hopeful" that the two sides could reach agreement and, in a surprise move in July, announced that he had decided not to authorize the construction of the B-1 bomber. By 1978, both sides were once more making progress toward SALT II. By the end of the decade, the chances for the approval of SALT II by the U.S. Senate were generally estimated to be about fifty-fifty.

The Soviet invasion of Afghanistan in early 1980 not only injured détente severely, but prompted President Carter to request a postponement of the Senate debate on ratification of the SALT II treaty. This was a realistic concession to a mood of rising militancy in the nation, even though, in the Carter administration's view, SALT II was needed more than ever now that relations between the superpowers were rapidly deteriorating. The president had to recognize the Senate's extreme reluctance to make a deal with the Soviet Union when that nation was crashing into a neutral country with a hundred thousand combat troops. Since the Soviet Union had apparently decided that the conquest of Afghanistan was more important than the salvaging of SALT, the superpowers were likely to move into a lengthy period of unchecked military competition. In short, the 1980s might resemble the 1950s, and a new cold war might replace détente.

DÉTENTE AND TRADE

Trade was to be an element of the fabric of détente from the very beginning. Henry Kissinger was not so naive as to believe that trade per se with the Soviet Union would forge the bonds of peace. As a historian, he knew that the nations that had gone to war against each other in Europe had also been the closest trading partners. History—especially Russia's—provided little assurance that trade ensured peace. But Kissinger believed that the Soviets needed American trade, technology, and credit, and hence he hoped that, once having become dependent upon these capitalist benefits, the Soviet Union might become more conscious of what it would lose by a return to confrontation. Besides, trade was a vital element in Kissinger's linkage concept.

Kissinger's assessment of the Soviet position in 1972 was essentially correct. Not only had American overtures to China made the Soviet leadership eager to quicken the momentum of détente, but serious shortages in vital sectors of the Soviet economy had made a rapid trade expansion with the United States highly desirable. Moreover, the Soviet leaders faced immense problems in developing the vast resources of oil, gas, and minerals located in Siberia. For this, American capital and technology were needed. And finally, in a time of poor domestic harvests, the Soviets wanted access to the American grain market.

On the American side, the timing, too, was favorable. Nixon and Kissinger had benefited from some Soviet help on the Indochina problem and anticipated future favors in this vital area of concern. In February 1972, the Soviet Union informed the United States that it was willing to reopen negotiations, suspended for twelve years, on the repayment of the outstanding Soviet World War II lend-lease debt.

This Soviet initiative triggered a flurry of activity, making 1972 a record year for Soviet-American agreements. In July, the superpowers signed an accord that made it possible for the Soviet Union to purchase $750 million of American grain. In August, it was announced that the Soviet purchases would exceed the $1 billion mark. It was also revealed that the Occidental Petroleum Company had concluded a $3 billion arrangement for the exploitation of Siberian natural gas. In October, the negotiations on the lend-lease issue were successfully concluded with a Soviet agreement to settle the outstanding debt by paying $722 million over twenty-nine years.

Progress, however, was not destined to be smooth. A comprehensive trade agreement that Nixon and Kissinger signed with the Soviet Union in October 1972 ignited a debate in the United States on the entire issue of détente. In the first place, the Soviet grain purchases contributed to a dramatic rise in food prices in the United States, and angry American consumers were complaining bitterly about the "great Russian grain robbery." Second, and more important, the trade agreement of October 1972 had granted the Soviets most-favored-nation status. This meant, in effect, the restoration of normal trade relations, which had been suspended at the height of the cold war, in 1951.

Senator Henry M. Jackson led the forces that were skeptical

about détente in general and were reluctant to grant most-favored-nation status to the Soviet Union without getting something in return. What Jackson sought, however, was not a concession in the economic field but a commitment from the Soviet government on free Jewish emigration from the Soviet Union. To this end, he proposed an amendment to the Soviet trade bill. This demand touched off a bitter and protracted conflict between Kissinger and Jackson over the merits of détente, a conflict that was exacerbated greatly by the outbreak of war in the Middle East in October 1973.

Jackson and his followers attacked Kissinger's concept of détente, claiming that it was a kind of one-way street in favor of the Soviet Union. The Russians, he argued, were always getting the better bargain. "We sell the Soviets cars," exclaimed a critic of détente in a Detroit plant, "and they sell us parking places in Siberia." In addition, the critics maintained, the Soviet Union had violated the spirit of détente by encouraging the Arab assault on Israel in October 1973. Instead of consulting with the United States and looking for ways to stave off the conflict, the Soviet leadership had aided and abetted Egypt and Syria in mounting their surprise attack. It was plain that the Russians were reaping the benefits of détente but not living up to their obligations. Hence, the United States should insist on a major concession: the lifting of restrictions on Jewish emigration from Russia to Israel.

Kissinger strenuously opposed the Jackson amendment to the Soviet trade bill, not because he approved of Soviet domestic policies, but because he thought that the stipulation was inappropriate and counterproductive. Its use denied the possibility, in his opinion, of normal commercial contacts so long as certain basic ideological conflicts remained unresolved. As he put it in 1974:

> Thus, the major impact of the continued denial of most-favored nations status to the Soviet Union would be political, not economic. Most-favored nations status was withdrawn in 1951, largely as a political act. Our unwillingness to remove this discrimination now would call into question our intent to move toward an improved relationship.

In short, if the United States rattled the skeletons in the Soviets' political closet, the Russians would probably respond in kind. Once the skeletons emerged from both closets, détente would be endangered. And as Kissinger never tired of pointing out, the overriding goal of détente was the avoidance of nuclear war. Besides, the Soviet attitude toward the leading capitalist nation had changed. Khrushchev had come to the United States in 1959, saying "we shall bury you." Yet when Brezhnev visited the United States in 1973, not a word was said about the burial of capitalism. Instead, Brezhnev's approach was more along the lines of "We want to borrow you." Trade, in Kissinger's opinion, could serve to promote political détente only if trade was in fact kept politically neutral.

The Kissinger-Jackson feud ended inconclusively. Kissinger had to settle for a trade act that required periodic review of Soviet Jewish emigration by Congress, on whose approval the continued Soviet most-favored-nation status would depend. At the same time, Congress placed a limit of $300 million on government loans and guarantees that could be granted to Russia without specific congressional approval. The result of these steps was an angry Soviet rejection, in January 1975, of the entire trade agreement on the grounds that such interference in Soviet internal affairs could not be tolerated. Nevertheless, Soviet-American trade continued, though at somewhat more modest levels.

In the summer of 1975, the Russians again entered the American market to buy large quantities of grain. A deal was concluded under which, beginning in October 1976, the Soviets agreed to buy a minimum of 6 million and a maximum of 8 million metric tons of wheat and corn each year for five years. Kissinger tried to introduce linkage into this business partnership. Specifically, he attempted to link grain with oil and thus to drive a wedge between the Soviet Union and the Arabs. The Soviet Union, however, agreed to sell the United States only a small amount of oil at prices slightly below those charged by the oil cartel.

The trade relations between the United States and the Soviet Union made Kissinger's approach to détente a subject of intense domestic controversy. Détente was no longer discussed solely by strategists of power politics; it now affected the daily economic lives of millions of Americans. Farmers wanted greater exports to the Soviet Union, resulting in higher prices for their products; consumers hoped for lower food prices and criticized the Soviet grain purchases; and politicians suddenly had to become sensitized to these crosscurrents in American politics. In this debate, Henry Kissinger preferred to deal with the question of Jewish emigration through quiet diplomacy. He pointed out that 35,000 Jews had left the Soviet Union for Israel in 1973 but that the rate of emigration had turned down sharply in 1974 and 1975 because the Soviet Union would not accept such humiliating conditions. In his judgment, it was a serious mistake to try to influence Soviet practice in domestic matters. He thought that it would be far better to try to induce changes in Soviet foreign policy. He did, in fact, attempt to use American grain sales in 1975 as a lever on Soviet foreign policy when he sought Soviet acquiescence to his diplomatic step-by-step initiatives in the Middle East. But he remained convinced that any attempt to change the domestic behavior of the Soviet Union would have a boomerang effect. Linkage, in short, was a concept that was meaningful only in international diplomacy. If misapplied to internal policies, it would set back, rather than advance, the process of détente.

What Richard Nixon and Henry Kissinger did with trade in 1972, Jimmy Carter undid in 1980. Stung by the invasion of Afghanistan, the president imposed a grain embargo on the Soviet Union, withholding 17 million tons of wheat, corn, and soybeans that had been scheduled to be shipped to Russia. To limit the damage at home, the administration decided to buy the unfulfilled grain contracts from farmers and exporters. In addition, it announced a stepped-up gasohol program and extra support loans to farmers. All high technology sales to the Soviet Union were suspended and Soviet fishing rights in American waters were severely curtailed. The United States decided to boycott the 1980 Olympics scheduled to be held in Moscow and urged its allies to do the same. The administration also pointedly paid court to the Soviets' bitter foes, the Chinese. On a trip to Peking, Defense Secretary Harold Brown suggested that the United States and China might seek "complementary actions" to counter Soviet expansionism. China responded immediately by offering to increase its grain purchases from the United States.

The grain embargo was not without its strong critics. Most of Jimmy Carter's opponents in the presidential race shared the view that the United States had "aimed a shot at the Russians and hit the American farmer instead." America's allies, with the exception of Britain, were not enthusiastic. Some, like Argentina and Brazil, would not go along at all. It appeared that the economic brunt of the embargo would have to be borne by the United States. At any rate, the "economic track" of détente seemed almost dead by 1980.

THE TESTING OF DÉTENTE DURING THE 1970S

For Henry Kissinger, the pursuit of détente could not be confined to the bilateral Soviet-American relationship. SALT and trade were important building blocks, but they were not enough. Should the Soviet Union tamper with the overall equilibrium in other parts of the world, stability—Kissinger's prerequisite to peace—would be in jeopardy. Thus, the Soviet-American relationship, in Kissinger's mind, was analogous to the hub of a wheel. Action at the rim would automatically be transmitted to the center. Détente, to Kissinger, was always a global proposition.

Détente was tested quite severely on at least six occasions in different parts of the world. In 1970, the Soviets supported a Syrian drive into Jordan and threatened to upset the balance in the Middle East; at almost the same time, they tried to build a nuclear submarine base at Cienfuegos, in Cuba; in 1971, in the India-Pakistan confrontation over Bangladesh, the Soviet Union and India were military allies in Indira Gandhi's dismemberment of Pakistan; during the entire Indochina war, the Soviet leadership supplied Hanoi with vital war matériel; in October 1973, during the Arab-Israeli conflict, the Soviet Union threatened unilateral intervention on the Arab side, which triggered a global military alert on the part of the United States; and in 1975, the Soviet leadership and Castro's Cuba gave considerable support to one of three political groups fighting for control in Portugal's former colony, Angola. Kissinger's responses to these six challenges are well worth examining.

For Kissinger, the Middle East had always been a dual problem. On one level, there was the deep and violent conflict between Israel and her Arab neighbors. By 1970, three wars had been fought and the festering wounds had not healed with the passage of time. Each side had done things that the other could neither forgive nor forget. Superimposed upon the Arab-Israeli conflict was the ever-present threat of a Soviet-American confrontation, since, over the years, the United States had supported the Israeli cause, while the Soviet Union had sided with the Arabs.

In the summer of 1970, Kissinger's sympathy for Israel and his concern for the maintenance of an overall Soviet-American balance coincided, when the Soviet Union, in a dramatic and unexpected move, decided to support a Syrian invasion of Lebanon and Jordan with advisers, air power, and tanks. Kissinger viewed the Soviet move as a potentially disastrous disruption of global equilibrium. He reasoned that if the Soviet Union succeeded in emplacing radical Arab governments in Lebanon and Jordan, Saudi Arabia's vast oil reserves might be vulnerable to similar encroachments. Israel would then be encircled and might be driven into the sea, with the global balance shifted, perhaps irrevocably, in Russia's favor.

Kissinger concluded that a move should be made without delay to expel the Soviet military presence, especially Soviet combat pilots and combat personnel, from the Middle Eastern scene. He recommended to the president that, unless the Syrian tanks were withdrawn from Jordan, Israel should be encouraged to intervene on the side of King Hussein. When Israel's Ambassador Yitzhak Rabin asked Kissinger whether the United States would come to Israel's aid if the Soviet Union escalated its support to Syria, Kissinger prevailed on Nixon to promise such American support. When Israel reported that Syrian tanks were "pouring across the Jordanian border" and that Hussein was fighting for his life, Kissinger climbed another step on the escalation ladder. Israeli forces would move against Syria in Jordan, he warned, unless the Syrians withdrew; if Egyptian or Soviet forces then moved against Israel, the United States would intervene against *both*. "You and your client started the war," Kissinger curtly told Soviet Ambassador Dobrynin, "and you now have to end it."

Kissinger's crisis management was successful. The Soviet Union called off the Syrian invasion. Kissinger, though pleased, decided to warn the Soviet leadership not to strain the fragile fabric of the developing détente. "Events in the Middle East and in other parts of the world," he declared on September 16, 1970, "have raised questions of whether Soviet leaders as of now are prepared . . . to forgo tactical advantages they can derive from certain situations for the sake of the larger interest of peace." It seemed that the Soviet answer to Kissinger's question was negative because at that very moment, half a world away, the Soviet Union was constructing a nuclear submarine base on the southern coast of Cuba, in clear violation of an understanding reached by President John F. Kennedy and Premier Nikita Khrushchev after the missile crisis of 1962.

It began almost like a replay of the missile crisis. A U-2 spy plane, flying over Cuba in September 1970, photographed a soccer field near the naval base of Cienfuegos. Cubans do not play soccer, but soccer is the Soviet national sport. Further pictures revealed that a Soviet nuclear submarine base was under construction at Cienfuegos. The 1962 agreement between Kennedy and Khrushchev had permitted Soviet defensive military installations. In Kissinger's view, a nuclear base was clearly offensive and would constitute yet another threat to global balance. He recommended that the president take a firm stance on the matter. Nixon agreed with Kissinger.

Kissinger, unlike Kennedy, decided to use quiet diplomacy. He arranged a private meeting with Dobrynin and informed the Soviet ambassador that the United States was aware that Russia was constructing an offensive base in Cuba. Unless the construction was stopped immediately, Kissinger warned, the new détente would be imperiled. Two weeks later, construction slowed down, and soon thereafter, it stopped completely. Apparently, Brezhnev was not willing to follow in the footsteps of his predecessor, whom he had described six years earlier as a "hare-brained schemer." Besides, the prospects of SALT, technology, and trade far outweighed the value of a naval base in Cuba. Thus, once again, Kissinger tested détente by a combination of diplomacy and force, and once again, the combination worked.

In August 1971, one month after Kissinger's trip to China, Prime Minister Indira Gandhi of India and the Soviet leadership signed a twenty-five year friendship treaty, which had all the earmarks of a military alliance. The pact, which, in the words of an Indian parliamentarian, "put some meat into India's vegetarian diet of nonalignment," was intended as a clear warning to Pakistan and as a deterrent against the possibility of Chinese intervention in the escalating conflict between Mrs. Gandhi and Yahya Khan, the president of Pakistan.

Yahya Khan was then engaged in a brutal civil war with the Bengalis of East Pakistan, who were separated from West Pakistan by one thousand miles of hostile Indian territory. He had decided to cancel the results of an election that would have given the presidency of Pakistan to a Bengali, Sheik Mujibur Rahman. The Easterners had rebelled, and the result was a West Pakistani campaign of reprisal so pitiless that 10 million Bengalis fled for their lives into neighboring India. Mrs. Gandhi, weighing whether it was cheaper to feed 10 million starving Moslem refugees or to go to war against Yahya Khan in the hope of dismembering India's traditional enemy, decided on the latter course. On December 1, 1971, she issued an ultimatum in which she demanded that Yahya Khan withdraw all his forces from East Pakistan. Yahya Khan ordered an air strike against India. The air strike not only turned out to be a fiasco but gave Mrs. Gandhi the necessary pretext for ordering the Indian army to march on Dacca, the capital of East Pakistan.

Kissinger had watched the events on the Indian subcontinent with growing concern. He believed that Mrs. Gandhi intended to destroy Pakistan and that, if she succeeded, India and the Soviet Union would completely dominate the subcontinent. Hence, in order to balance the Soviet-Indian alliance, the United States would have to side with Pakistan. Nixon agreed. In fact, as the "Anderson Papers" revealed later, Kissinger "got hell from the President every ten minutes for not being tough enough on India." The United States "tilted" toward Pakistan because Kissinger and Nixon believed that Mrs. Gandhi intended not only to detach East Pakistan from the West, but to dismember her old rival altogether. Even though State Department officials, in particular Undersecretary of State Joseph Sisco, disagreed with this analysis, Kissinger's view finally prevailed. He accused India of aggression and warned the Soviet Union that détente might be jeopardized if the Soviet-Indian offensive continued. A naval task force of eight ships, led by the nuclear aircraft carrier *Enterprise*, was dispatched to the Bay of Bengal. It was "gunboat diplomacy" in nuclear form. When there was no immediate response from Moscow, Kissinger declared that, unless the Soviet Union began to exercise a restraining influence on India very soon, the plans for the president's trip to Moscow might be changed and "the entire United States-Soviet relationship might well be reexamined."

The Soviet leadership, unwilling to jeopardize the Moscow summit, apparently decided to restrain India. At any rate, the war ended on December 16, with Pakistan split into two separate states. Kissinger claimed that his warning to the Soviet Union had prevented Mrs. Gandhi from dismembering West Pakistan, as well. Sisco doubted whether she ever had such plans and many critics now began to accuse Kissinger of siding with a corrupt dictatorship against the world's largest democracy, and ignoring, in the process, the human tragedy of 10 million helpless Bengali refugees who had been the victims of Yahya Khan's brutality. Moreover, the critics pointed out, the Soviet-backed democracy won and the American-supported dictatorship lost, which did not exactly enhance American prestige throughout the world. Kissinger himself was so depressed by this episode that he briefly considered resignation. But he held on to his conviction that his policy of toughness against the Soviet Union had preserved stability on the Indian subcontinent.

An analysis of the Indochina war reveals that the United States tested the limits of détente far more than did the Soviet Union. Nixon and Kissinger decided to mine Haiphong only a few days before they were to visit Moscow in May 1972, and yet Brezhnev chose not to cancel the summit talks. Later that year, the Soviets applied pressure on Hanoi and cut back arms deliveries to their ally. These moves compelled the North Vietnamese leadership to make its first serious concessions to Kissinger in Paris. And even the bombings of Christmas 1972 did little to disrupt détente. In Brezhnev's calculus of power, the fear of China and the hope for arms control agreements, technology, and trade with the United States were overwhelming practical considerations. Détente conferred some very real benefits that the ideological alliance with Hanoi simply could not match. Kissinger's belief that China was the key to Russia and that Russia was the key to an Indochina settlement made sense in 1972 and 1973. Hanoi's final victory in 1975 stemmed more from its own enormous staying power and from Saigon's total military collapse than from Soviet violations of détente. On the whole, the Soviet Union showed remarkable restraint during the final years of the Indochina war.

The record is more mixed if one examines Soviet policy in the Middle East. There is no doubt that the Soviet leadership supplied the arms that made possible the Egyptian-Syrian surprise attack on Israel in October 1973. Moreover, the Soviets were definitely aware of the impending attack but chose not to warn the United

States. This was clearly in violation of Nixon's and Brezhnev's 1973 pledge to consult with each other if potentially dangerous situations arose. Two weeks later, however, when, with American help, the Israelis had turned the war around and had entrapped 100,000 Egyptian soldiers, Brezhnev threatened the United States with "unilateral steps" in order to prevent an Arab military defeat. In response, Kissinger recommended that the president announce a general "alert" of American military forces. Backed up by this show of force, Kissinger resorted to diplomacy. "If the Soviet Union and we can work cooperatively," he said, "first, toward establishing a cease-fire, and then toward a durable settlement in the Middle East, then détente will have proved itself." Shortly thereafter, the Soviet Union and the United States agreed upon a face-saving formula through the United Nations. Once again, Kissinger had talked the Russians out of a confrontation after having alerted American military forces to prepare for one. And once again, the two superpowers returned from the nuclear brink to the safer terrain of détente.

Kissinger's "step-by-step" approach to a Middle Eastern settlement in 1974 and 1975 remained virtually an American monopoly. The two disengagement agreements between Israel and Egypt and between Israel and Syria were triumphs of Kissinger's personal diplomacy. And the Sinai agreement reached by Israel and Egypt in September 1975 was yet another success for Kissinger. The Soviet Union grudgingly acquiesced in Kissinger's diplomatic solo performance. It had little choice because only the United States, by exerting pressure on Israel, was in a position to recover territories for the Arabs, while the Russians could do nothing more than supply the weapons for another war. Besides, the triangular policy with China was still effective and the lures of SALT, technology, and trade still proved too great for Brezhnev to resist.

Thus, for two years, the United States was the peacemaker in the Middle East and the Soviet Union was largely confined to the sidelines. And while the quest for peace continued, Kissinger was able to dominate Middle East diplomacy and yet maintain détente with Russia. Only when the step-by-step approach ran out of steps and the Palestinian question moved to center stage, in late 1975, did Kissinger's diplomatic monopoly end.

Thus, in the Middle East, détente was strained by both the Soviet Union and the United States. The Soviet Union tested it in times of war, Kissinger through his unilateral diplomacy of peace. On several occasions détente was bruised, but it managed to survive, though its critics gained in influence and power, especially in the United States.

The testing of détente was extended to the African continent in 1975, when the Soviet Union backed one of three political factions contending for the control of Angola, which had just gained its independence from Portugal. Calculating that the memory of the Indochina war and congressional aversion to a new American involvement in a civil war would probably deter the United States from intervening in Angola, the Soviet Union supported the Luanda faction with war matériel and 12,000 Cuban combat soldiers.

Though by that time Congress had severely circumscribed Kissinger's power in virtually every area of foreign policy, he nevertheless attempted once again to apply the leverage of linkage. He declared that the conclusion of a SALT II agreement might be in jeopardy and also added that trade concessions that he had recommended for the Soviet Union might founder on opposition in the Congress. Once again, he was quite explicit about the need to preserve détente, stating that there was "no question that the overall relationship [would] suffer if we do not find an adequate solution to the Angola problem."

This time, however, the Soviet leadership was no longer quite so eager for trade with the United States since it had been able to satisfy many of its needs through purchases in Japan and Western Europe. Besides, Gerald Ford, who faced an election in 1976, needed an arms pact at least as much as Brezhnev did. Most important, the Russians could readily see that Kissinger's leverage was limited by congressional opposition. As the Soviet-backed faction edged closer to military victory, Kissinger, in deepening frustration, pleaded with the Congress to match the aid provided by the Soviet Union and Cuba. The Congress refused flatly, and Gerald Ford accused the legislative body of "having lost its guts." Finally, in February 1976, the Organization for African Unity (OAU) placed its official approval on the Soviet-backed Luanda faction by recognizing it as the official government of Angola. Once again, détente had undergone a strenuous test as both the Soviet Union and the United States had violated each other's assumptions about its meaning. The Soviet leadership had always regarded the support of "national liberation movements" as permissible within the confines of détente and was therefore somewhat baffled by Kissinger's response. Kissinger, in turn, believing that détente meant the avoidance of such confrontations in peripheral areas, had been ready to back diplomacy with force.

In 1975, the Soviet Union took the initiative in Europe. That summer, thirty years after the end of World War II, the heads of thirty-five nations met in Helsinki, Finland, and signed a declaration that committed them to "broaden and deepen" the process of détente. Specifically, the conference ratified the postwar frontier in Europe, a goal that had long been sought by the Soviet Union. The signatories also pledged not to resort to force in disputes among themselves and to increase trade and other contacts between East and West. Unofficially, Helsinki ratified the principle of permanent spheres of influence in Europe for the Soviet Union and the United States. Kissinger welcomed the Helsinki accord because it helped to institutionalize the principle of equilibrium in Europe and thus would stabilize détente in the geographic area that had once been the very center of the cold war.

The record of the six occasions on which détente was tested in peripheral areas during the 1970s suggests that the mixture of diplomacy and force worked quite successfully, particularly when combined with linkage. When, in 1970, the Soviet Union tested détente in Jordan and in Cuba, it applied diplomacy and force in a way that allowed withdrawal before Soviet prestige had become irrevocably involved. In the Middle East, once again, after the "alert" of October 1973, Kissinger offered a face-saving device through the United Nations. In the Indochina war, the use of linkage resulted in quite extraordinary Soviet restraint; only in Bangladesh and in Angola does the evidence seem negative. But it was in 1980 that the entire fabric of détente was in serious jeopardy.

AFGHANISTAN

During the opening days of 1980, the Soviet Union did something it had never done before: it used its own troops to invade a neutral country.

As close to a hundred thousand troops smashed into Afghanistan, President Carter announced that his "opinion of the Russians ha[d] changed more drastically in the last week than in the previous two and a half years." Describing the invasion as "a quantum jump in the nature of Soviet behavior," and the most serious crisis since the Second World War, the president announced an embargo on grain and high technology products against the Soviet Union. In his State of the Union address in January 1980, he declared that the United States would use armed force, if necessary, to repel any Soviet assault on the Persian Gulf region. This new "Carter Doctrine" thus extended the NATO alliance concept to the Middle East. Containment now included all regions of vital strategic or economic interest to the United States. Suddenly, all the détente effort of the 1970s seemed in jeopardy. 1980 seemed more like 1950. What was behind these shattering events and did perception play a role in them?

The evidence suggests that the Soviet leadership made its move based partly on objective considerations of strategy and power balance, but also partly on its perceptions of what the United States might or might not do.

The "objective" factors apparently were the following: Moscow's primary purpose was probably to tighten its control over a rebellious border state. The tide of Islamic fervor which had already shaken Iran was now threatening Afghanistan. Unless it was checked quickly, it might spread across the border into Soviet Central Asia and stir unrest among the Soviet Union's fifty million Moslems. Second, the invasion was probably part of a long-range strategy to gain influence over Pakistan, Iran, and other Persian Gulf nations. It might ultimately place the Soviet Union in the strategic position of controlling Western oil supplies. Finally, Moscow probably intended to send a message to Peking that it was prepared to resort to force if its border interests were threatened.

Perceptions of American intent probably also played a role. In the first place, the Soviet leadership had apparently concluded that SALT II had little chance of winning approval during an election year. Moreover, since NATO had decided in December 1979 to deploy in Western Europe, by the mid-1980s, new atomic-tipped missiles capable of striking targets in the Soviet Union, SALT was simply not all that important any longer. Second, Moscow may have reached the conclusion that the United States was so distracted by Iran that it would not act strongly on Afghanistan. After all, the fifty American hostages held captive in Teheran by Iranian militants had dominated America's attention for two months. And, finally, one might venture the following speculation: When the United States, during the 1960s and early 1970s, had more than half a million combat troops fighting in Vietnam, and had mined Haiphong and bombed Hanoi, the Soviet Union had not cancelled SALT I. In fact, ten days after the mining of Haiphong Harbor in May 1972, Richard Nixon and Henry Kissinger arrived in Moscow to meet with Leonid Brezhnev in a summit meeting to sign the first strategic arms limitation treaty between the superpowers. Why, then, should the United States overreact if the Soviet Union took advantage of an opportunity that came its way in 1980? It is entirely possible that the Soviet leadership underestimated the American response to Afghanistan in a way not dissimilar to Nikita Khrushchev's underestimation of John F. Kennedy's response to Soviet missiles in Cuba.

A dispassionate Olympian view of the Afghanistan invasion might conclude that when it comes to testing détente through intervention, the superpower score is very close to even. The United States intervened in Vietnam, Cambodia, and the Dominican Republic, and the Soviet Union intervened in Hungary, Czechoslovakia, and Afghanistan. It is true that Afghanistan was a neutral country, but Cambodia was, too. Unfortunately, however, when passions are inflamed, such Olympian views enjoy little popularity. Empathy gives way to an "us-and-them" psychology. The lessons of the Cuban missile crisis are forgotten. No one places himself in the other fellow's shoes. The terrible swift sword is unsheathed on both sides as the arms race gathers momentum once again. But one must also be honest with oneself and ready to admit one's own mistakes. Afghanistan and Vietnam do not cancel each other out. Two wrongs do not make a right; they remain two wrongs. If we realize this truth, right will not lead to self-righteousness and strength will not congeal into rigidity. The door would remain open for a renewal of détente. Afghanistan would then not be the prelude to Greek tragedy; it would be yet another temporary darkness in man's unceasing struggle toward light.

Chapter Fourteen

—•◆•—

Out of the Night

Under the first term of Ronald Reagan's presidency, the Soviet-American relationship deteriorated to a level not seen since the days of the Cuban missile crisis. During the détente years, there was little talk of nuclear war. Instead, the two nations pursued a pragmatic, businesslike relationship. Ten years later, however, in 1983, a television version of nuclear holocaust was watched by 100 million frightened Americans. In my university classes in New York City, more than half of the students expected to perish in a nuclear war before the year 2000. The unthinkable had become possible once again. What had happened?

In order to help us comprehend this turn of events, a brief analysis of Ronald Reagan's background and perceptions of America and Soviet Russia is essential.

On July 17, 1980, Ronald Reagan was concluding his acceptance speech as the Republican party's nominee for president of the United States.

"Four times in my lifetime," he declared, "America has gone to war, bleeding the lives of its young men into the sands of beachheads, the fields of Europe, and the jungles and rice paddies of Asia. We know only too well that war comes not when the forces of freedom are strong, but when they are weak. It is then that tyrants are tempted." And then, his eyes misty with tears, he added: "I'll confess that I've been a little afraid to suggest what I'm going to suggest. I'm more afraid not to. Can we begin our crusade joined together in a moment of silent prayer?" After fifteen seconds of silence, he lifted his head and said softly: "God bless America."

Six months later, at the age of 70, Reagan became the fortieth president of the United States. Looking back on the inaugural

244

ceremony, he confided to his speechwriter: "I've never been filled with such a surge of patriotism. It was hard not to cry during the whole thing. Well, it was cold, but it was so moving. I was crying frozen tears."[1]

The presidency of Ronald Reagan was to become a celebration of traditional American values: self-reliance, free enterprise, liberty, morality, religion, hard work, patriotism, and anticommunism. In the words of one friendly biographer, Ronald Reagan embodied "all twelve traits of the Boy Scout Law: he was trustworthy, loyal, helpful, friendly, courteous, kind, obedient, cheerful, thrifty, brave, clean, and reverent."[2] Sometimes, in Reagan's view, to go forward was to go back into the past.

Born three years before World War I in a small town in Illinois, young "Dutch" Reagan fought hours of solitary battles with lead Civil War soldiers while his older brother played games with other boys.[3] The Civil War was still a living memory when Reagan was a boy and veterans survived in most Illinois towns and villages. The arch on Main Street celebrated the memories of other young Americans—some only twelve years older than young Ron—who had fallen on the battlefields of Europe. There were heroes all around him.

"I'm a sucker for hero worship," Reagan wrote in 1977, listing the books that had made a deep impression on him as a boy.[4] His favorite boyhood author had been Edgar Rice Burroughs, who wrote about the improbable exploits of Tarzan of the Jungle. During his inaugural address, the new president cited the example of an American army private who had died in France during World War I. The dead soldier had left behind a diary with the words "My Pledge" written on the fly leaf. Underneath, he had written: "America must win the war. Therefore I will work, I will save, I will sacrifice, I will endure, I will fight cheerfully and do my utmost, as if the issue of the whole struggle depended on me alone." Ronald Reagan's heroes had always been heroes.[5] What are the origins of this quintessentially American figure?

[1] Lou Cannon, *Reagan* (New York: Putnam, 1982), p. 18.

[2] Frank Van Der Linden, *The Real Reagan* (New York: Morrow, 1981), pp. 25–26.

[3] Cannon, *op. cit.*, p. 18.

[4] *Ibid.*

[5] *Ibid.*, p. 20.

Ronald Reagan's father, Jack, was a rebellious first-generation Irishman who made his living as a shoe salesman and who had a weakness for drink. In a poignant passage from his memoirs, *Where's the Rest of Me?*, Reagan recalls how, on one winter night, he found his father dead drunk, lying on his back on the front porch: "Seeing his arms spread out as if he were crucified—as indeed he was—his hair soaked with melting snow, snoring as he breathed, I could feel no resentment against him."[6] Yet the man had character. On one occasion, after a full day of selling, father and son checked into the only hotel in a small Illinois town. "You'll be comfortable here," the innkeeper confided to Jack Reagan, "we don't let Jews in here." Infuriated, the older Reagan left the hotel and he and his young son spent the winter night in their car. "He came home with pneumonia," Reagan recalls about his father in his autobiography, "and later had the first of his heart attacks that eventually caused his death."[7]

Nelle Wilson Reagan was "a natural practical do-gooder" who devoted her life to her alcoholic husband and her two sons, as well as to her charitable duties and goodwill trips. "My mother was always finding people to help," Reagan writes. In her spare time, however, she took the two children to the theater and encouraged young Ron to take drama classes in high school. Although deeply committed to the Protestant work ethic, Nelle Reagan always found time for beauty and regeneration.

In the opinion of one perceptive biographer, Reagan's childhood instilled in him a deep fear of dependency and a fierce commitment to autonomy and self-reliance.[8] Living in fear of his father's uncontrolled behavior may have placed an extraordinary premium on self-mastery in his own life and in the life of the nation. It is true, of course, that most Americans cherish freedom and independence as much as Reagan does, but they do not share his exaggerated fears that only fundamental changes at home and abroad can preserve these values. His alcoholic father may have left him with little room for moderate feelings about self-mastery and dependency. People were either fully free or they were wholly

---

[6] Ronald Reagan, *Where's the Rest of Me?* (New York: Duell, Sloane, Pearce, 1965), p. 17.

[7] Van Der Linden, *op. cit.*, p. 40.

[8] Robert Dallek, *Ronald Reagan: The Politics of Symbolism* (Cambridge: Harvard University Press, 1984), p. 16.

unfree. There was no middle ground. In Theodore White's words, "Reagan is no intellectual, but he has ideas and these ideas, simple and stubborn, are compulsive for him."[9] Thus, "the ideology of individual freedom, conventional morality, patriotism, and passionate anti-communism reflected Reagan's deepest emotions."[10] The welfare state symbolized dependency at home, and Soviet totalitarianism stood for its malignant expression and threat from abroad.

Reagan's first chance to become a hero in public presented itself during his freshman year at Eureka College. When the school ran out of funds and the president proposed a drastic reduction in courses that juniors and seniors needed for graduation, young Reagan presented a strike plan that ultimately forced the president to resign. "Hell," Reagan recalled, "with two more lines I could have had them (his fellow students) riding through every Middlesex village and farm without horses yet."[11] The students won and "Eureka got back into the business of education."[12] Young Reagan had not only struck a blow for freedom, but had discovered that his words could inspire a crowd.

Reagan's need to be the "good guy" and the hero manifested itself with great consistency in his career as movie actor. Biographer Lou Cannon points out that in Reagan's fifty-three films, he played the part of the villain only once. And he repeatedly expressed regret that he ever made that picture.[13]

In light of the preceding, it is not surprising that Reagan's earliest political idol was Franklin Delano Roosevelt. In his youth, Reagan was a very emotional New Dealer. Roosevelt's exhortation, made in the depth of the Depression, that the nation had "nothing to fear but fear itself" probably appealed to Reagan less as an economic message than as a call for courage and self-renewal. FDR, after all, had overcome a crippling personal dependency and helped the nation regain its self-confidence. In Reagan's psyche, Roosevelt might have been the heroic father young Ron had never had.

[9] Theodore White, *America in Search of Itself* (New York: Harper & Row, 1982), pp. 384–386.

[10] Dallek, *op. cit.*, p. 58.

[11] *Ibid.*, p. 18

[12] *Ibid.*

[13] Quoted in Dallek, *op. cit.*, pp. 19–20.

Even though as president, Ronald Reagan no longer approved of Roosevelt's New Deal programs, "his style, his metaphors, and his speeches were the offspring of FDR's."[14] On the deepest level, Reagan probably resonated with Roosevelt because he shared with him an affinity for rescuing others from dependency and defeat.

In the speech that put him on the political map—his keynote address on behalf of Barry Goldwater in 1964—Ronald Reagan used Roosevelt's metaphors. "You and I have a rendezvous with destiny," he told his audience. "Either we accept the responsibility for our own destiny or we abandon the American Revolution."

When, in the late 1940s, Reagan began his career as a radio sportscaster in Davenport, Iowa, he discovered how important it was to be liked. It was not enough to be a hero, one had to be a nice guy, too. This was the beginning of his public style—an amazing combination of crusading zeal leavened by a nonaggressive conciliatory personal manner. Unlike Woodrow Wilson or Barry Goldwater, who were unable to compromise, Reagan always sensed with the intuition of the actor when he was in danger of losing his audience. Shortly after World War II, for example, he joined a number of liberal causes, including the United World Federalists. When these causes became unpopular and he suspected that they were being exploited by Communists, he quickly made an about-face and, with equal zeal, became a conservative. As an actor, he was extremely active in the Screen Actors Guild and believed that he had personally prevented a Communist takeover of the movie industry.[15] Yet, and this is a critical point, he never engaged in the red-baiting and character assassinations that many of his colleagues pursued at the time in order to save their own careers. In fact, he helped remove the name of Nancy Davis—the future Mrs. Reagan—from a Hollywood blacklist because he believed her to be a loyal American. Thus, Reagan was never trapped into rigidity by his crusading convictions. His personality saved him from that fate. That is why it is quite possible to disagree violently with Reagan's ideas, while still liking the man personally. And that is why, as president, Ronald Reagan would walk away from failures without apparent damage to his popularity. Heroes who are nice guys are more easily forgiven. It was better to be a flexible heroic

[14] Cannon, *op. cit.*, p. 32.
[15] Dallek, *op. cit.*, p. 23.

FDR than a Woodrow Wilson, who was ready to stand or fall by his crusade.

This personal "grace under pressure" was never more evident than after the president was shot and wounded in 1981. "Honey, I forgot to duck" became a classic, as did the statement made to his doctors before surgery that "they better be Republicans." Less well known, but even more impressive, is the story recounted by one of Reagan's biographers of how the hospitalized president, still weak from surgery, got down on his hands and knees to mop up some spilled bathwater, so that his nurse would not get into trouble.[16]

And thus, this American folk hero rode to the rescue of California in 1967 and to the rescue of his country in 1981.

In light of this background, it is not surprising that Ronald Reagan brought to the presidency an extremely negative view of the Soviet Union. Of all American presidents, his perception was probably the darkest and his rhetoric the harshest. A few examples will serve to make the point. In his first press conference in 1981, Reagan called the USSR a nation ruled by men who "reserve unto themselves the right to commit any crime, to lie, to cheat." A few months later, he told an audience of West Point cadets that the Soviet Union was an "evil force." And in March 1983, in an address to a conference of Christian fundamentalists in Orlando, Florida, the president referred to the USSR as the "focus of evil in the modern world . . . an evil empire."[17]

Not only was the Soviet Union evil, but it would not last much longer. "The West won't contain Communism, it will transcend Communism," the president told the graduating class of the University of Notre Dame in 1981. He continued, "Communism is a bizarre chapter in human history whose last pages are even now being written." And in June 1982, Reagan declared before the British Parliament that "the march of freedom and democracy (would) leave Marxism-Leninism on the ash heap of history." The Soviet experiment was in the process of full decay.

Ronald Reagan seemed more interested in seeing the USSR in the dustbin of history than actually seeing the country for himself.

---

[16] Cannon, *op. cit.*, p. 406.

[17] Speech to the National Association of Evangelists, Orlando, Florida, March 8, 1983.

When Leonid Brezhnev died in 1982, after eighteen years of rule, the president did not see fit to attend his funeral. And when his successors, Yuri Andropov and Konstantin Chernenko died, once again Reagan chose not to go to Moscow. At age seventy-four, Ronald Reagan had yet to visit the Soviet Union for the first time in his life.

In August 1984, Ronald Reagan made an interesting slip that may have revealed his deep-seated anti-Communist mind-set.

While testing his voice before a radio broadcast, he jokingly made the following off-the-record announcement: "My fellow Americans, I am pleased to tell you I just signed legislation which outlaws Russia forever. The bombing begins in five minutes."

To dismiss this example of presidential playfulness as merely tasteless humor may be a bit too generous. Nor, on the other hand, did it prove that the president was a warmonger. What the slip probably did reveal was a profound unconscious prejudice against the Soviet Union. All the more reason why a visit to Russia might have been useful and might even have served as a corrective.

Not only did the American president perceive the Soviet Union as an "evil empire," but he tended to regard leftist movements in the Third World as tentacles of the USSR. Guerrillas in El Salvador and the Sandinistas who ruled Nicaragua were both direct extensions of Soviet ambition. Poverty and social inequality were seen as far less important causes for unrest in those areas than Soviet revolutionary subversion. Hence, in El Salvador, Reagan supported the government against guerrillas, and in Nicaragua he supported guerrillas against the government. The president's perceptions of communism did not allow for nuances and shadings. It was "us against them," good against evil. In Ronald Reagan's universe, Joseph Stalin had never died.

The Soviet leadership probably hoped at first that Ronald Reagan would turn out to be another Richard Nixon: tough in his rhetoric, but pragmatic in his actions. Brezhnev, in his final year, was quickly disabused of this notion. Hence, fearful that the United States might try to detach Poland from the Soviet orbit in a "rollback policy" reminiscent of John Foster Dulles, Brezhnev used a Soviet-trained Polish general to declare martial law in Poland and to outlaw the Solidarity union.

On September 1, 1983, a dreadful tragedy occurred that no

doubt confirmed the perceptions of the American president. The Soviets shot down a Korean airliner on a night flight to Seoul with a loss of 269 civilian passengers. Even though the plane had over-flown Soviet air space for more than two hours, and the decision to destroy it had apparently been taken by a regional Soviet commander without Politburo authorization, the barbarism of this act went a long way to poison Soviet-American relations even further. Self-righteous "explanations" about "American spy planes" and the "sanctity of Soviet air space" only increased American wrath. Name-calling reached a peak after this catastrophe. President Reagan and Secretary of State George Shultz both described the USSR as an international outlaw. Andrei Gromyko, a senior Soviet diplomat, not only failed to apologize for this example of mass murder, but announced that the Soviet Union would do it again if its air space were violated. Thus, the Amerian leader's devil image and the Soviet leadership's wooden-headedness combined to drag the relationship to its lowest ebb since the bleakest days of the cold war.

Three weeks after the Korean disaster, Yuri Andropov, the former KGB boss who now ruled the Soviet Union, delivered a major policy statement. In this document, Andropov in effect accused Reagan of killing détente. "Even if someone had any illusions about the possible evolution for the better in the policy of the present U.S. Administration," Andropov declared, "the latest developments have actually dispelled them."[18] A few weeks later, Soviet diplomats and "Americanologists" such as Georgi Arbatov began to compare Ronald Reagan to Adolf Hitler. The door-slamming and bridge-burning rhetoric continued on both sides, almost to the time of Andropov's death in February of 1984.

Beginning in early 1984, the president, apparently for domestic and political reasons, adopted a somewhat more conciliatory tone. In his State of the Union address in January 1984, he "reached out" to the Soviet Union. Yet, he made a gross historical error. "Our two countries have never fought each other," he declared. Apparently, he had never heard of the American intervention in 1918, designed to bring down the new Soviet regime of V. I. Lenin. And again in May, in a speech before the Irish Parliament, he appealed to Moscow to reduce tensions.

[18] Foreign Policy Statement by Yuri Andropov.

Yet a great deal of damage had been done. Neither side had found the courage to say "I am wrong" on a single issue. Worst of all, both sides were to blame for endangering the future of the planet and of generations yet unborn, for this breakdown in diplomacy had spilled over into the vital area of arms control.

When two countries despise and distrust each other as thoroughly as the United States and the Soviet Union did in the early 1980s, diplomacy itself becomes militarized. Arms control then becomes not a genuine search for reductions, but a competitive jockeying to gain an advantage over the adversary. Every proposal contains a "joker" which makes the package unacceptable to the other side. The result is not reduction, but mutual escalation.

The Soviet Union's greatest fear during the early 1980s was that the United States would implement a 1979 NATO decision to place more than 500 Pershing and Cruise missiles into Western Europe in order to balance Soviet SS-20 missiles, which were aimed at Western European targets. In late 1981, President Reagan proposed the so-called "zero option," offering not to deploy the American missiles if the Soviets dismantled theirs. After two years of intensive bargaining, the Soviets rejected the "zero option," claiming that it would still leave French and British nuclear missiles aimed at the Soviet Union and thus give NATO a net advantage. Even a much publicized "walk in the woods" near Geneva in late 1982, by Paul Nitze and Yuli Kvitsinsky—the two main arms negotiators—was not able to break the impasse.

In early 1984, the United States began to deploy the Pershings and Cruises in several European countries. Reagan declared that the United States had to have something to bargain with, apparently expecting the Soviets to negotiate more intensively at the table. Instead the Soviet team simply walked out and broke off all negotiations.

In the matter of controlling strategic intercontinental missiles, the president proposed a START program which stalled almost immediately. He also pushed vigorously for two new arms initiatives: First he proposed deployment of the MX missile, which he named the "peacekeeper." The MX is an intercontinental missile equipped with ten warheads, each of which can carry several hundred times the explosive power of the bomb dropped on Hiroshima and each of which can be released in flight at different times and at different targets. It was difficult for the Soviets not to perceive the MX as a first-strike weapon. Second, in early 1983, the president gave an address, quickly dubbed the "Star Wars" speech, in which he advocated placing laser beam stations in space designed as shields to abort a possible Soviet missile attack. Reagan described this "Strategic Defense Initiative" as purely defensive. His hope was that it would ultimately render nuclear weapons obsolete. Scientists were divided over whether the SDI was technologically feasible. The concept was immediately attacked by the Soviet leadership, which perceived the "shield" as a thinly disguised American plot to hit the USSR first without suffering a retaliatory strike. Yet another Reagan plan to "build down" nuclear arms by trading in two obsolete weapons for each new one was rejected by the Soviet Union as a design to modernize the American arsenal, not to reduce it.

By 1984 there were no negotiations between the two superpowers on virtually anything, including arms control. Konstantin Chernenko, Andropov's successor, apparently remembering the American boycott of the Moscow Olympics in 1980, decided to boycott the American Olympics in Los Angeles in 1984. The atmosphere was as icy and dangerous as it had been in the darkest days of the cold war.

Neither side had reason to be proud of its record in the early 1980s. The American president was a crusader who shunned the pragmatism and more businesslike approach of most of his predecessors. All three Soviet leaders—Brezhnev, Andropov, and Chernenko—responded with a good deal of sanctimonious rigidity. Neither side was able to say the liberating phrase: "You have been wrong, but I too have made mistakes," or to echo the words of President John F. Kennedy of a quarter century before: "Let us begin."

President Reagan's landslide electoral victory in November 1984, however, was to become a turning point in U.S.-Soviet relations. Apparently eager to leave behind him a legacy of peace, the president agreed to reopen a new dialogue with the Soviet Union. In January 1985, Secretary of State George P. Shultz and Soviet Foreign Minister Andrei Gromyko met in Geneva and agreed to begin negotiations on all aspects of offensive, defensive, strategic, intermediate, and space weapons. "It's my hope that this week's meeting in Geneva, while only a single step, is the beginning of a new dialogue between the United States and the Soviet

Union," the president declared.[19] "The Soviet Union is prepared to go its part of the road," the Soviet foreign minister responded. At a news conference in Washington, the president was asked if the agreement to resume arms control negotiations with the Soviet Union might lead to a new era of détente. "Yes," replied the man who had, in effect, removed the term from the White House lexicon. "We would welcome such a thing as long as it was a two-way street."[20] What accounts for the differences between Reagan I and Reagan II?

In the first place, the president did not really change his mind on the MX or on Star Wars. He remained convinced that only American strength had made the Soviet Union return to the negotiating table. It was his belief that in order to sign a good treaty with the Russians, one had to be prepared to have no treaty at all. Therefore, a policy based on military strength had to be continued. Yet, with an eye on the history books, the president now became concerned about his image. Unlike Lyndon Johnson, who destroyed his presidency in the jungles of Vietnam, Reagan never risked his popularity. His need to be a "nice guy" and a winner as president of the United States was as powerful as his need to be a hero in the movies of his past. Hence, when his foreign policy became unpopular, as it did in Lebanon, or when his rhetoric toward the Soviet Union became so harsh that nuclear war seemed a real possibility, the president pulled back. He removed the American marines from Beirut and "reached out" to the Soviet Union. In the spring of 1985, he extended an invitation to Mikhail Gorbachev, the new Soviet leader, to visit the United States. This flexibility enabled him to walk away from failures with very little damage and to be reelected by a landslide. Americans were more likely to forgive mistakes made by "nice guys" with whom they could identify than blunders made by stubborn men prepared to stand or fall on principle. Reagan thus became a kind of "Teflon President," nothing bad would stick to him. His shallow knowledge of foreign policy often snared him into serious errors, but he was never trapped as Lyndon Johnson was. The crusader and the actor inhabited his soul in equal measure.

Reagan II from 1985 to 1988 was a very different man from Reagan

[19] *The New York Times,* January 13, 1985.
[20] *Ibid.*

I. The catalyst of that change was Mikhail Gorbachev, who, at fifty-four years of age in 1985, was the first Soviet leader younger than the Soviet state itself.

The relationship between these two men ushered in a new détente between the superpowers that went far beyond that of the Nixon-Brezhnev years. It led to five summits, in Geneva, Reykjavík, Washington, Moscow, and New York; the first arms reduction treaty in history; a Soviet pullout from Afghanistan, and a pronounced turn for the better in Soviet-American relations.

The reasons for these remarkable developments were complex. Reagan faced a growing concern for his historical legacy and a first exposure to a pragmatic, reasonable, and even likable Soviet leader. Gorbachev had an overriding need to modernize a backward economy and thus divert money and brainpower from a top-heavy military sector. The results of this fortunate conjunction of personalities and objective factors were far-reaching. They hold out the promise of an end to the cold war.

For decades, Americans had perceived Soviet leaders as aging men waving feebly from the Kremlin walls or scowling at the United States while saying, "*Nyet.*" During Ronald Reagan's first term, Comrade Death became a growing embarrassment to the Soviet Union. As Brezhnev, Andropov, and Chernenko died in rapid succession, Red Square began to resemble a giant funeral parlor. But when, at last, in March 1985, Andrei Gromyko nominated "that man with the nice smile who has iron teeth" to the most powerful post in the Soviet Union, that of General Secretary of the Communist party, a spring thaw began to melt the glacial ice of decades. A child of the post-Stalin generation was now at the helm of the Soviet Union: Mikhail Gorbachev, who, with a beautiful and outspoken wife by his side, was to become a kind of Communist John F. Kennedy.

Born in 1931, young Mikhail did not have an easy childhood. As a youngster, he lived through several years of Nazi occupation and worked as a combine driver on a state farm. When Stalin's reign of terror came to an end in 1953, Gorbachev was a law student at Moscow University. As a young party apparatchik, he attracted Nikita Khrushchev's attention through his competence and efficiency in the Stavropol region. After Khrushchev's demise, he was promoted by Leonid Brezhnev, moved to Moscow, and soon became a member of the Central Committee of the Communist party. After Brezhnev's death, Yuri Andropov co-opted him as a special protégé, as did Konstantin Chernenko a year later. After the latter's death in March 1985, the remaining members of the old guard in the Kremlin decided not to bet against the actuarial tables any longer and took a chance on young Gorbachev.

The new Soviet leader moved quickly to consolidate his personal power. His principal rival for the top job, Leningrad Party boss Giorgi Romanov, went into sudden retirement. By mid-1985, Gorbachev had embarked on his double-track policy: economic modernization and reform at home and arms reduction with the United States abroad. On November 21, 1985, Reagan and Gorbachev met for the first time face-to-face in Geneva. The meeting was cordial, and the two men agreed that a nuclear war could never be won and must never be fought. At the same time, Gorbachev announced his plans for a dramatic restructuring of Soviet society, or *perestroika*, in an atmosphere of greater political openness, or *glasnost*. These two Russian words were to become symbols of a new Gorbachev era.

The most important element of Gorbachev's *perestroika* was to be economic modernization. The USSR, the new Soviet leader said, must become a *real* superpower. Implicit in that phrase was an amazing confession: Take away the Soviet Union's missiles and men under arms, and it would be a Third World country.

And, indeed, this was true. The Soviet economy was a dinosaur of inefficiency. In early 1986, for example, it was reported that the Soviet Union had exported 30,000 automobiles to Romania. A Romanian inspector, however, discovered to his chagrin that every key of each Soviet automobile fitted every ignition. Needless to say, the cars had to be shipped back to Russia. Stories of this kind convinced Gorbachev that, unless the bloated Soviet bureaucracy was streamlined and the economy modernized, the only country in the world that would continue to regard the Soviet Union with admiration might be Albania.

But the price of economic reform at home was arms control abroad. A breathing spell was needed from all-out military competition with the West. Hence, when Reagan and Gorbachev met for their second summit in Reykjavík, Iceland, in late 1986, Gorbachev decided to try a high-risk gamble. When alone with the American president, Gorbachev pulled four typewritten pages from his briefcase that outlined a sweeping proposal: The Soviet Union was prepared to destroy 50 percent of its strategic missiles if the United States would do the same and limit the testing of the Strategic Defense Initiative (SDI) to the laboratory. Reagan, who had expected a modest Soviet initiative limited to missiles in Europe, responded by rejecting the proposal, since, in his view, it would kill the SDI.

Suddenly, almost overnight, the initiative in arms control had passed to the Soviet Union. For decades the Americans had said yes and the Russians had said *nyet*; now, for all the world to see, a Soviet leader came up with creative arms control proposals, and the Americans were rejecting them. One leading scholar offers a good analysis of this reversal:

> Americans used to come to the table as if arms control were poker, with the U.S. as the dealer, while the Soviet Union played it as plodding defensive chess. Gorbachev changed all that. In terms of poker, he shuffled the deck, dealt himself new cards, upped the ante, bluffed and called. In terms of chess, he played with the aggressive, unorthodox, intuitive style of the new Soviet champion, Gary Kasparov.[21]

The collapse of the Reykjavík Summit did not stop Gorbachev. Believing that the SDI might ultimately be killed by the American Congress anyway, for technological and financial reasons, he now began to concentrate on a more modest objective: the signing of an intermediate-range nuclear forces (INF) treaty with the United States.

Actually, this "zero option" had originally been President Reagan's idea. As early as 1981, Reagan had proposed the elimination of an entire class of Soviet missiles in exchange for the withdrawal and destruction of the American missiles then deployed in Europe. Brezhnev had rejected the idea, but now, by 1987, it became the centerpiece of a third superpower summit to be held in Washington. To Gorbachev, the "zero option" made sense. It had long been an objective of Soviet policy to prevent NATO from surrounding the Soviet Union with nuclear missiles. Brezhnev had permitted this to happen. Gorbachev would get the missiles out.

Gorbachev's visit to Washington in December 1987 was a historic turn for the better in the forty-year struggle between the two

---

[21] Strobe Talbott et al., *Mikhail S. Gorbachev: An Intimate Biography* (New York: Signet, 1988), pp. 10, 11.

superpowers. Reagan and Gorbachev signed the first Soviet-American disarmament treaty in history. Sixteen hundred Soviet missiles and four hundred American missiles, all stationed in Europe, were consigned to the scrap heap under rigorous on-site verification procedures that made cheating next to impossible. Gorbachev agreed to this asymmetry in order to compensate for the vast superiority of Soviet conventional forces in Europe. Even though the total number of 2,000 missiles to be destroyed added up to only 4 percent of their combined arsenals of approximately 50,000, both men described the INF treaty as an auspicious beginning.

When it was all over, President Reagan declared that the meeting had "lit the sky with hope for all people of goodwill." Cold war rhetoric was giving way to frank discourse and personal rapport. Neither man forgot the vast ideological differences that separated them, but both staked out common ground on which to build for the future. The person closest to Ronald Reagan—his wife Nancy—probably described this evolving relationship better than anyone:

> There is good chemistry between the two men. They can talk candidly now and they do. They enjoy the one-on-one. I know Ronnie likes it, and Chairman Gorbachev likes it. They both understand there are big differences like Afghanistan and human rights. But they know where that point is beyond which they do not press each other. When they get there, they cool it.[22]

Ronald Reagan himself admitted to a change of heart before Gorbachev left Washington. In a television interview, Reagan recalled the Marxist goal of a one-world Communist state. But then he added: "All right, we now have a leader who is apparently willing to say that he is prepared to live with other philosophies in other countries."[23]

Rapprochement with the United States was not the only foreign policy task Gorbachev had set for himself. The other was rapprochement with his Eastern European allies, most of whom still remembered Khrushchev's invasion of Hungary, Brezhnev's invasion of Czechoslovakia, and the crushing of the Solidarity

---

[22] *Ibid.*
[23] *The New York Times*, May 29, 1988.

Union in Poland. Gorbachev traveled extensively in these countries, promoting *perestroika* and *glasnost* and pronouncing Stalin a
criminal. His efforts enjoyed a moderate success in these countries, and new jokes began to surface. In Poland, for example, the
story made the rounds that the Soviet government had issued a
commemorative stamp of Joseph Stalin. There was a problem with
the stamp, however: it did not stick very well because people kept
spitting on the wrong side. In Czechoslovakia, someone asked the
question: "What is the definition of a string quartet?" Answer:
"The Leningrad Symphony Orchestra after a tour of the United
States."

In East Germany, on the other hand, Stalinism was still so
deeply rooted that Gorbachev's new book, *Perestroika*, was not
translated into German. The authorities feared that Gorbachev's
recommendations for reform were so far-reaching that they might
threaten the stability of the entrenched Communist regime in
East Germany.

Ronald Reagan, for his part, had begun to realize that the
Soviet Union was a real place with real people, not an abstraction
from the memory of a movie actor who had grown up during the
times of Lenin and Stalin. Impressed by yet another Gorbachev
concession—a military pullout from Afghanistan—Reagan decided, for the first time in his life, to see Soviet Russia for himself.
In May 1988, the seventy-eight-year-old president and his wife
visited Moscow. During this fourth summit, the emphasis was not
on arms control but on human rights. The American president
spoke about freedom of speech, religion, and emigration, and met
with prominent dissidents as well. His hosts were not thrilled at
being lectured to in their own country, and Georgi Arbatov, the
Kremlin's leading Americanologist, wondered out loud how President Reagan would respond if Chairman Gorbachev were to set
up a field kitchen in New York City and ladle out soup to New
York's homeless. Yet, even though the two leaders struck sparks off
one another, the cordiality of their relationship remained unim-
paired.

There was a bit of progress on arms control as well. The United
States Senate ratified the INF Treaty on the eve of the Moscow
Summit by an overwhelming vote of 93 to 5. This vote strengthened the hands of both leaders, even though little headway was
made on the main objective, which was to cut Soviet and Amer-

ican strategic arsenals in half. Verification obstacles, such as permitting Soviet inspectors access to missiles stationed on American submarines, prevented a breakthrough on a Strategic Arms Reduction Treaty (START).

Nonetheless, both leaders agreed that progress had been made. Gorbachev announced that "the age of disarmament ha[d] begun." And President Reagan retracted his statement made five years earlier that the Soviet Union was an "evil empire." When queried by reporters why he had changed his mind, the president responded that the "evil empire" belonged to "another time, another era" and that Gorbachev was "a serious man committed to serious change."

On balance, perhaps the most important result of the first four summits between the two leaders was this: Both men declared at the first summit in 1985 that nuclear war was no longer a viable option for the superpowers, and by the time of their fourth meeting in Moscow three years later, they meant it.

Mikhail Gorbachev's farewell visit to Ronald Reagan in New York in December 1988 was no doubt his most dramatic. In an eloquent and audacious speech before the United Nations, the Soviet leader offered a sweeping vision of a "new world order" for the twenty-first century, including specific initiatives on a variety of Western concerns such as Afghanistan, emigration, and human rights. Most compelling was a unilateral decision to reduce, within two years, the total Soviet armed forces by 10 percent; withdraw 50,000 troops from Eastern Europe; and cut in half the number of Soviet tanks in East Germany, Hungary, and Czechoslovakia. What was memorable about Gorbachev's address was not only the package of specific proposals but also his departure from the shopworn slogans and ideological dogmas that had driven Soviet foreign policy for more than half a century. "Today the preservation of any kind of closed society is hardly possible," he declared.

This statement was put to the test the very day after Gorbachev uttered it, when a powerful earthquake hit Soviet Armenia, destroying several cities and killing more than 50,000 people. The Soviet leader immediately returned to his homeland to lead the rescue effort. Significantly, however, with *glasnost* well entrenched, the magnitude of the disaster and its consequences were relayed promptly to the West, and Moscow accepted help from abroad—even from the United States, which it had not done since the days of World War II. This reaction stood in sharp contrast to Moscow's response to the Chernobyl nuclear disaster of March 1986, during which the Soviet Union had shrouded itself in its traditional secrecy. Not surprisingly, the American response to the catastrophe in Soviet Armenia was open-hearted and generous. In 1986, the world was suspicious and angry; in 1988, it shared in the grief and helped as best it could.

As American leaders were quick to point out after they studied Gorbachev's speech, troop and tank reduction proposals still left the Soviet Union with a sizable margin of superiority in conventional military strength over the NATO countries. But what was perhaps more important than these numbers was the growing conviction in the United States that Gorbachev was not just seeking a breathing space but rather was actually seeking a fundamental change in the Soviet system. The big question in the West about the Soviet leader was no longer "Is he sincere?" but rather "Can he last?"

And, indeed, the philosophical base of Mikhail Gorbachev's speech made one wonder whether a Soviet leader could indeed have spoken those words. The following statements from his United Nations address could easily have been made by an American president. Here are some that are worth quoting:

> The use of threat of force no longer can or must be an instrument of foreign policy. . . . All of us, and primarily the stronger of us, must exercise self-restraint and totally rule out any outward-oriented use of force. . . . It is now quite clear that building up military power makes no country omnipotent. What is more, one-sided reliance on military power ultimately weakens other components of national security.

> It is also quite clear to us that the principle of freedom of choice is mandatory. Its nonrecognition is fraught with extremely grave consequences for world peace. Denying that right to the people under whatever pretext or rhetorical guise means jeopardizing even the fragile balance that has been attained. Freedom of choice is a universal principle that should allow for no exceptions. . . . As the world asserts its diversity, attempts to look down on others and to teach them one's own brand of democracy become totally improper, to say nothing of the fact that democratic values intended for export often very quickly lose their worth.

> What we are talking about, therefore, is unity in diversity. . . . We are not abandoning our convictions, our philosophy or traditions, nor do

we urge anyone to abandon theirs. But neither do we have any intention to be hemmed in by our values. That would result in intellectual impoverishment, for it would mean rejecting a powerful source of development—the exchange of everything original that each nation has independently created.

We are, of course, far from claiming to be in possession of the ultimate truth.[24]

Not only did President Reagan and President-elect George Bush warm up to Gorbachev, but so did the American people. According to a Gallup Poll, 65 percent of the respondents believed that the Soviet Union was undergoing major rather than cosmetic changes, and 76 percent believed that Moscow was now more likely to live in peace with its neighbors.[25] Perhaps most important, Americans began to perceive the Soviet leader as a real human being, not a cardboard figure saluting from the Kremlin Wall. As one New Yorker put it, "To me, he is more like a human being than the other people who have held power there. He showed more of a human side when he went home where he belonged to deal with the Armenian earthquake. He didn't go with politics." [26]

Roy Medvedev, the dissident Soviet historian, observed that Gorbachev's speech was the best of any world leader since John F. Kennedy. And indeed, there were parallels: the wit, the crowd appeal, and a latent dread that this man was risking too much and might be pushing his luck.

For forty years, the United States had proposed initiatives and successive Soviet leaders had scowled and said *nyet*. Now, Mikhail Gorbachev was proposing sweeping initiatives and the United States, delighted but taken aback, was saying maybe. By the time Ronald Reagan left office and President George Bush was sworn in, the entire choreography had changed.

By 1989, the pace of change accelerated as Communist regimes began to topple like ninepins all over Eastern Europe. In June, Lech Walesa's Solidarity Union won the first free election in Eastern Europe in forty years. Hungary followed suit as Imre Nagy, the prime minister who had presided over the failed revolt of 1956, received a hero's funeral and church bells tolled across the coun-

[24] *Time*, December 19, 1988, p.18.

[25] *The New York Times*, December 12, 1988.

[26] *The New York Times*, December 12, 1988.

try. In November, East Germany ceased to exist as the infamous Berlin Wall came down. Two weeks later, half a million Czechs converged in the heart of Prague, waving banners reading "Down with Communism." They succeeded as Václav Havel, a dissident playwright who had spent five years in Communist jails, became the nation's popular leader. And in December, Romania had its day when the people executed the tyrant Ceauşescu. Even Bulgarians and Albanians demanded their freedom. By 1990, no Communist governments remained in Eastern Europe and only four survived elsewhere: North Korea, Vietnam, China, and Cuba. The Communist military alliance known as the Warsaw Pact was disbanded and NATO, its Western counterpart, adapted its objective from military deterrence to political and economic integration.

There is no doubt that without the catalytic force of Mikhail Gorbachev none of this could have happened. When the old-line Communists appealed to the Soviet Union for help against their own peoples, Gorbachev made it abundantly clear that no Soviet tanks would roll in their defense as they had in Hungary in 1956 and again in Czechoslovakia in 1968. When the peoples of Eastern Europe realized this, there was nothing left to stop them; 1989 and 1990 became the years of people power.

Though utterly diverse in their cultures and heritages, Poles, Hungarians, Germans, Czechs, Romanians, Bulgarians, and Albanians seemed to follow the same script as they turned on their jailers. Some images of upheaval became unforgettable: Lech Walesa at confession outside the Lenin shipyards in Poland; Imre Nagy's posthumous rehabilitation in Budapest; Germans dancing atop the crumbling Berlin Wall; Czechs carpeting Wenceslas Square in Prague under swirling snow in their "velvet revolution"; and the Romanian flag with the hammer and sickle gouged out flying over the parliament building in Bucharest. People chanted "Freedom" in half a dozen languages. They did not always win, however. In Beijing there was another, more melancholy image: a lone man armed only with courage, facing down a column of tanks near Tiananmen Square. There, the old guard crushed the student protesters who had come to demand democracy. Still, 1989 was the year the Communist god failed in Eastern Europe. When it was over, the people had changed the course of history.

Gorbachev had not begun his journey in 1985 as the gravedigger of communism, but as a reformer. His concepts of *glasnost* and *perestroika* were designed to make the Communist system more decent and more efficient, not to dismantle it. Yet, in 1990, he began to be overtaken by events in his own country. The three Baltic republics of Lithuania, Latvia, and Estonia reminded Gorbachev of the fact that they had been forcibly annexed by Stalin in 1940. They now demanded their freedom. Later that year, in October, Germany was reunified after more than forty years of division. That historic event, too, would have been impossible without the cooperation of Mikhail Gorbachev, who acquiesced not only in Germany's continued membership in the European Community but in NATO as well.

At long last, the cry for freedom reached the epicenter of communism, Moscow itself, when the Russian parliament under its freely elected leader, Boris Yeltsin, declared its sovereignty. Suddenly, there were two Moscows: Moscow, the capital of the Soviet Union under Gorbachev as president, and Moscow, the capital of the Russian Republic under its own president, Boris Yeltsin.

History will probably show that the defection of Russia was the death knell of the Soviet Union. After all, the Russian Republic comprised 70 percent of the Soviet people and 70 percent of the USSR's resources. To that extent, Russia was the Soviet Union and when Soviet communism lost its very homeland, it was truly doomed.

In August 1991, in a desperate coup, eight hard-line Soviet Communists tried to turn back the clock. They managed to arrest Gorbachev but missed Yeltsin, who defied them by leaping on a tank and barricading the Russian parliament against the Soviet military. Three days later, the putschists gave up and people danced in the streets of Moscow and Leningrad. For the first time in their history, the Russian people, like the Eastern Europeans before them, had taken their freedom.

A chastened Gorbachev returned from his exile in the Crimea and promptly resigned from the Communist party. Soon, statues of Lenin came down all over the country. Leningrad was renamed St. Petersburg. The three Baltic states received their sovereignty, and the Soviet Union itself began to disintegrate as each of its twelve remaining republics demanded its freedom. Ukraine, the USSR's second-largest republic, declared its independence on December 1, 1991. Gorbachev now was president of an entity that existed as little more than a shadow of its former self. The old Soviet Union was fast becoming history.

On December 22, at a historic conference at Alma-Ata, the capital of Kazakhstan, eleven of the twelve remaining Soviet republics declared the Soviet Union dissolved and reconstituted themselves as the Commonwealth of Independent States. Georgia, the single holdout, did attend as an observer. On Christmas Day, Gorbachev, realizing that history had passed him by, reluctantly resigned his post as president. That same day, official burial rites took place in Moscow as the hammer-and-sickle flag of the USSR was lowered from the Kremlin and the red-white-and-blue emblem of the Russian people was hoisted up to take its place. The Soviet Union was no more.

Mikhail Gorbachev's miscalculation had been his belief that reform could be controlled from above. At some point, reform became revolution and assumed its own life. In the end, the dominant force he unleashed was the masses—vast crowds of students, workers, soldiers, peasants—in Moscow, Berlin, Warsaw, Budapest, Prague, Bucharest, and Sofia, united by the common goal of unloading their Communist masters and asserting their democratic liberties.

The cold war, too, was over. Only one superpower remained now, the United States. Or did it? The end of the cold war had overtones of cosmic irony. Over a period of forty years, at the cost of a 100,000 lives in Korea and Vietnam and trillions of dollars expended on deterrence, the United States had won. Yet the victor had bankrupted itself in the process. America had become the world's biggest debtor nation. As the Soviet Union went down in economic chaos and its people struggled for survival, there was to be no Marshall Plan. Japan and Germany, whom the United States had rescued after World War II, had now become its creditors.

With the glue of communism gone, nationalism became the driving force all over Eastern Europe. In Yugoslavia, it erupted into full-fledged civil war. Deep in the former Soviet Union, there were danger signals. Armenia and Azerbaijan went to war even in the midst of an earthquake, and fighting erupted in Georgia as well. And though the pace of nuclear disarmament quickened dramatically, with the Americans footing the bill for the destruction of huge quantities of Soviet missiles, thousands of nuclear weapons did remain in Russia, under the control of Boris Yeltsin.

The torch had passed, an era had ended. A Russian student, reflecting on Gorbachev, put it rather aptly: "He couldn't give us sausage," he said, "but he gave us freedom. And anyone who believes that the former is more important than the latter will probably wind up with neither."[27]

Like the Biblical Moses, Mikhail Gorbachev had led his people through the wilderness to the promised land of freedom. His tragedy was that he was allowed to glimpse it, but not to enter.

Unlike Gorbachev, Boris Yeltsin embraced the new future without ambivalence or doubt. On January 2, 1992, he freed up food prices all over Russia. Privatization of many state enterprises followed, and, by spring, even land could be bought and sold freely and peasants could grow whatever crops they chose. Russia's antiquated infrastructure creaked to a virtual standstill and the new Russian parliament became the scene of heated controversy. The winter that twice before had saved the Russian people from foreign invaders this time became their adversary. Desperately, Yeltsin's Russia looked to the West for help to save its fledging democracy.

In March 1992, former President Richard Nixon, now an elder statesman of 79, addressed the challenge in a letter to President Bush:

> While the communists have lost, we have not won until we prove that the ideas of freedom can provide the peoples of the former Soviet Union with a better life. We must enlist the same spirit that won the defensive battle against communism to win the offensive battle to ensure the victory of freedom. We must mobilize the West to commit the billions of dollars needed to give Russia's reforms a fighting chance to succeed.[28]

Unless the West acted with generosity and speed, Nixon warned, Russia might sink back into despotism and a new cold war would erupt.

On April 1, the leaders of seven industrial democracies rose to the challenge by announcing a $24 billion one-year program to help propel Russia toward democracy, including a contribution

[27] *The New York Times*, December 24, 1991.
[28] *Time*, March 16, 1992.

from the United States of nearly $4.5 billion. In announcements from Washington and Bonn, President Bush and Chancellor Helmut Kohl presented the program as a way for the United States and its allies to prevent economic collapse in Russia and to stop a new authoritarianism from rising from the rubble of the Soviet empire. The $24 billion was to include a $6 billion fund to stabilize the ruble, $2.5 billion in debt rescheduling, $4.5 billion in aid from the International Monetary Fund, and $11 billion in food, medicine, export credits, and other aid. In June, Bush and Yeltsin met in Washington and agreed to reduce long-range nuclear warheads by one-half. Both men made economic recovery their top priority.

The Russian challenge was profound. A nation with a centralized command economy had undertaken a program to transform itself into a market economy. Decades of Communist inertia and mismanagement would not yield easily to such a radical transformation. A Russian student captured the moment nicely. "Communism," he said, "is the largest and most painful road from capitalism back to capitalism."

At year's end, Russia's first freely elected president faced a serious challenge from the Congress of People's Deputies, Russia's parliament consisting of more than 1,000 delegates assembled from all over the Russian Federation. By a narrow majority, the Congress demanded the resignation of Yegor T. Gaidar, Yeltsin's appointee to the post of prime minister. Gaidar, who had been the chief advocate of a rapid transformation toward a free market economy, was replaced by Viktor S. Chernomyrdin, a more conservative figure who declared that he did not want Russia to become "a nation of shopkeepers" and that Russia needed "a market, not a bazaar."[29] Yeltsin himself managed to retain his job as president. The Russian people clearly did not wish to change course, but they wanted to slow down the tempo a bit. Little wonder. After seventy-five years of Communist dictatorship, there was little to guide Russia's leaders in their struggle toward democracy and a free market economy. The process could not be reduced to economic formulas because at its core was the search for a new way of thinking, an entirely new identity. And that search would entail a transition period between the collapse of inherited structures

[29] *The New York Times*, December 21, 1992.

and the growth of new ones, between a nostalgia for the enforced security of the past and the promise of freedoms as yet only vaguely understood.

In the larger perspective of history, Russia had been the object of two of the most extraordinary experiments in modern history. The first was the attempt to build a Communist society. The second is the effort—currently underway—to undo the enormous damage of the first, and to return Russia and the other splinters of the Soviet empire to the mainstream of history.

Perhaps the most important dividend of the demise of Soviet communism was the emerging amity between the new Russia and the United States. Now that the distorting lenses of Marxism-Leninsm were removed, Russians and Americans enjoyed a veritable honeymoon. Boris Yeltsin repeatedly affirmed his friendship for America. The era of Soviet vetoes in the UN Security Council was over. Russians remembered that the United States had been an ally in World War II and that the two countries had never been at war with one another. America was no longer the enemy; it had suddenly become a role model.

The most concrete manifestation of this new Russo-American amity was no doubt the signing of the START II Treaty by Presidents Bush and Yeltsin. On January 3, 1993, in Moscow, the two leaders, "recognizing the new realities that have transformed the political and strategic relations between the parties," put their names to the most sweeping disarmament treaty in modern history: They agreed to eliminate almost three-fourths of their nuclear arsenals, reducing the total number of strategic warheads from 22,500 to a considerably safer 6,500.[30] President-elect Bill Clinton gave his full support to the agreement. If the proposed cuts are carried out, Russia will be down to 3,000 warheads and the United States down to 3,500, roughly their levels in the 1960s before the advent of multiple-warhead missiles (MIRVs). In Yeltsin's view, the objective could be reached even earlier if the United States would be willing to contribute to the costs of the scrapping process.

By early 1993, there were still some serious obstacles to be overcome. Both Moscow and Washington made it clear that the missiles stationed in Kazakhstan, Byelorussia, and Ukraine, which

---

[30] *The New York Times*, January 4, 1993.

were included in the START II Treaty count, would have to be destroyed as well. Of these, Ukraine, uneasy about its far more powerful Russian neighbor, might wish to retain some of its nuclear arms. This problem may be a harbinger of things to come: the possible proliferation of nuclear weapons to splinter states that might be less responsible than was the former Soviet superpower. The only solution to this challenge would be a UN Nuclear Nonproliferation Treaty with enforcement capability.

The new Russo-American friendship was tested once again in the spring of 1993 when President Yeltsin, increasingly frustrated by the Russian legislature's efforts to slow down his economic reform program, plunged the country into a constitutional crisis. Yeltsin went over the heads of the legislators to the Russian people, demanding a popular referendum on his rule on April 25, 1993. This vote of confidence pitted the first popularly elected Russian executive in a thousand years against a parliament of legislators, most of whom had been appointed during the Communist era. The newly elected American president, Bill Clinton, promptly placed his support behind Yeltsin. Fearful that a Russian relapse into communism or a collapse into chaos might trigger a second cold war, Clinton met with Yeltsin in a "first aid summit" in Vancouver, British Columbia, in early April, exhorted him to win, and pledged $1.6 billion intended to show "immediate and tangible" support for the Russian president's economic reform program. Ten days later, at an emergency meeting in Tokyo, the world's seven leading industrial nations, including the United States, committed themselves to $28 billion in aid to Russia. Mindful of their earlier $24 billion pledge made in 1992 under the Bush administration, most of which had never actually been disbursed because of too stringent lending conditions, the seven Western nations agreed to funnel most of the new funds through the World Bank and the International Monetary Fund under considerably easier terms. Yet care was taken to save Boris Yeltsin's face and also to reassure American voters. In the words of the new secretary of state, Warren Christopher, "The U.S. effort to aid reform in Russia (was) in no way a program of charity, in no way a handout."[31] Christopher then urged even larger amounts of aid in the future, warning that "the world (would) be a considerably

[31] *The New York Times*, April 16, 1993.

more dangerous place if Mr. Yeltsin does not prevail."[32] The United States had placed itself squarely on the line for democracy and economic reform in Russia.

On April 25 democracy won a significant victory when the Russian voters expressed their confidence in Mr. Yeltsin's leadership as well as in his economic reform program by a sizeable majority. However, they did not endorse an early election to replace Mr. Yeltsin's major adversary, the Russian parliament. And in June, Yeltsin clashed again with the legislators when he tried to build a new Russian constitution with a strong presidency based on the model of France under Charles de Gaulle. Hence, the battle over who rules Russia was likely to continue.

These problems, grave though they may be, should not make us lose sight of the enormity of recent events. The cold war was over at long last. The West had won on a scale not even imagined by its most ardent visionaries. The Soviet Union, considered by most Americans a permanent fixture of the international landscape, had ceased to exist. Friendship and goodwill had begun to replace suspicion and hostility even though the recession weighing on the United States had made concrete help rather meager. The timing, in that sense, was poor. Russia would have to rediscover her soul with only little help from the outside. Yet, for the first time in her tortured history, the Russian nation was groping for a way to govern itself freely. Despite the terrible economic adversity in evidence all over the former Soviet Union, there was nonetheless a birth of freedom. The fear had gone; the terror had lifted. Russia had come out of the night.

[32] *Ibid.*

Part Three

THE ROLE OF PERCEPTION IN RUSSO-CHINESE RELATIONS

Chapter Fifteen

China and the Soviet Union: Perception and Reality

Machiavelli would have taken considerable pleasure in the dynamics of Sino-Soviet-American triangular relations in our time. During the 1950s, China and the Soviet Union were allies, and the United States feared the menace of a monolithic Sino-Soviet threat. In the 1960s, after the Cuban missile crisis had ushered in a détente between the Soviet Union and the United States, China began to fear the specter of Soviet-American collusion. And in the 1970s, the Soviet leaders began to worry that the Chinese and Americans might be getting along too well. Each of the three powers has had its turn at being frozen out by the other two.

During the early 1980s, as Soviet-American détente congealed into ice, Sino-American relations became increasingly warm. A relationship that had been based for an entire generation on fictions, anxieties, and fears once again showed signs of returning to a sense of reality. Needless to say, beasts did not turn into beauties overnight, and stubborn objective differences, such as the disposition of Taiwan, remained. However, the leaders of the two nations at last began to fashion their policies less on fears and more on facts.

Today, the Russo-Chinese relationship is cordial. Military posturing on both sides has given way to trade, economic, and even military cooperation. This turn for the better is largely due to the demise of the Soviet Union and the policies of Deng Hsiao-ping,

Mikhail Gorbachev, and Boris Yeltsin. In this chapter, I shall analyze the major phases of Sino-Soviet relations: first, the origins of the split; second, historical relations since the split; and finally, the birth of a new détente, which has carried over into China's relations with post-Soviet Russia.

ORIGINS OF THE SPLIT

Despite the plethora of recent information on the Sino-Soviet split, it continues to be difficult to present a definitive analysis of the many forces in world politics and of the specific Chinese and Russian factors that led to the pivotal rupture. The actual course of events is obscured not only by the sheer complexity of the developments themselves, but also by the desire of each party, after the fact, to emphasize the negative role played by the other in the exacerbation of the situation. The following therefore constitutes a limited analysis of the best-documented elements involved.

Viewed in a historic context, a long-term tension rooted in the beginning of interstate relations can be identified. The Treaty of Nerchinsk, signed in 1689 between Russia and the Manchu government, was the first Western-style border agreement in which a Chinese government participated. While the territorial disposition agreed upon at the time has since been hailed by the Chinese as "unequal," it is difficult to judge in retrospect the fairness of the agreement. What is evident is that, in the Chinese view, the treaties of Nerchinsk and Kiakhta marked the beginning of processes of foreign intercourse and incursion that were to culminate in the humiliating parcelization of China into spheres of influence by a number of foreign powers in the nineteenth century.

This historical experience has subsequently affected not only the self-image of China, but also presumably its perception of the Soviet Union. One would hesitate to extrapolate unduly from historical experience, yet it is more likely that relations with the Soviet Union were affected by these contacts in which the character, intentions, and power of that state were judged from the perspective of a China which was evolving from the "Middle Kingdom" to a semi-colony. Recent clashes between China and Russia both on the Ussuri River and on the border of Sinkiang-Kazakhstan were on one level a perpetuation of this interstate tension.

In addition to the nationalist tensions arising from China's experience as a weakened state, vulnerable to foreign pressures, a new historical tension was introduced with the founding of the Chinese Communist Party in 1921, together with the expansion of the Comintern into China. During this period, little mentioned in later accounts of the "split," the new Soviet government's two-pronged policy of assisting Sun Yat-sen in the formation of a unified Kuomintang (National People's Party) and army, and at the same time pressing its "United Front" tactics on the naissant CCP, was evidence for certain Chinese Communist leaders of the limits of Soviet support. The Shanghai Massacre of 1927 not only convinced the remaining CCP leaders of the perfidy of Chiang Kai-shek's Kuomintang (KMT), but also resulted in an increased sensitivity to the interdependence of Russian and Communist-Comintern interests in China.

While there is insufficient information to determine exactly what Soviet assistance was given to the CCP during the period of the early Soviets, such as Kiangsi and during the years in Yenan, even covert aid was generally assumed to have been minimal. The CCP had taken the path of peasant revolution about which Stalin was certainly less than enthusiastic, while the Soviet government, itself in the midst of domestic turbulence and the threat of war, had gone so far as to enter into a nonaggression pact with the KMT government, presumably as proof of its support for the Allied cause in the Pacific. By the time the CCP government had come into power in China in 1949, the Soviet government had two apparent credits: it was Communist, and it had assisted in the takeover of the northeast by surrendering Japanese troops in its occupied territories to the CCP rather than the KMT. Yet, even this one substantive gesture had been marred by the Soviet removal of entire plants from Manchuria, for the return of which the Chinese government would have to pay.

Although the People's Republic of China (PRC) government had little reason for fraternal feelings toward the power to the north and, in fact, had sufficient grounds to suspect strongly its ultimate intentions, the Chinese leadership quickly moved to cement relations with the Soviet Union. A protracted mission to the Soviet capital in 1950 led to the expressed statement that henceforth China would "lean to one side." Two basic factors seem to have determined this policy position which was to persist until

1959: the Chinese analysis of their own domestic imperatives and their sensitivity to the authority of the Communist movement, as embodied in Stalin.

On a purely nationalist level, China was a country that had suffered from decades of war, with consequent large-scale political and economic disruption. Although the Chinese leadership had, as a result of its wartime experiences, a good deal of faith in its ability to organize the population to begin the tasks of reconstruction, economic and technical assistance nonetheless appeared vital for the restoration and development of the Chinese nation. While in the long run such aid might have been forthcoming from other sources, both the urgency of the problem and the preferred methods for dealing with Chinese restructuring mitigated against gambling on alternative possibilities. While the United States had indeed refused to use its own troops to support the failing cause of the Chiang Kai-shek government, the extreme wariness of both the United States and the PRC toward each other made any détente between these two states unlikely in the volatile, developing cold war environment. A tentative effort to effect a rapprochement with the United States, made by Mao Tse-tung and Chou En-lai toward the end of the war through a visit to Washington, was rebuffed. More fundamentally, the climate prevalent in the United States in 1950, particularly the feeling that China had "been lost" to communism, virtually foreclosed reconciliation.

The Chinese perception of a Communist Russia and of Stalin reinforced this assessment of Chinese needs and options. A Communist China that was not allied with or even dependent upon the Soviet Union could only have been seen as a challenge to the Soviet role as the center of world communism, especially after the defection of Tito's Yugoslavia. By accepting the need for close relations between the two states, the Chinese apparently hoped to avoid sabotage against their efforts at national reconstruction, and to gain recognition for the acceptance of their own unorthodox road to power. Finally, whatever his past record in the Chinese case, Stalin was the political heir of Marx and Lenin, the leader of the first Socialist state—a man of great power and influence in the Chinese view—whose success in furthering the interests of Russia and of communism had endowed him with great authority in the eyes of the leaders of the fledgling state.

Association with the Soviet Union was thus desirable on

grounds of both ideology and circumstance. While the Chinese leadership had a positive view of its capabilities, it was at the same time extremely sensitive to the vulnerability of its position. Not only was economic expediency an important consideration, but the Chinese position as a state bordering on the Soviet Union made the situation all the more sensitive. Although the CCP leadership had good reason to be suspicious regarding the intentions of the Soviet leaders, they nonetheless were highly sensitive both to Stalin's position as the sage of world communism, to the legitimacy which the new régime could gain from such an alliance, and to the power and capabilities of the Soviet Union vis-à-vis China. In the same manner, in the Soviet view an association with the new Chinese state was both a practical way of defending its flank, somewhat countering increasing American influence in Asia, and of bringing a potentially unorthodox ideological brother under the wing of Soviet leadership. While the Soviet Union was convinced of its own overwhelming advantage in the event of any contretemps with the new state to the south, an equally overwhelming desire to consolidate both its border regions and its leadership within a united socialist bloc dictated a policy sympathetic to the maintenance of a Communist Chinese government. The suspicions and misperceptions between China and the United States that became so evident in the steps leading to involvement in the Korean War further underlined the objective convergence of Soviet and Chinese policies during the early 1950s.

As the Sino-Soviet relationship evolved, however, tensions quickly resurfaced, resulting both from changes within the two countries and from developments in the perceptions of the two leaderships of the course that international policies was taking. Even in the beginning, Soviet aid terms were not noticeably generous. As the Chinese government began to implement its programs successfully and consequently to gain in self-assurance regarding its ability to govern, the unwillingness of the Russians to pass on the technological know-how that might increase Chinese independence rankled progressively more. Chinese awareness of Soviet unwillingness to assist in the progressive achievement of the self-reliance of the Chinese state was eventually to be a crucial factor influencing the decision to risk a break with the Soviet Union. The importance of this factor is highlighted by the importance that the Chinese have subsequently given to the charge that in June 1959 the Soviet Union reneged on a pledge to assist China in acquiring nuclear capability.

The rise of Khrushchev, the shock of de-Stalinization, and the events in Poland and Hungary were to assist in casting the Soviet Union's leadership role in a new perspective. Although Khrushchev did not have, in the Chinese view, the authority of Stalin, he was the leader of the center of the Communist movement and of China's most powerful ally. But as the process set in motion by de-Stalinization came to fruition with uprisings in Eastern Europe, the Chinese leadership saw its own forecasts coming true, with a consequent great diminution in respect for the authority and even the legitimacy of Khrushchev as the ideological torchbearer of communism. The Chinese view of the dilution of Soviet "orthodoxy" encouraged embarkation on the Great Leap Forward as a Chinese road to communism, and this was understood by both parties as a declaration of independence from the Soviet Union's prerogative to lead.

By 1959 a number of incipient tensions between the two states had surfaced. In the first place, Khrushchev in July of that year had made evident his condemnation of the instrumentality of communes in a speech in Poznan, Poland, in which he expressly endorsed the collective as opposed to the communal approach to agricultural organization. Furthermore, at that time there was a crisis within the CCP itself, which resulted in the dismissal of P'ing Teh-huai, the Chinese Minister of Defense, a Politburo member, who was subsequently accused of having attempted to exert pressure on the course of Chinese domestic policy through discussions with various Soviet military leaders.

Although it is difficult to ascertain whether or not P'ing Teh-huai was, in fact, guilty of conspiring with elements of the Soviet leadership, it is nonetheless illuminating that the Chinese saw such contacts as threatening the continued pursuance of the Great Leap Forward. In fact, at this time each party began to appear sensitive to contacts between "dissident" elements within it own leadership group and leaders of the other state, as symbolized by the P'ing Teh-huai case. The recurring charges of mutual interference in each other's internal affairs indicated that other tensions between the two states both reflected and were exacerbated by the need to balance various interest groupings within the respective party leaderships. The attitudes of the Chinese military establishment may well have been particularly salient, as it has since been charged that every minister of defense to date had supported a policy of rapprochement with the USSR in the interest of a modern sophisticated defense system. It is thus possible to hypothesize that, by 1959, the Soviet Union had come to appear as a threat to the Maoist leadership group, both through its obvious disapproval of China's independent policy course and through its possible link with the "dissident" members of the Chinese leadership.

Finally, in the same year, Khrushchev stepped up his movement toward détente with the United States, a development that the PRC leadership perceived as being contrary to Chinese interests. The Chinese reaction to the Soviet posture on peaceful coexistence and the "spirit of Camp David" in 1959 is illustrative of the dynamics involved. Not only did the shift in posture from confrontation to coexistence reinforce Chinese doubts regarding the character of their former ally, raising questions about the limits of Soviet opportunism; in addition, the Soviet Union's desire to deal with its former enemy made its intentions vis-à-vis China even more suspect, especially with the latter reembarking on a more independent domestic course.

From the perspective of the Russian leadership, the Chinese alliance became increasingly burdensome as the Soviet Union moved into an era of peaceful coexistence. Not only did it become increasingly difficult to cement coordination in the security field between the two, but it had become more difficult and more burdensome to rationalize the shifts in Soviet policy in terms of orthodox Communist ideology and Chinese interests. At one and the same time, the Soviet leadership was being asked to condone the pursuance of a policy course outside of that proven by the Soviet experience while simultaneously adhering to a posture in international relations that would brook no deviance from the previous posture of confrontation.

In the Chinese view, several aspects of the relationship between itself and the Soviet Union had become increasingly evident in the course of events since 1950. First and perhaps foremost, the Chinese had become convinced of their ability to govern the PRC on a Chinese and Communist basis. In 1950 they had only been able to draw on their limited experience in mobilizing national sentiment during the Sino-Japanese War. By the early 1960s, however, they had become increasingly convinced of their capacity to meet the needs of the developing Chinese nation. With this self-assurance came an increased impatience with the attitude of Soviet tutelage.

Although there is no general agreement about whether the Great Leap Forward was initiated in a mood of optimism on the basis of past performance or as a result of dissatisfaction with accomplishments to date, it is evident that by this time the Chinese leaders had made a judgment that the Soviet model was insufficient for China's long-term development needs. Not only was the amount of actual economic assistance limited and a debit to be repaid, but an increasing recognition of the differences between the Soviet and the Chinese economic situations had occurred. As the Chinese strove to meet the demands of an overwhelmingly agricultural and underdeveloped society, they found the Russian experience and attitude increasingly irrelevant to their own problems. Even the debacles of the Great Leap were insufficient to convince the Maoist leadership that an independent course was not both desirable and necessary, if only to assure their own dominance within the CCP.

Finally, although the alliance had served the purpose of eliminating a military threat to the north, it seemed to have little effect on China's strategic position vis-à-vis its other borders. Closely tied with the Chinese desire for an independent nuclear capability, which would have greatly contributed to its importance as a regional power and therefore had been valued for its own sake, there was also the Chinese experience with the actual intentions of the Soviet Union when China was threatened by another nuclear power. Both during the Korean War and during the Taiwan Straits Crisis of 1958, the United States had threatened to use nuclear weapons against China. The fact that the Soviet Union had not made explicit a security guarantee of its own, but had instead requested that it be allowed to establish various types of military installations on Chinese territory, made not only the intentions but also the capabilities of the USSR as an ally suspect. While the PRC leadership had, if anything, overestimated Soviet capabilities in the post-Sputnik era, experience had apparently indicated that Soviet power would be severely restrained in any situation relating to the United States. Hence, during the entire period when a hostile U.S. alliance system posed the primary threat to Chinese security, the value of the "Soviet connection" seemed severely restricted.

As far as can be ascertained, by 1962 the "split," as it is now known, had become a fact. Within the historic intercourse between the two states, and the experiences of the brief decade or so of close alliance, lay most of the elements that were to continue to plague later attempts to improve relations between the two states.

BILATERAL RELATIONS SINCE THE SPLIT

Following the withdrawal of Soviet advisers from China and the more or less complete rupture of interparty relations between the two states, Sino-Russian intercourse continued to be marked by almost unremitting hostility, only superficially affected by the resumption of interstate negotiations. Both states continued to harbor an extreme distrust with regard to the intentions of the other. Each regarded itself as being both Communist and successful in developing its own natural resources and natural power position.

Each saw the other as trying to make explicit its adversary's limited capacity to influence both Communist and developing nations. While the PRC saw Russian military capabilities as being primarily oriented against China, the Soviet leadership saw the developing Chinese nuclear capability as being directed, first and foremost, against the Soviet Union.

The Great Proletarian Cultural Revolution in China marked a pause in the period of hostility between the two countries. Although there was in fact a continuation of the strident Chinese charges against the Russian leadership, probably reflecting an awareness of increased national vulnerability in a period of divisiveness and general upheaval, the force of the PRC's position was greatly diminished by its blatant disregard for all foreign relations and its "image" in general, as China turned in upon itself.

Beginning in 1969, in contrast, the increasing normalization of China's relations with a broad spectrum of states, its subsequent representation in the United Nations in 1971, and its increasingly active role in issues of global magnitude ushered in a new phase in bilateral relations characterized by an increase in competition and, hence, potential tension between the two states. Crucial to the increase in perceived competition was a necessary upgrading in the

USSR's assessment of the character, intentions, and capabilities of the PRC leadership, which appeared increasingly to be both willing and able to play the role of a major actor. At the same time, and particularly suspicious in the Soviet view, the only substantive signs of progress on bilateral relations were the exchange of ambassadors in 1970 and the beginning of negotiations regarding the demarkation of borders following clashes in the Ussuri area. As far as can be determined, these negotiations did not in fact settle outstanding territorial problems between the two states, but merely reopened an instrumentality of communication.

The bilateral relations between China and the Soviet Union continued to be marked by an almost irrational fear of the other's intentions and by a very rational knowledge that each was increasingly focusing its military capability on the other. Although neither apparently had anything really substantive to gain through upgrading the confrontation with the other, each gave the appearance of being a state which, because of its fears of encirclement, was pathologically unable to deal with an immediate neighbor of any power whose intentions and future actions were not highly predictable.

These limits to the desire to normalize bilateral relations further, particularly on the Chinese side, were made apparent in Leonid Brezhnev's address on the occasion of the fiftieth anniversary of the USSR. In this speech the Soviet leader stated that he could only view the Chinese allegation that they were disturbed by some threat emanating from the Soviet Union as being hypocritical, insofar as China had not replied to the USSR's proposal, repeatedly made since 1960, "to assume clear, firm, and permanent commitments ruling out an attack by one country on the other." Brezhnev went on to say that having neither territorial nor economic claims on the PRC, the Soviet Union wanted to see China a flourishing socialist power and to work shoulder-to-shoulder with her for peace, against imperialism, but that "when this is to come about depends on China herself." In fact, the making public of this Soviet proposal, obviously seen as a means of countering Chinese intransigence and hence an instrument of pressure, would support the view that the Soviet leadership was indeed the more interested of the two parties in achieving some type of détente. Nonetheless, in the same "leak," Brezhnev gave some indication of the price which the Soviet Union would exact.

For example, he singled out China's "great-power designs" as basic to "the line of fighting the USSR and, in effect, the entire Socialist community, which they continue to regard as the main obstacle. . . ." Brezhnev implied that the existence of an independent "Communist" power amounted to "continuous attempts to split the Socialist camp and the Communist movement, to foment discord among the fighters for national liberation, to range the developing countries against the Soviet Union and the other Socialist states." While this was never made explicit, it seems that only by joining with the other socialist states in recognizing the ultimate predominance of Soviet leadership in the foreign policy sphere could the Chinese leadership remove this perceived Soviet threat to socialist unity. In addition, the manner in which the Soviet leader characterized Chinese foreign policy pointed to the Russians' extremely ambivalent feelings with regard to Chinese détente with the United States. On the one hand, "it amounts to undisguised sabotage in an effort to limit the arms race and the struggle for disarmament and for a relaxation of international tension." Yet on the other hand, "it amounts to unprincipled alignments on anti-Soviet grounds with any, even the most reactionary, forces." From such a characterization it is evident that the Soviet leadership objected to any restraints placed upon its movements toward détente to the Western world, but that simultaneously, it viewed the apparent Chinese thrust toward normalizing its relations with the United States and other nonsocialist states, especially Western European countries, as being "anti-Soviet."

The Chinese leadership, in turn, may well have wished that a hostile nuclear power did not exist on its northern border, but as a state that had been subject to nuclear threats when aligned with that power, it was understandably suspicious of the overall value of any such guarantees. Even if the Chinese were willing, for the sake of concentrating on domestic developments, to forsake the acquisition of an independent nuclear capability, their security imperatives would have rendered such a decision unrealistic. Moreover, the fact that by 1973 the Soviet Union had massed close to fifty divisions on the Chinese border and had stationed troops in Outer Mongolia did little to allay Chinese suspicions.

In his report to the Tenth Party Congress in July 1973, Chou En-lai attacked the Soviet "fascist dictatorship" and asked the following question:

Must China give away all of the territory north of the Great Wall to the Soviet revisionists in order to show that we favor relaxation of world tension and are willing to improve Sino-Soviet relations?

Brezhnev replied, during a speech in Tashkent in September, that the Chinese leadership had not responded to the Soviet proposal for a nonaggression pact tendered the previous year in which both countries would promise not to attack each other by land, sea, or air "with any type of weapons" nor to threaten to attack. The Chinese leadership, in turn, responded by asserting that a nonaggression pact would be meaningless unless it became part of an overall settlement of outstanding issues between the two states, particularly the border issue.

In essence, it seems that the Chinese simply had little faith in Soviet intentions and probably considered Soviet military guarantees as marginal in value. The Soviets, in turn, were aware of their own vast military superiority and China's awareness of that fact. Most fundamentally, however, the more confident China grew as a national power, the less likely it was that she would ever again subjugate herself to an alien tutelage, Russian or otherwise.

The deaths of Mao Tse-tung and Chou En-lai did little to improve relations between Russia and China. In 1979, their successor Deng Hsiao-ping made the crucial decision to alter Mao's policy and to set China's course on the road to modernization. As the United States recognized the PRC officially, China moved even farther away from Russia. In 1980, she let a thirty-year friendship treaty lapse and broke off talks on improving ties with Russia. Instead, she seemed determined to use her new relationship with the United States to exert pressure on the Soviet Union for the recovery of Chinese territories. China and the United States came close to being partners in alliance. In Sino-Soviet relations, on the other hand, a complete about-face had occurred: from being close allies in 1950, these two nations had become adversaries by the year 1980. This was the price Soviet Russia had to pay for not undoing what czarist Russia had done more than a century before.

The ending of the Vietnamese war did not lack in irony. In 1978, Vietnam, now a Communist nation backed by the Soviet Union, invaded Cambodia, backed by China. Cambodia was virtually dismembered in the process. In 1979, China returned the compliment by invading Vietnam. In short, by the end of the decade, China and the Soviet Union were fighting a proxy war in Asia.

Soon after the American withdrawal from Vietnam, the only wars in Asia were those waged by Communists against other Communists.

The Soviet invasion of Afghanistan in 1980 proved to be a major watershed event in Asia. Not only did it move the United States much closer to China, but it further deepened the hostility between China and the Soviet Union. The Chinese leadership perceived the Soviet intervention near the Chinese border as a direct threat to its security. Mao Tse-tung's successors had obviously been proven right in their analysis of Asia: the Soviet Union proved to be a far greater threat in the long run than the United States.

In historical perspective, it is important to remember that the decade of the 1950s was the only period in the entire history of Chinese-Russian relations in which the two nations were closely allied. This ten-year aberration from a century-long pattern of national tension and territorial competition and even tutelage was in essence a response to a common enemy that, temporarily, was perceived as the greater threat: the United States. As this threat seemed to recede into the distance, the traditional animosities between China and Russia resurfaced and the relationship reverted to the more familiar historical enmity.

THE BIRTH OF A NEW DÉTENTE

During Ronald Reagan's first term, the United States and China came closer together than they had ever been since the victory of Chinese communism. Conversely, the distance between the United States and Russia became greater than it had been since the years of Stalin and the cold war. These dramatic changes, of course, affected the Sino-Soviet relationship as well.

From the Soviet perspective, the icy relations with the United States prompted a desire for "détente" with China. Moreover, the military stalemate in Afghanistan and the simmering crises in Poland and Eastern Europe in general awakened fears of a "two-front" conflict. In China's view, the top priority for the 1980s was the modernization of her economy. To achieve this goal, China needed peace on her borders and a breathing spell with Moscow. Thus, both countries were ripe for a tactical rapprochement with each other by the early 1980s.

Accordingly, in November 1982, Foreign Minister Huang Hua went to Moscow to attend Brezhnev's funeral and, following a lengthy meeting, Soviet Foreign Minister Andrei Gromyko announced that he was "quite optimistic" about the prospects for improving Sino-Soviet relations. The Soviets responded by offering talks about possible troop reductions along the border. The Chinese agreed to negotiate but cautioned that, in their judgment, "the talks would last a long time; they would be marathon talks."

In December 1984, China announced the signing of four new cooperation agreements with the Soviet Union, including the first long-term trade pact that the two Communist powers had negotiated in twenty-five years. Both Soviet and Chinese officials commented on the warm atmosphere that prevailed during the negotiations. One Soviet official even compared the situation to President Nixon's visit to Moscow in 1972, a trip that he said was important more for the fact that it had occurred and for its friendly atmosphere than for any notable political breakthroughs. "Now," Soviet First Deputy Prime Minister Ivan V. Arkhipov said, "our side has come, and although we have not overcome the big problems, the atmosphere has been changed."[1]

The principal reason for the new détente was the priority placed on domestic economic reform in both countries. Both Deng Hsiaoping in China and Mikhail Gorbachev in Russia began to pursue a peaceful international climate that would make it easier for them to divert resources to the industrial, agricultural, and consumer sectors. The Chinese welcomed Gorbachev's declared willingness to rely less on the threat of use of force in foreign policy. In their view, Gorbachev was making concessions on three issues that had inflamed Sino-Soviet relations in the past: (1) he was pulling out troops from Afghanistan; (2) he was reducing Soviet troop and missile deployment on the Chinese border; and (3) he no longer supported Vietnam's incursion into Cambodia. Moreover, the Soviet leader looked with admiration at China's economic reforms. After all, Deng was doing successfully what Gorbachev was hoping to achieve with *perestroika*. Hence, first gradually, and then with increasing speed, tensions on the Sino-Soviet border gave way to trade as Russians and Chinese in numerous border towns discov-

[1] *The New York Times*, December 30, 1984.

ered that they shared common interests. As one Soviet official put it: "Business is booming: we manufacture what they want, they grow what we want."

In 1988, Strobe Talbot, an American journalist, was permitted to tour the Sino-Soviet border. He vividly described what went on in Mudanjiang, a small Russian town on the Chinese border. Chinese and Soviet officials were traveling back and forth, comparing shopping lists, displaying wares, and negotiating barter deals. Since both countries had nonconvertible currencies and neither wanted to expend precious reserves of hard currency, no money changed hands. The Chinese supplied vegetables and textiles; the Soviets sent back cement, fertilizer, pharmaceuticals, and electrical machinery. Chinese traders made room in their sample cases for bottles of Mao-tai, not to sell, but to lubricate negotiations with the Russians. In the meantime, the Russians poured the Mao-tai, not from traditional samovars, but from colorfully decorated thermos bottles imported from China. A Chinese restaurant was doing a lively business, staffed and supplied from across the river. A group of Chinese fruit growers was welcomed by a brass band. As their spokesman put it: "Our Soviet neighbors would like to learn to produce melons the way we do here."[2]

Officials on both sides agreed that the volume of trade went up as military tensions went down. In 1969, Mao Tse-tung had ordered the urban populations of Northern China to dig tunnels and to store grain in preparation for a Soviet nuclear attack. Two decades later, the vast network of tunnels beneath the streets of Harbin was converted into a subway, and bomb shelters now serve as underground hotels and shopping centers.

All this is not to say that all tensions were eliminated along the Sino-Soviet border. Powerful military installations continued to exist, albeit at reduced levels. Perhaps one reason why the Sino-Soviet cold war never erupted into a major conflict was the fairly accurate perception each nation had of the other's military power. The Chinese had always been aware that they were no match for the vastly superior Soviet military apparatus, and the Soviets had learned sufficiently from history, including recent American history in Vietnam, the possible calamitous consequences of a major land war in Asia. And, at present, this realism is being strength-

[2] *Time*, July 18, 1988.

ened by "rice roots" and "grass roots" trading contacts by ordinary Chinese and Russian citizens along the world's longest border. The catalyst of this new détente no doubt was Mikhail Gorbachev. His reform program dictated peace not only with the United States but with China as well. Ronald Reagan changed his mind about the Soviets and so did Deng Hsiao-ping. One could now do business with the Russians. Sample cases began to displace military hardware on all sides. The banks of the Ussuri River, once the scene of bloody fighting between Chinese and Russians, now became the setting for brisk barter between profit-minded neighbors.

In May 1989, Mikhail Gorbachev visited Beijing, the first Soviet leader to do so in thirty years. He and Deng Hsiao-ping agreed to normalize relations. According to their joint communiqué, military forces along the Soviet border would be reduced to levels commensurate with "good-neighborly relations"; negotiations on a variety of boundary disputes would be pursued; and both sides would work to settle the Cambodia problem.

The Sino-Soviet summit was all but drowned in the clamor of the Beijing student uprising. Copies of Gorbachev's speech to the Chinese people were late in circulating because the copy-machine repairman was out demonstrating in Tiananmen Square with a million other protesters. To these huge crowds in Beijing, Mikhail Gorbachev had become the symbol of democracy. A strange twist of fate, indeed, that few Americans would have predicted.

The demise of Soviet communism and the ascendancy to power of Boris Yeltsin in Russia did not undermine the new Russo-Chinese détente. In fact, in 1992, Russia, badly in need of hard currency, sold weapons to China, including missile guidance technology. The Chinese were rumored to resell these weapons for a handsome profit to Iran, North Korea, and Pakistan. In December 1992, Yeltsin visited Beijing and signed twenty-four agreements with the Chinese covering cultural, trade, and scientific exchanges, food credits, the construction of a nuclear power plant, and the reduction of troops along the Russo-Chinese border. "Let's talk less and do more,"[3] Yeltsin said to his hosts before he left Beijing. And so, Russia's new capitalist president sold weapons to his Chinese Communist hosts so that they could both make some money for their countries. *Sic transit gloria mundi.*

[3] *The New York Times*, December 19, 1992.

A Communist historian was once defined as a man who accurately predicts the past. In China, Marx, Lenin, and Mao are no longer demigods. In Russia, Stalin is a criminal today and Brezhnev a mediocre bureaucrat. How will future historians judge Deng, Gorbachev, and Yeltsin? Only time will tell, of course. But I shall hazard a guess that history will judge them by a higher standard, that of granting democracy to their peoples. In that light, Deng Hsiao-ping falls far short of Gorbachev and Yeltsin. By crushing the Beijing uprising and failing to move on from economic to political reform, he permitted history to pass him by. The last Soviet leader and the first freely elected Russian president, on the other hand, saw history's challenge, accepted it, and did their best to meet it.

Chapter Sixteen

"Through a Glass, Darkly; but Then Face to Face"

As we conclude this study, it is difficult to avoid a feeling of sadness. Why do people behave like this? Why such blindness? Why such stubbornness? Why does it take humanity so long to travel from misperception to reality? Can we learn anything from the tragic past so that it might serve as a prologue for a better future?

These are difficult questions. History is humanity's great laboratory. But it does not yield its secrets easily. As the knowledge of a person's past gives us some clues about his future, history provides us with some clues about a nation's future. It never repeats itself exactly. If it can teach us anything at all, it teaches through analogy, not identity. But by what mental processes do we select the right analogy? What lessons do we choose to select from the myriad of events of the past? The answer is that we choose those that we *perceive* as meaningful. Perception, thus, is crucial.

Let us now, toward the end of the book, make an attempt at definition. Perception in world politics may be defined as the total cognitive view a nation holds of itself and of others in the world. As such, it includes, of course, both reality and distortion. There is little doubt that many nations much of the time see themselves and others the way they really are; but, as the examples in this book have shown, it is equally clear that some nations some of the time see themselves and others in partially distorted or even totally distorted ways. Hence, I have tried to isolate from the composite picture of reality and illusion the elements of illusion, and then I have attempted to determine what effects these have had on decisions of national policy.

In this endeavor, it has been useful to consider four different dimensions of perception in world politics. First, there are nations' self-images; how do national leaders perceive themselves? The question, "Who do they think they are?" may be posed in a spirit of genuine inquiry. Second, one must consider a nation's perception of the nature and character of its counterplayer. How does a national leader view another nation's intentions toward itself? What, in other words, does it expect to happen? And finally, how well do nations perceive one another's objective power and capabilities?

Four dangers must be guarded against in any perceptual approach to world politics. First, nations are clearly more than groups of people living on pieces of territory. Large political entities cannot be dealt with in the same manner as individuals. Hence, wherever possible, I have tried to focus on the perceptions of individual leaders or of small groups whose actions were accessible to empirical analysis. Second, nations probably exist more in time than in space. Thus, I have adopted a historical approach and dealt with three nations only: China, Russia, and America. It is hoped that by thus limiting the breadth of the analysis, I have gained in depth. Third, there often exists a fine distinction between perception and judgment. Policy decisions often include both elements, and the task of separating them is frequently difficult, if not impossible. Finally, it is worth pointing out again that, in the mosaic of world politics, perception is only one part of the pattern. I believe that we have found a key to one riddle, but I know that there are many keys yet to be found for the other unsolved riddles.

What, now, are the major insights that are revealed by my six examples in Chinese-American relations? In all of recorded history, the most rigid and enduring self-image was probably that held by Imperial China. For over two millennia, it saw itself at the center of the universe and as the hub of virtue, learning, and civilization. This image of itself excluded the possibility of learning anything from anybody else, since one could learn nothing from barbarians. The empire was self-contained and self-sufficient, and foreign barbarians were thought to inhabit small islands separated from civilization by "intervening wastes of sea."

It is probably not enough to say that the Chinese had false perceptions of the early Americans with whom they came in contact. It may be more accurate to say that they had no concept at all to account for the strange new phenomena they were encountering. The first meeting with the West must have been an experience comparable to an invasion from a hostile foreign planet. The early attempts to fit the Western powers into the long-familiar pattern of tributary relationships doomed Imperial China from the start. Its decision to give the barbarians the right to try their own citizens on Chinese soil in order not to sully its hands was the beginning of extraterritoriality in China. And to meet foreign firepower with pronouncements of superior virtue was to invite the dismemberment of the empire through military force. Thus, China's self-image prevented it from learning anything at all for half a century; and when at last the image cracked, it was already too late.

Before the first encounters between China and the United States, American perceptions of China were marked by respect and veneration. With physical contact, however, this respect quickly gave way to a kind of benevolent contempt. The Americans came to regard the Chinese as wards in their own country. By 1900, the barbarians perceived the Chinese as heathens to be civilized, and Imperial China now perceived the barbarians correctly—as the agents of its destruction.

As the Nationalist revolution engulfed China, first under Sun Yat-sen and then under Chiang Kai-shek, the perceptual relationship between China and America underwent significant changes. While Americans continued to regard themselves as benevolent guardians of China, they now perceived Chiang Kai-Shek as not only the hero and future hope of China, but also as a steadfast friend of the United States and an enemy of communism—in short, as an ally in a global moral battle. It could never be admitted that the anti-Western passions of the new revolutionary China also extended to the United States; nor could it be admitted that the wartime alliance with Chiang Kai-shek was more an outgrowth of the power balance of the time than a common crusade against the forces of evil. Alliance had to be made synonymous with friendship. And finally, Americans tenaciously refused to see that nationalism and communism in China had been born in the same anti-Western mold. Chiang Kai-shek, the Christian general, was endowed by America with all those qualities that were considered virtuous and moral. In return, the United States fully expected to be regarded with similar enthusiasm and respect.

When Mao Tse-tung's communism emerged victorious from the Chinese civil war, Americans, burdened with the Chiang Kai-shek image of the past, were unable to deal pragmatically with the new situation. They could not suddenly abandon a heroic Christian leader who for so long had been perceived as America's trusted friend. Nor, however, could they save him from disaster. Hence, many Americans found refuge, if not comfort, in the myth of China's loss through the machinations of subversives in the American government itself. The denouement of China had been so unthinkable that only treason could explain it. Thus, the extravagant American image of Chiang Kai-shek contributed substantially to America's failure in China. Ironically enough, the object of this image also felt abandoned and betrayed by his former ally. And on the Chinese mainland, America was suddenly confronted with a new and fiercely hostile presence.

The Korean War became the great watershed in Sino-American relations. On the American side, it marked the death of the image of China as the heroic underdog and the birth of a new image— that of a hostile and menacing power to be reckoned with. The Chinese Communists, in turn, learned to perceive the United States as their archenemy, bent on their destruction.

The most crucial perception on both sides during the Korean War no doubt was that of the enemy's intent. General MacArthur firmly believed that the Chinese Communists neither would nor could intervene in Korea. He perceived the soldier of the People's Liberation Army of 1950 in the same way that he had perceived the defeated Chinese Nationalist soldier of 1949—with considerable disdain. The Chinese, on the other hand, were convinced that MacArthur, in his drive toward the Yalu River, would not stop at the border but would invade China itself. Hence, military intervention was seen as the only possible recourse.

Once the Chinese intervention had occurred, MacArthur's image of China's power began to play a decisive role. When the Chinese infiltrated 200,000 men into North Korea and dealt Mac-

Arthur's army a devastating blow, the American general was unable to accept this fact. And when the Chinese broke contact temporarily before striking again, MacArthur ascribed this move to their need for rest. The old images died hard, and MacArthur blundered into the trap of his own misperceptions. The tenacity with which Americans held on to their old images was exemplified in official State Department declarations to the effect that the war was not being waged against the Chinese people, but only against their Communist leaders. Since no one knew how this distinction could be put into effect on the battlefield, it was soon abandoned. But it demonstrated the utter incapacity of many Americans to admit that the Chinese Communists had secured a genuine power base and a measure of popular support.

The old images, in short, helped prevent a more pragmatic policy, helped prevent Americans from seeing a massive Chinese intervention coming, and ultimately almost led to disaster on the fields of battle in Korea.

Perception has also had a tragic impact on the war in Indochina during both the French and American phases. After the Chinese intervention in the Korean War, American leaders expected a similar intervention on the side of Ho Chi Minh. Even though the Chinese never intervened in armed combat, this expectation led to policy decisions of the gravest consequence. France, whose presence in Indochina before the Communist victory in China had been perceived by the United States with considerable misgivings, now became the defender of the West in Asia. The perceptions that America entertained of communism in Europe were automatically transferred to the Asian scene. The United States began to fight a war by proxy in Indochina. Military aid to France increased by leaps and bounds until by 1954 the United States was paying over half the cost of the Indochinese war.

American perceptions of Ho Chi Minh also underwent dramatic changes. In 1946, most Americans had seen him as a nationalist resisting the incursions of French colonialism. By the time of the Korean War, he had become, in the view of most American leaders, a puppet of Chinese communism. A man had to be either a nationalist or a Communist but could not really be both. The towering shadow of Mao Tse-tung was seen to hover over the figure of Ho Chi Minh.

Thus, the Indochinese war, which had begun as a local nation-

alist uprising with Communist leadership cadres, was now perceived by the United States as a mortal test of will between a
Communist monolith and the forces of the free world. When the
showdown came between France and Ho Chi Minh at Dienbienphu in 1954, a massive military intervention by the United States
was averted by the narrowest of margins.

China's perception of hostile intent by the Americans was as
one-dimensional as that of the United States. The Chinese saw
themselves in deadly peril. American aid to France had to be
balanced with Chinese aid to Ho Chi Minh. A vicious circle was
created in which the border line between real and imaginary
threats tended to blur and finally disappear altogether. A spiral of
Hobbesian fear was set in motion. Each side vividly felt the terrible
fear it had of the other but could not enter the other's counterfear
or even understand why it should be particularly nervous. The
stage was thus set for an even more tragic encounter.

As the American presence in Indochina displaced that of
France in the late 1950s, and as this presence gradually changed to
a massive military intervention of half a million men during the
1960s, American perceptions again were crucial. American leaders
remained the prisoners of their coldwar images at the very time
when communism had in fact ceased to be monolithic and was
breaking up into political and ideological fragments. They continued to see the shadow of China looming over North Vietnam.
Mutual perceptions of both character and intent now became true
devil mirror images. Each side compared the other's declarations
to those of Hitler. Both evoked analogies to Munich in their own
need to stand up against each other. Both saw themselves as the
torchbearers of truth and justice in the world.

Fortunately, however, both China and America by now had
developed a healthy respect for each other's military power. American leaders reiterated that they had no wish to encounter Chinese
troops in battle, and the Chinese made fewer references to Americans as paper tigers and exercised a policy of extreme restraint. Of
course, the split with the Soviet Union and the shock waves of the
Cultural Revolution probably made China less willing to risk war
with the United States. And equally, the deep divisions within
America over the Vietnamese war made her leaders most reluctant
to risk an even wider war with China. But it is altogether possible
that both China and America had learned to perceive each other's

power quite correctly in Korea and that this more realistic appreciation served as a restraining memory.

Finally, in 1971, after a generation of estrangement, the leaders of China and America decided to establish a relationship based less upon their fantasies and more upon the facts. By that time, many young people in the United States were better acquainted with the landscape of the moon, which they had seen on television, than with mainland China, and many young Chinese perceived an America that had no resemblance whatsoever to reality. The process of détente that followed the China visits of Henry Kissinger and President Richard Nixon began to mitigate the most flagrant misperceptions and distortions that had plagued the Sino-American relationship. But a century of tutelage and a generation of bitter enmity could not be washed away so simply by visits, cultural exchanges, the opening of liaison offices, trade relations, or even a common membership in the United Nations. For two thousand years, China had perceived herself as the center of civilization and all others as barbarians. Then, for a hundred years, the "barbarians" treated the Chinese as inferior wards in their own country. But of all the major Western nations, only the United States refused to have anything whatever to do with China for more than twenty years after the ascendancy of Mao Tse-tung to power. The challenge of the future became plain: for the first time in their histories, China and America would have to learn to deal with one another not only on the basis of reality, but equality as well.

After the death of Mao Tse-tung, China embarked on a course of modernization. Inevitably, she was drawn closer to the United States and moved even farther away from the Soviet Union. The Soviet invasion of Afghanistan in 1980 turned China into virtually an unofficial member of NATO. Within a single generation, the threat of Soviet Russia had turned two enemies into near allies. The Americans now perceived the Chinese as natural partners in their new containment policy against the Soviet Union. And the Chinese were determined now to use American barbarians against the Russian barbarians.

It was under Deng Hsiao-ping that the Chinese were told to "improve communism through capitalism." Maoism became a thing of the past. Peasants were encouraged to make profits, and joint ventures with Westerners began to flourish. A stock exchange opened its doors in Shanghai, and Chinese students flocked to the United States by the tens of thousands. Modernization could simply not proceed on the Communist model. In Deng's telling phrase: "It doesn't matter what color the cat is so long as it catches mice." During the 1980s, the Chinese rediscovered the profit motive and did so with a vengeance. After all, China had been Communist for only thirty years and merchant-minded for three thousand. Americans and Chinese became economic partners once again, and business deals began to displace angry military rhetoric.

Ronald Reagan visited China, and he and Deng Hsiao-ping exchanged cordial toasts. True, China was a long way from becoming a democracy. Political reform lagged far behind economic reform, and political dissidents still languished in Chinese prisons. But Americans no longer looked down on Chinese as coolies or as Communist aggressors; and Chinese no longer regarded Americans as menacing barbarians. Realistic perceptions displaced the distortions of the past, as tourists took the place of soldiers. At long last, Chinese and Americans came to regard each other as equals.

In June 1989, China lurched back into darkness when Deng Hsiao-ping crushed the Beijing uprising with terrible brutality. Americans, too, were estranged from China as they watched an Orwellian scene of purges and executions. I cannot help but think, however, that after the old men of the Mao generation are gone, democracy may have another chance. Deng Hsiao-ping's formula of economic reform without political freedom is destined to be transitory. Somewhere in that vast nation of a billion people, a Chinese Gorbachev may be waiting in the wings.

I believe that the students who were prepared to give their lives for democracy in China will not be forgotten. Their voices will be heard again all over the land. Freedom, once aroused, will rise again and yet again until it is victorious. In my mind's eye, I see that student carrying that banner into the future: "Give us democracy or give us death." China's future will not be death; it will be democracy.

The most significant misperception in the relations between the young American republic and czarist Russia occurred on the American side. When Catherine the Great and Czar Alexander II embarked on policies that happened to be helpful to the United

States, the Americans assumed, without any evidence whatsoever, that Russia's policy was fashioned in response to American desires. The truth was that the fate of the United States was a matter of complete indifference to czarist Russia.

When Catherine the Great refused to lend troops to King George III to crush his rebellious subjects, the American revolutionaries assumed that the czarina's refusal stemmed from her affection for the American fighters for independence. When Czar Alexander sent his fleet to New York and San Francisco during the American Civil War, the North assumed that the ships had come for the purpose of helping the Union cause. And when the czar sold Alaska to the United States, the Americans purchased it as a debt of gratitude for past Russian favors.

Actually, in all these cases, the czars followed the dictates of their national interest. The fact that these interests happened to converge with those of the Americans was purely coincidental. The czars never considered the Americans as very important. In fact, in comparison with the European powers, the United States was perceived as virtually irrelevant.

When, under Czar Nicholas II, American and Russian interests began to diverge and ultimately to collide, the Americans went to the other extreme. Even though Nicholas' policies had as little to do with the United States as those of his predecessors, the Americans—once again relating these policies to themselves alone—overreacted in the opposite direction. Affection now turned to suspicion, and romanticism gave way to hatred. Thus, the consequence of basing policy on legends rather than on facts was naiveté and lack of balance.

The tragedy of the Russo-American encounter in 1917 was that both Wilson and Lenin perceived each other and their nations with a total lack of empathy. Wilson attempted to fit the events in Russia in 1917 into the framework of the American experience and Lenin perceived the United States through the prism of Marxism alone.

On the American side, there probably was no experience that could have equipped the American people to perceive the Bolshevik Revolution for what it really was: a political and social upheaval of earth-shattering proportions that remade an entire society. The American Revolution had not been marked by excessive violence, and the Civil War had been fought and won to preserve a union, not to destroy it and supplant it with a new political order. Thus, the absence of any comparable historical experience probably doomed the United States to misperceive completely the revolutionary process in Russia. There was simply nothing in the American experience to relate it to. The reports about the events in Russia that were written in the summer of 1917 by David R. Francis, the former grain merchant, and by Elihu Root, the elderly statesman who "did not like filth," demonstrate this total lack of empathy in its starkest form. The expectation that democracy, American style, would flourish in Russia and that such self-government would lead to renewed Russian enthusiasm for World War I demonstrated how little the American leaders understood the revolutionary forces that were reshaping the Russian nation.

Lenin and Trotsky, on the other hand, perceived the United States so much through Marxist lenses that the reality of America was completely lost to them. Their absolute commitment to Marxism made for distortion a priori. America had to be adjusted to fit the Marxist categories. Perception thus took place within a closed and predetermined system. Moreover, to the Bolsheviks, nothing mattered but their revolution. They could not conceive that it could have appeared otherwise to anybody else. Even the fact that a world war was in progress was of little consequence to them.

Thus, with equal egocentricity, Americans and Bolsheviks perceived themselves as secular crusaders for the good life on earth and saw each other as anathema. Each made a distinction between the other's "good people" and "evil government" and saw the latter as a transitional phenomenon to be removed from the face of the earth with all possible speed. Hence, even though in 1920 there were few objective causes for conflict between America and Russia, these perceptions had made the two nations into mortal enemies.

The years preceding the establishment of diplomatic relations between the United States and the Soviet Union illustrate the tenacity with which negative images and stereotypes can live on, despite the growing impact of objective forces that point in the direction of flexibility and change.

Throughout the decade of the twenties, Americans took great delight in using Russia as a mirror of their own accomplishments. By the thirties, the tables had turned and Russia now used America as a mirror of its own successes. When Lenin adopted the NEP,

Americans saw this decision as the triumph of capitalism in Russia. When the Great Depression overtook America, however, Stalin perceived it as "the first swallow of the impending spring" of communism. Both nations saw only what they wished to see, and new facts were conveniently adapted to fit the perceptions.

It took the catastrophe of the Depression to make Americans somewhat more receptive to new facts. Suddenly, the United States discovered that it needed the Russian market for its goods. The Russians in turn discovered that they needed the American goods. And both Russia and America began to realize that they shared a common interest in defending themselves against the rising menace of Germany and Japan.

What is striking is that it took the two nations so long to establish diplomatic relations in the absence of any major objective power rivalries between them. The negative images that each maintained about the other no doubt retarded the process toward rapprochement. Had this rapprochement come earlier and had it been more solid, perhaps the rise of the Axis powers might have been stemmed and the disasters that followed might have been averted. When the war made allies of America and Russia, the old images prevented real trust and genuine collaboration. And no doubt these images—latent and beneath the surface though they were—came to the fore again at war's end and hastened the coming of the cold war.

The fate of Germany after World War II is a fearful example of the evolution of a vicious perceptual spiral. Both Russians and Americans distorted incoming information to fit their images of the other's hostile intent. With every step up the spiral, the prophecy came nearer to fulfillment, until the image became fact. The result was a divided Germany, half of it rearmed and integrated into the North Atlantic Treaty Organization and the other half equally rearmed but committed to the Warsaw Pact.

It is amazing how many formulas came to grief on these mutual perceptions of hostile intent. Both the Pleven Plan and the EDC on the Western side and proposals for free all-German elections and an all-European security pact on the Soviet side failed to be accepted. Americans perceived Soviet offers as ruses, transparent maneuvers, or baited traps. Russians saw American initiatives as aggressive designs, capitalist tricks, or imperialist expansion. Each side, of course, saw its own moves as purely defensive.

The greater danger in this cold war struggle lay in the possibility that the extreme images of hostile intent that each side held of the other might have driven the spiral of suspicion and countersuspicion to the desperate side of a preventive war. If each side had continued to believe that the other was its mortal enemy, this view might have influenced behavior to such a point of rigidity and compulsiveness that the inevitable conflict could have become a self-fulfilling prophecy. It took a near catastrophe to introduce a larger measure of reality into the relations of the superpowers—the Cuban missile crisis of 1962.

In essence, the story of the Cuban crisis is the story of the two most powerful men in the world, who first saw what they wished to see but were able to correct their misperceptions and thus pull back from the edge of nuclear destruction.

President Kennedy at first perceived Premier Khrushchev as a prudent statesman who would never take the gamble of placing offensive missiles in Cuba. Ambiguous evidence was adjusted to this desire to see Khrushchev as a man of peaceful intent. Thus, Soviet ships with large hatches, riding high in the water on their way to Cuba, were dismissed as lumber ships. When the truth was revealed, the American leadership was taken by complete surprise.

Premier Khrushchev, on the other hand, first perceived the American president as irresolute and weak. After all, Kennedy had seemed to lack resolve in the crises of the Berlin Wall and the Bay of Pigs. Hence, Khrushchev was convinced that he could place offensive missiles in Cuba and Kennedy would take no forceful action. Thus, before the crisis erupted into the open, both leaders saw what they wanted to see. As a result, Kennedy lowered his guard in Cuba and Khrushchev shipped his missiles.

During the acute stage of the crisis, self-images played a crucial role. It is striking how much emphasis Kennedy placed on appearances. He admitted, in fact, that the missiles had to be removed, not because they made America weak, but because they made her *appear* weak. They symbolized an unacceptable challenge to the American will. Thus, if America did nothing, the president said, she would "be dead."

Fortunately, Kennedy was equally concerned with the Soviet leader's self-image. He knew that Khrushchev would not withdraw the missiles if this forced *him* to appear weak. The pledge not to invade Cuba was Kennedy's recognition of this truth and bears testimony to the American leader's gift of empathy. "The final lesson of the Cuban missile crisis," in Robert Kennedy's words, was "the importance of placing ourselves in the other country's shoes." ·

Both men changed their perceptions in response to mortal danger. While this is a sad reflection, it is also true that lesser minds, when confronted with such peril, tend to hold on to their misperceptions with redoubled tenacity. Even people of great intelligence, when confronted with disaster, often use this intelligence not to question their false images, but instead to shore them up. Intelligence alone, as the Cuban missile crisis shows, is no guarantee for survival in the nuclear age. Great moral courage, a respect for facts, and above all, a gift for empathy are also needed.

After the Cuban missile crisis, the two superpowers slowly moved beyond the cold war. By the 1970s, a fragile détente had come into existence, partially because of changes in the global power balance; détente drew the two superpowers toward rapprochement. Moreover, there was the personality of Henry Kissinger. His role was of such significance in the evolution of détente that it merits special attention.

Henry Kissinger differed from most American diplomats in the sense that his policies were based on doctrine and deliberate design rather than on the more pragmatic day-to-day approach that had been typical of American diplomacy. This doctrine, which rested on three main pillars, emerged very clearly in Kissinger's first book, A World Restored, which was a study of the Congress of Vienna of 1815. The reason Kissinger undertook this study was that he was interested in the manner in which the European diplomats of the early nineteenth century secured the peace of Europe for 100 years. He found three answers to this question. First, to be secure, a peace must be based on a negotiated settlement with all sides in equilibrium rather than on a victor's peace. Everybody is a little bit unhappy, but no one is completely unhappy. Thus, no one will try to overthrow the settlement through yet another war, and the relative insecurity of each guarantees the relative security of all. Second, a victorious power, in order to have peace, will not attempt to annihilate the vanquished but will coopt it into the established order by giving it something of its own substance. Thus, the victor decontaminates the defeated of its revolutionary ardor and transforms it subtly from a "have not" into a "have" nation. Third, in the absence of a globally controlled system, the best guarantor of peace is balance and, hence, a balancer is essential. This balancer will seldom ask the question, Who is right and who is wrong? but rather, Who is weak and who is strong? By adding weight to the "lighter" side whenever an imbalance occurs, the balancer restores equilibrium and thus maintains peace.

Kissinger's policy, in fact, was a process of transplanting these three concepts into the modern world. The first principle was adopted in the Middle East, where the October War of 1973 ended in a stalemate. The second principle was applied to the Soviet Union, which received gigantic credits from the United States, and unlike Mr. Khrushchev, who in 1959 talked about "burying" capitalism, Mr. Brezhnev began to be engaged in "borrowing" from capitalism. Kissinger's hope was that, subtly and over time, a community of economic interests would be established between the capitalist and Communist worlds. Third, the president's trip to China created a triangle between the Soviet Union, China, and America, in which Kissinger attempted to place the United States into the role of balancer, where it would be wooed by both China and the Soviet Union.

One may agree or disagree with Kissinger's approach to diplomacy. But it is impossible to ignore the fact that his approach was based on a consistent philosophic doctrine that evolved over a quarter century of reflection and experience. There is little doubt, however, that this policy reduced the dangers of nuclear war through accident or misperception between the United States and the two great powers of the Communist world.

The Soviet invasion of Afghanistan in 1980 dealt a severe blow to détente. For the first time in their history the Soviets had used combat troops to invade a neutral nation. Would the United States be able to remember that the Soviet Union had not abandoned détente a decade earlier when the United States had made an "incursion" into Cambodia, another neutral Asian country? Or would there be another cold war?

There is little doubt that Ronald Reagan's "devil-images" of the Soviet Union contributed substantially to the resumption of the cold war during the early 1980s. His description of the USSR as "'the focus of evil in the world" probably served to reinforce the negative and often rigid behavior that became typical of Soviet leaders toward the United States. Soviet comparisons of Reagan to Hitler no doubt deepened the abyss that separated the two superpowers. Only the rising fear of nuclear catastrophe and the domestic imperatives of a presidential election cooled down the heated rhetoric and injected a degree of pragmatism into U.S.-Soviet relations. The resumption of arms control negotiations held out the hope that one-dimensional stereotypes might once again be tempered by the reality principle.

And then came Mikhail Gorbachev. His *glasnost* and *perestroika* policies triggered détente with the United States and led to the first Soviet-American disarmament treaty in modern history. His insistence on far-reaching reforms at home dictated much calmer, more peaceful foreign policies abroad, both toward America and China. He insisted that political reforms precede economic restructuring, unlike the Chinese, whose priorities were the reverse. His visit to the United States in 1987 encouraged Ronald Reagan to visit Russia for the first time ever in 1988. By that time, Reagan had changed his mind about the "evil empire" and had developed a genuine liking for the Soviet leader. And the American people followed suit, as even hard-boiled New Yorkers cheered the general secretary when he visited their city and also shared in his grief when he had to return home abruptly to deal with the aftermath of a horrendous earthquake.

As reality displaced distortion, after the death of the Soviet Union in 1991 and the ascendancy of Russia's first freely elected president, Boris Yeltsin, Americans and Russians rediscovered memories of old-time friendships in the war against Japan and Germany. As official hostility began to melt away, they also discovered that they shared more similarities than differences. And they began to wonder why they had hated and feared one another for so long. After all, they had never fought a major war. On the contrary, they had been allies in the century's most devastating conflict. And so, at long last in early 1993, they decided to scrap almost three-fourths of their nuclear arsenals in the most sweeping disarmament treaty in modern history and the United States took the lead in providing aid and credits to the new Russian democracy. Why, then, this long twilight struggle that had edged them so close to the nuclear abyss for forty years? Why indeed? Perhaps the answer must be sought in the terrible distortions of Communist ideology which forced almost every Russian to wear Marxist glasses. Shortly after the ideology conquered Russia, it perceived the United States as its enemy even though there were no objective grounds for such hostility. And when the distorting ideology died at last in 1991, trust and friendship were restored with amazing speed.

There are junctions in history when a single human being can change its course. Men like Hitler and Stalin, steeped in hatred, prejudice, and misperceptions, changed it for the worse. But there are men who try to free their nations of ideologies and stereotypes that have outlived their times. Such leaders know that unless they do so history will simply pass them by and lead them to oblivion. Such men change history for the better, and sometimes they even turn the minds of other leaders away from misperception to reality. Mikhail Gorbachev and Boris Yeltsin are such men. They freed the mind and soul of the Russian people and ended the cold war.

* * *

Our fifteen case studies have demonstrated that false images affect policy, often disastrously. But perhaps an even more significant conclusion emerges from the case studies: people do not easily abandon misperceptions through rational analysis but do so primarily through trauma and catastrophe. Most national leaders will not examine their prejudices and stereotypes until they are shaken and shattered into doing so. People, in short, learn and grow largely through suffering.

As a comment on the human condition, this observation is both accurate and tragic. As a comment on our political condition in the modern world, it is many times more tragic since it involves the entire human race, not just a few people. If we examine the lead time before wars, we will see that it has become shorter and shorter. In Napoleonic times, national leaders had months; in 1914, they had weeks; in 1962, Kennedy had just thirteen days. In the 1990s we may have only hours. Under such conditions, rationality and self-analysis become absolutely essential.

It is, of course, a truism that our perception of the truth is all we have to go on. We cannot postpone a diplomatic decision until all the facts are in, until maturity of judgment has developed and historical perspective has illuminated the situation. We must decide and act *now* even though we may be aware that our vision may be blurred. We cannot but act on incomplete knowledge and so can never prove that our vision is correct. Once all the facts are in, foreign policy has become history. In this sense, the diplomat's task is a trying and cruel one, and the scholar, who does not have to face this existential imperative, should extend a measure of empathy and tolerance.

Nevertheless, the nuclear age demands that diplomats must constantly strive to improve the accuracy of their perceptions. In this light, the crucial question that now confronts us is this: What can be done to make sure that the reality principle governs Chinese-American, Russo-American, and Russo-Chinese relations? Reality is complicated enough, and everything must be done so as not to render it even more complex by adding to it our unsubstantiated misperceptions. How can we eliminate or at least minimize the pernicious influence of stereotypes and misperceptions that have dominated relations among these three great nations for so long? Toward this end, I shall now advance a number of concrete suggestions.

First, national leaders should guard against the dangers of psycho-logic: the tendency to see what they want to see and to respond to situations, not on the basis of empirical evidence, but on the basis of their subjective wishes. The wish must never create policy; only facts can do so.

In Indochina, for example, many Americans who felt that it was important for the United States to win the war also felt that a meaningful victory was in fact possible. Conversely, many Americans who felt that a defeat would not seriously endanger American security also felt that victory was in fact impossible. In both cases, the chances are considerable that at least part of the basis of these views was related to psycho-logic and not to the substance of the evidence. Psycho-logic greatly influenced the thinking of hawks as well as doves in Vietnam policy.

Similarly, many Americans, understandably incensed at the Soviet invasion of Afghanistan, selectively forgot that a decade earlier the United States had half a million combat troops fighting ten thousand miles away in Asian jungles. Nonetheless, détente held then; Gorbachev proved détente could be built again.

One cannot, of course, simply tell diplomats not to misperceive. But one can guard against psycho-logic by including in the leadership group people with different temperaments and outlooks. This is what President Kennedy did when he pondered the alternatives during the Cuban missile crisis. It takes leaders with strong egos, however, to encourage others to tell them not what they want to hear, but what they ought to know. President Johnson was not temperamentally equipped to do this. He tended to surround himself with people who shared his perceptions of the world. A wise leader, on the other hand, will make sure to include at least a "devil's advocate" or two in his inner circle.

Second, and related to psycho-logic, is the all-too-human tendency to ignore conflicting evidence and to give more weight to supporting evidence once a decision has been made. Psychologists describe this phenomenon as reduction of cognitive dissonance. It is simply the temptation to rationalize a decision by listening to those who support it and ignoring those who oppose it. Usually, the more difficulty the policy maker has in reaching a decision, the greater will be the tendency to justify it afterward. President Johnson's justification of his Vietnam policy, following the decision to Americanize the war, and his tendency to surround himself with advisers who supported that policy, were classic examples of dissonance reduction, or more simply put, of reassuring himself that he had made the right decision.

Wise leaders do not reduce such dissonance but remain receptive to it and encourage it. They tend to resist internal pressures toward a consistent mental picture. They always remain open to new evidence that might become a new objective basis for a change in policy.

Third, policy makers often transfer an image automatically from one place to another or from one time to another without careful empirical comparison. Thus, Americans transferred their image of monolithic communism from Europe to Indochina, where the actual situation was entirely different. When images are transferred from past to present, they usually become analogies. Facile analogies to Munich or to Hitler, which were used at different times by American, Soviet, and Chinese leaders, often served as seductive symbols for their peoples but did not necessarily have a realistic basis. Mature policy makers know that each challenge to their nations has its own distinct reality. While there may be similarities to past events, there are also differences. Diplomats must remain conscious of both.

Fourth, mature diplomats will take care not to fall into the traps that their egos might ensnare them in. They will not view their nations as central to another nation's policy—witness the errors of the young American republic in its relations with czarist Russia. They will not mistake alliances for friendship when there is little or no friendship—witness American errors vis-à-vis Chiang Kai-shek. Mature diplomats will not try to explain every phenomenon abroad in terms of their own historical experience—witness Wilson's explanation of the Russian upheavals in 1917 or Lenin's explanation of America. Wise leaders admit the possibility that new concepts must be learned in order to assimilate new experiences. Imperial China's failure to do so led straight to her destruction. Moreover, diplomats must make an effort at all times to keep perspective on themselves.

Fifth, policy makers must be able to change their perceptions of themselves and others without the dreadful catalyst of war. It is a tragic commentary on the human race that it took a Great Depression, a major war is Asia, and a close brush with atomic holocaust to bring such changes about. Wise leaders will decontaminate their policies of shopworn slogans and base decisions on realities, not on anachronistic ideologies or on fictions. Such policy makers will encourage their people to use their minds to learn new facts, not offer up their bodies in defense of shadows.

Mikhail Gorbachev was such a leader. Since his appearance, war among the world's three great powers has become remote. I could not have made this assertion in previous editions of this book.

Of all the virtues that a world leader in the postatomic era must possess, perhaps the greatest is a gift for empathy. It is no longer enough to understand another nation with one's mind; one must learn to feel its essence with one's soul. This is how Kennedy and Khrushchev successfully averted a holocaust over Cuba. This is how Henry Kissinger helped to fashion détente with Russia and China. And this is how Mikhail Gorbachev and Ronald Reagan related to one another. That people can learn to act like this gives one hope for our survival.

All of us must leave the garden of our misperceptions and venture forth into the larger world. As Sigmund Freud discerned so brilliantly, ancient myths are not fairy tales but glimpses of deep psychological truths. Why were Adam and Eve expelled from the

Garden of Eden? Because they had tasted the fruit of the Tree of Knowledge of Good and Evil. They had not become *less* by doing so but *more*. "And the Lord God said, Behold, the man is become one of us, to know good and evil." The Fall was not merely an act of rebellion; it was also an act of maturity.

The myth of Eden records the painful fact that each person must leave the garden in order to become fully human. The overtones of woe with which this myth has echoed down through the ages testify to the reluctance and the pain with which wisdom—and hence full humanity—is born. We *yet* have to accept our Fall.

Since the last edition of this book appeared, I have become an optimist. Hence, as I promised then, I have retitled my book *Nations at Dawn*. And I am grateful to have been witness to Russia's journey out of the night.

Selected Bibliography

CHAPTER TWO

Dulles, Foster Rhea. *China and America*. Princeton: Princeton University Press, 1946.

Fairbank, John K. *Trade and Diplomacy on the China Coast*. Cambridge: Harvard University Press, 1953.

Fairbank, John K. and Teng, Ssu-yu, Eds. *China's Response to the West: A Documentary Survey*. Cambridge: Harvard University Press, 1954.

Isaacs, Harold R. *Images of Asia*. New York: Capricorn Books, 1962.

Ricci, Matthew. *China in the Sixteenth Century: The Journals of Matthew Ricci: 1583–1610*. Translated by Louis J. Gallagher, S. J. New York: Random House, 1953.

Tan, Chester. *The Boxer Catastrophe*. New York: Columbia University Press, 1955.

CHAPTER THREE

Borg, Dorothy. *Historians and American Far Eastern Policy*. New York: Columbia University Press, 1966.

Chiang Kai-shek. *China's Destiny*. Edited by Philip Jaffe. New York: Roy Publishers, 1947.

Schram, Stuart. *Mao Tse-tung*. New York: Simon and Schuster, 1966.

Tsou, Tang. *America's Failure in China, 1941–1950*. Chicago: University of Chicago Press, 1963.

Tuchman, Barbara W. *Stilwell and the American Experience in China, 1911–1945*. New York: Macmillan, 1971.

Wright, Mary C. *The Last Stand of Chinese Conservatism*. Stanford: Stanford University Press, 1957.

CHAPTER FOUR

Griffith, Samuel B., II. *The Chinese People's Liberation Army*. New York: McGraw-Hill, 1967.

MacArthur, Douglas. *Reminiscences*. New York: McGraw-Hill, 1964.

Panikkar, K. M. *In Two Chinas*. London: Allen and Unwin, 1955.

Spanier, John. *The Truman-MacArthur Controversy and the Korean War*. Cambridge: Harvard University Press, 1959.

Truman, Harry S. *Years of Trial and Hope. Vol. II: Memoirs*. Garden City, N.Y.: Doubleday, 1956.

Whiting, Allen S. *China Crosses the Yalu*. Stanford: Stanford University Press, 1960.

CHAPTER FIVE

Bator, Victor. *Vietnam: A Diplomatic Tragedy*. Dobbs Ferry, N.Y.: Oceana Publications, 1965.

Fall, Bernard B. *The Two Vietnams*. New York: Praeger, 1964.

Gurtov, Melvin. *The First Vietnam Crisis*. New York: Columbia University Press, 1967.

Hinton, Harold C. *China's Relations with Burma and Vietnam*. New York: Institute of Pacific Relations, 1958.

Isaacs, Harold R. *No Peace for Asia*. Cambridge: M.I.T. Press, 1967.

McAlister, John T. *Vietnam: The Origins of Revolution*. New York: Knopf, 1969.

CHAPTER SIX

Eisenhower, Dwight D. *Mandate for Change, 1953–1956*. Garden City, N.Y.: Doubleday, 1963.

Fitzgerald, Frances. *Fire in the Lake*. Boston: Atlantic, Little, Brown, 1972.

Geyelin, Philip. *Johnson and the World*. New York: Praeger, 1966.

Halberstam, David. *The Best and the Brightest*. New York: Random House 1972.

Hersh, Seymour. *The Price of Power*. New York: Summit, 1983.

Karnow, Stanley. *Vietnam*. New York: Penguin Books, 1984.

Kissinger, Henry. *White House Years*. Boston: Little, Brown, 1979.

———. *Years of Upheaval*. Boston: Little, Brown, 1982.

Zagoria, Donald S. *Vietnam Triangle*. New York: Pegasus Press, 1967.

CHAPTER SEVEN

Bonavia, David. *Verdict in Peking: The Trial of the Gang of Four.* New York: Putnam, 1984.

Butterfield, Fox. *China: Alive in the Bitter Sea.* New York: Times Books, 1982.

Fairbank, John K. *China Perceived: Images and Policies in Chinese-American Relations.* New York: Knopf, 1974.

————. *The United States and China.* Rev. ed. Cambridge: Harvard University Press, 1975.

Harding, Harry. *China's Second Revolution: Reform After Mao.* Washington, D.C.: Brookings, 1987.

Hsu, Immanuel C. Y. *China Without Mao.* New York: Oxford University Press, 1983.

Kane, Anthony J., Ed. *China Briefing.* Boulder, Colo.: Westview Press, the Asia Society, 1988.

Kissinger, Henry. *White House Years.* Boston: Little, Brown, 1979.

Lampton, David M. and Keyser, Catherine H. *China's Global Presence.* Washington, D.C.: American Enterprise Institute, 1988.

Mancall, Mark. *China at the Center.* New York: Free Press, 1984.

Pye, Lucian W. *Mao Tse-tung: The Man in the Leader.* New York: Basic Books, 1976.

Salisbury, Harrison E. *The New Emperors: China in the Era of Mao and Deng.* Boston: Little, Brown, 1992.

Yahuda, Michael. *Toward the End of Isolationism: China's Foreign Policy After Mao.* New York: St. Martin's Press, 1984.

CHAPTER EIGHT

Bailey, Thomas A. *America Faces Russia.* Ithaca: Cornell University Press, 1950.

Farrar, V. J. *The Annexation of Russian America to the United States.* Washington, D.C.: W. F. Robert Company, 1937.

Golder, Frank A. "The Russian Fleet and the Civil War." *American Historical Review* (July 1915).

————. "Catherine II and the American Revolution." *American Historical Review* (October 1915).

Hecht, David. *Russian Radicals Look to America, 1825–1894.* Cambridge: Harvard University Press, 1947.

Ulam, Adam B. *In the Name of the People.* New York: Viking, 1977.

Zabriskie, E. H. *American-Russian Rivalry in the Far East, 1895–1914.* Philadelphia: University of Pennsylvania Press, 1946.

CHAPTER NINE

Baker, R.' S. and Dodd, W. E. *The Public Papers of Woodrow Wilson, 1917–1924.* New York: Harcourt, Brace 1927.

Filene, Peter G. *Americans and the Soviet Experiment, 1917–1933.* Cambridge: Harvard University Press, 1967.

Jessup, P. C. *Elihu Root.* 2 vols. New York: Dodd, Mead, 1938.

Kennan, George F. *Russia Leaves the War.* Princeton: Princeton University Press, 1956.

————. *The Decision to Intervene.* Princeton: Princeton University Press, 1956.

————. *Russia and the West Under Lenin and Stalin.* Boston: Little, Brown, 1961.

Strakhovsky, Leonid I. *American Opinion About Russia.* Toronto: University of Toronto Press, 1961.

CHAPTER TEN

Bailey, Thomas A. *America Faces Russia.* Ithaca: Cornell University Press, 1950.

Banghoorn, Frederick C. *The Soviet Image of the United States.* New York: Harcourt, Brace, 1950.

Beloff, Max. *The Foreign Policy of Soviet Russia, Vol. I, 1929–1936.* Oxford: Oxford University Press, 1947.

Filene, Peter G. *Americans and the Soviet Experiment, 1917–1933.* Cambridge: Harvard University Press, 1967.

————, Ed. *American Views of Soviet Russia, 1917–1965.* Homewood, Ill.: The Dorsey Press, 1968.

CHAPTER ELEVEN

Feld, Werner, *Reunification and West Germany-Soviet Relations.* The Hague: Martinus Nijhoff, 1963.

Halle, Louis J. *The Cold War as History.* New York: Harper & Row, 1967.

Kennan, George F. *Russia and the West Under Lenin and Stalin.* Boston: Little, Brown, 1961.

McCullough, David. *Truman.* New York: Simon and Schuster, 1992.

Moore, Barrington, Jr. *Soviet Politics—The Dilemma of Power.* Cambridge: Harvard University Press, 1950.

Rapoport, Anatol. *The Big Two: Soviet-American Perceptions of Foreign Policy.* New York: Pegasus, 1971.

Schlesinger, Arthur M., Jr. "Origins of the Cold War." *Foreign Affairs* (October 1967).

CHAPTER TWELVE

Allison, Graham T. *Essence of Decision: Explaining the Cuban Missile Crisis.* Boston: Little, Brown, 1971.

Hilsman, Roger. *To Move a Nation.* Garden City, N.Y.: Doubleday, 1967.

Kennedy, Robert F. *Thirteen Days.* New York: Norton, 1969.

Kissinger, Henry A. *Nuclear Weapons and Foreign Policy.* New York: Harper & Row, 1957.

Schlesinger, Arthur M., Jr. *A Thousand Days.* Boston: Houghton Mifflin, 1965.

Sorensen, Theodore. *Kennedy.* New York: Harper & Row, 1965.

CHAPTER THIRTEEN

Bradsher, Henry S. *Afghanistan and the Soviet Union.* Durham, N.C.: Duke University Press, 1983.

Khrushchev, Nikita S. *Khrushchev Remembers.* Boston: Little, Brown, 1974.

Newhouse, John. *Cold Dawn: The Story of SALT.* New York: Holt, Rinehart and Winston, 1973.

Stoessinger, John G. *Henry Kissinger: The Anguish of Power.* New York: Norton, 1976.

Ulam, Adam B. *The Rivals: America and Russia Since World War II.* New York: Viking, 1971.

Zagoria, Donald, Ed. *Soviet Policy in East Asia.* New Haven: Yale University Press, 1982.

CHAPTER FOURTEEN

Bialer, Seweryn and Mandelbaum, Michael. *The Global Rivals.* New York: Knopf, 1988.

Brzezinski, Zbigniew. "The Cold War and Its Aftermath," *Foreign Affairs* (Fall 1992).

Gorbachev, Mikhail. *Perestroika: New Thinking for Our Country and the World.* New York: Harper & Row, 1987.

Hough, Jerry. *Russia and the West: Gorbachev and the Politics of Reform.* New York: Simon and Schuster, 1988.

Kennan George F. "Communism in Russian History," *Foreign Affairs* (Winter 1991–1992).

Stoessinger, John G. *The Might of Nations: World Politics in Our Time.* 10th ed. New York: McGraw-Hill, 1993.

Talbot, Strobe and Editors of *Time. Mikhail S. Gorbachev: An Intimate Biography.* New York: Time, 1988.

CHAPTER FIFTEEN

Clubb, Edmund O. *China and Russia: The Great Game.* New York: Columbia University Press, 1977.

Leong, Sow-Theng. *Sino-Soviet Diplomatic Relations, 1917–1926.* Honolulu: University of Hawaii Press, 1976.

Salisbury, Harrison E. *War Between Russia and China.* New York: Norton, 1969.

Schwartz, Benjamin I. *Chinese Communism and the Rise of Mao.* Cambridge: Harvard University Press, 1951.

Schwartz, Harry. *Tsars, Mandarins, and Commissars.* Philadelphia: Lippincott, 1964.

Short, Philip. *The Dragon and the Bear: Inside China and Russia Today.* New York: Morrow, 1983.

CHAPTER SIXTEEN

Aron, Raymond. *Peace and War.* New York: Doubleday, 1966.

Freud, Sigmund. *Civilization and Its Discontents.* London: Hogarth Press, 1953.

Fromm, Erich. *The Anatomy of Human Destructiveness.* New York: Holt, Rinehart and Winston, 1973.

Kennedy, Paul. *The Rise and Fall of the Great Powers.* New York: Random House, 1987.

Morgenthau, Hans J. *Politics Among Nations: The Struggle for Power and Peace.* 6th ed. New York: Knopf, 1985.

Schell, Jonathan. *The Fate of the Earth.* New York: Knopf, 1982.

Stoessinger, John G. *The Might of Nations: World Politics in Our Time.* 10th ed. New York: McGraw-Hill, 1993.

———.*Why Nations Go to War.* 6th ed. New York: St. Martin's Press, 1993.

INDEX

Index